THE

CONSERVATIVE

AFFIRMATION

BOOKS BY WILLMOORE KENDALL

Baseball: How to Play It and How to Watch It
John Locke and the Doctrine of Majority Rule
A Communist Party in Action (A. Rossi)
    translated with an introduction
China: An Area Manual for Psychological Warfare
    with David N. Rowe
Czechoslovakia: An Area Manual for Psychological Warfare
    with David N. Rowe
The Social Contract (J.-J. Rousseau)
    translated with an introduction
Democracy and the American Party System
    with Austin Ranney
War and the Use of Force
    with Mulford Q. Sibley
El Hombre Ante La Asamblea
El Oso y el Dragón
The Committee and Its Critics (with the staff of *National Review*)
El Occidente ante el Comunismo

THE
CONSERVATIVE
AFFIRMATION

by WILLMOORE KENDALL

GATEWAY EDITIONS • CHICAGO

Gateway Editions is an imprint of Regnery Gateway, Inc.
All inquiries should be directed to Regnery Gateway, Inc., 940 North
Shore Drive, Lake Bluff, IL 60044

Manufactured in the United States of America.

Library of Congress Cataloging in Publication Data
Kendall, Willmoore, 1909-1967.
    The conservative affirmation.

    Originally published: Chicago : Regnery, 1963.
    Includes bibliographical references and index.
    1. Conservatism. 2. Liberalism. 3. United
States—Politics and government—20th century.
4. Political science—Book reviews. I. Title.
JC571.K39 1985   320.5'2   85-5517
ISBN 0-89526-811-6 (pbk.)
ISBN 0-89526-591-5 (hardcover)

To Nellie
who invented it
and Yvona
who barreled it through

Contents

Introduction

When *The Conservative Affirmation* was first published in 1963, one
reviewer, a friend and admirer of Willmoore Kendall, wrote that the
title was "a singular piece of impudence," noting that the book's working title, *What is Conservatism, and other Anti-Liberal Essays,* would have
been more appropriate to its iconoclastic contents. The legend of
Willmoore Kendall, the knockabout polemicist who had an uncanny
ability to infuriate not only Liberals but also his fellow Conservatives,
has been growing steadily over the years since "the boy wonder of
Oklahoma" graduated from university at age eighteen and launched
himself into the war of ideas. Dwight MacDonald, a left-leaning jour-
nalist, once described him as "a wild Yale don who can bring an argument into the shouting stage faster than any man in town." Even
Francis G. Wilson, Kendall's dissertation adviser and an intimate
friend, writing in a scholarly evaluation of Kendall's contribution to
political science, held that his criticism "has . . . to be turntabled
from the negative to the positive" in order to fully appreciate his intellectual achievement. Kendall, it has been said, was a natural "agin-
ner," a loose cannon on the Conservative deck. The Kendall myth
eventually found its most concise expression in the title of a posthu-
mously published volume of his essays: *Contra Mundum*—Kendall
against the world.

Willmoore Kendall certainly contributed to the legend that he left
in his turbulent wake. Extremely brittle in his personal relationships,
it was said that when he worked as an editor at *National Review* he
was on speaking terms with only one staff member at a time, whose
identity changed each month. Many of Kendall's friends found themselves suddenly *persona non grata,* for little or no apparent reason.

And of course—most famous of all—Kendall's stormy relationship with Yale University, where in fourteen years he had never been promoted or given a raise, ended when, acting on his suggestion, the administration literally bought out his tenure rights for a sum in the tens of thousands of dollars.

Yet for anyone who turns carefully to the body of Kendall's work, with an openness to the spirit that animated it, the *Contra Mundum* myth, which threatens to obscure his real contribution, simply won't stand up. There is, for one thing, the testimony of dozens of his students, profoundly influenced by him and deeply grateful for the attention he bestowed on them so generously. For another, the Yale incident now appears differently in the light of the recent forced resignation of a conservative follower of Leo Strauss from the same Yale political science department. And that professor was just as popular with students as was Kendall.

More importantly, the notion of Kendall as a merely negative thinker misses the profoundly moral vision which undergirded his attacks on Liberalism. This psychologizing of Kendall, based as it is on the erroneous Marxist and Freudian belief that a man's ideas are merely a "superstructure" reflecting his emotional problems or social background, does not comprehend the deeper truth that a man's ideas ultimately shape his whole approach to the world. The historian George Nash has accurately referred to Kendall as "this strangely driven man." Kendall indeed had a demon in him, but it derived from the same sources that fuel the outrage of the great satirists. At root it is a moral force—the "savage indignation" of a Jonathan Swift—against hypocrisy, turpitude, and humankind's seemingly limitless complacency in the face of evil. Kendall had a rage for truth that constantly made distinctions (this often caused him to break with fellow Conservatives); he had no time for sentimentality, woolly thinking, or self-serving ideas. If he did not rise to the level of prophetic insight (how few are those who do), he nonetheless possessed a keen sense of the urgency of the West's spiritual and intellectual crisis. Perhaps Kendall's greatest virtue is that he constantly argued with himself; more than once in his mature years, he had the humility to "start over," changing his intellectual position in response to some challenge to his habits of thought. Describing the development of his former teacher, William F. Buckley, Jr. said:

> In 1949, he was rather cynical about the great truths . . . . Slowly,
> but inexorably, he has lost the cynicism he acquired as a preco-
> cious scholar at Oxford and as a young and gifted teacher in
> the turbulent 30's, to the point where he has become, in my opin-
> ion, one of the few fine and intensely moral figures of our time.

Vain though he was, Kendall's convictions were hard-won, at a
cost many men would not have the honesty or the integrity to pay.

To the end of his life, Kendall retained a fierce love for the rural
Oklahoma towns where he grew up, seeing them as traditional out-
posts of Christendom, however simple and inarticulate they might
be. In such communities men govern themselves by ordering their
souls in accordance with a higher law: they are the virtuous people
deliberating under God. Though Kendall was singularly free of the
belief in America as a "savior nation," he did believe that America
had a "mission": "to prove that self-government is possible." As
a boy Kendall traveled through these towns with his father, a blind
Methodist preacher. By reading to his father (he had learned to read
at age 2 by playing with a typewriter) and, later, engaging in endless
debates with him on every imaginable topic, Kendall developed his
masterful command of language and relentless, dialectical method of
argument. Like many prodigies, Kendall's time was divided between
the listlessness brought on by a lack of adequate stimulation, and fu-
rious activity. He graduated from high school at thirteen, and from
the University of Oklahoma at eighteen. After dabbling in journalism and studying Romance languages, Kendall obtained a Rhodes
Scholarship and left the plains for Oxford University.

Oxford proved a major turning point. Taking the Philosophy, Politics, and Economics course (P.P.E.), with the conservative R.G.
Collingwood as his tutor, Kendall acquired his passion for political
science. At Oxford he threw himself into late night disputations,
defending positions calculated to provoke his audience to exaspera-
tion and disbelief. But however much he posed as the wild man from
Oklahoma, Kendall was absorbing European culture and history, gaining a "polish" and "elegant civility" his students would never forget.

From the cloisters and quadrangles of Oxford, where Kendall had
flirted with Trotskyite Communism, he went to ideologically wracked

Spain on the eve of the civil war as a correspondent for the United Press. Like a fellow Trotskyite by the name of George Orwell, Kendall watched with horror as the Soviet Union intervened ruthlessly in the activities of the left-wing factions. This experience would help Kendall to see that J.S. Mill's model of the "Open Society" (which pictures society as something like an Oxford debating club), is utterly helpless when confronted by the brutal forces in the real world that have not the slightest regard for parliamentary rules of order—much less for the value of human life.

Kendall returned to America still a man of the Left, and applied himself to completing his Ph.D. at the University of Illinois. His dissertation was published as *John Locke and the Doctrine of Majority Rule*, a groundbreaking study which proved that for all of his talk about "individual rights," Locke believed that society is superior to the individual, and that the majority should be entrusted with maintaining individual freedom. In time, Kendall would revise considerably his ideas on Locke and majority rule, but unlike many conservatives, he remained a fervent majoritarian.

The next jolt Kendall received to his liberalism came during the controversy surrounding the Communist spy trials in the late 1940s and early 1950s. By this time a thoroughgoing anti-Communist, Kendall was shocked by the liberal expansion of "free speech" protected under the First Amendment to an almost meaningless level. The liberals seemed to be saying that society had no right to exclude from its ranks those who seek to overthrow it; in response to all this, memories of Spain may well have risen in his mind. Kendall was forced to reevaluate the corrosive skepticism at the heart of liberalism, a skepticism about man's ability to know truth and embody that truth in political institutions. He found himself a man of the Right.

The bulk of Kendall's mature career was taken up with his intensive study of the American political tradition. Academic orthodoxy, represented by Louis Hartz and his followers, insisted that America had always been liberal and buttressed its case by citing the equality doctrine of the Declaration of Independence and the so-called "natural rights" in the Bill of Rights. Against this thesis Kendall pointed out that the concept of equality was missing from the Constitution, and that the Bill of Rights was generally opposed and eventually

adopted largely as an act of conciliation. Far from establishing a plebiscitary democracy dominated by an activist president seeking to implement a "program," the Constitution clearly intended the legislature
to be supreme. Kendall argued that the liberals read into the minds
of the Framers intentions that they could not have had. The Constitution had been silent as to the relationship between the branches of
government, said Kendall, but from the beginning the Constitution
had been interpreted in the light of the "constitutional morality" put
forward in the *Federalist Papers*, a document he said had "biblical status" in the American political tradition.

Kendall's reading of the *Federalist Papers* and the "constitutional
morality" expounded by Publius may constitute his most lasting
achievement. The common interpretation of the Framers as modernists, heirs of Locke and Hobbes, who saw men as creatures of passion and erected a system that would set factions against each other,
according to Kendall is based on a shallow reading of the great documents of the Founding. Though Publius did want to frustrate dema-
gogically led "majority factions" from sweeping the legislature, and
did expect that a large republic, staggered elections, and other procedural methods would frustrate such factions, this accounts for only
part of Publius's vision. Citing passage after passage from the *Federalist Papers*, Kendall demonstrated that the legislature was to be made
up of virtuous men who were to arrive at the "deliberate sense of
the community." This "government by consensus," guided by a concern for the common good, would indeed be an expression of majority
rule, but it would be filtered through the virtuous representatives of
the people.

In the last years of Kendall's career, his interpretation of the American political tradition was strengthened by his reading of two scholars who had done pioneering work in restoring the practice of political
philosophy: Leo Strauss and Eric Voegelin. Kendall's contention that
the Framers were neither Lockeans nor self-seeking capitalists went
against the whole grain of the political science profession, locked as
it was (and still is) into the "behavioral" and quantitative studies bequeathed to it by positivism and pragmatism. Strauss and Voegelin
broke free from this positivist quagmire by showing that its roots lay
in the modernist refusal to accept metaphysical truth. Whereas the

classical-biblical worldview believed that man and society were bound to order themselves by the natural law, the modernists, beginning with Descartes and Machiavelli, denied a higher law and based their political ideas on the manipulation of men whom they saw as ruled only by their passions. Given these insights into the gulf separating the "ancients" from the "moderns," Kendall was able to show that the Framers were in fact continuous with the older, natural law tradition. After studying Strauss and Voegelin, Kendall declared that he had to reeducate himself. For a man who often discussed American institutions without referring to European history or the classical-biblical philosophical tradition, this was an act of genuine humility. It added a new dimension to his political thought.

Kendall's complex but powerfully argued understanding of the American political tradition lies behind the issues he confronts in *The Conservative Affirmation*. Kendall was not a book writer; his restlessness precluded that. But he was a brilliant essayist, zeroing in on a specific topic and applying to it his seemingly inexorable dialectical skills. The first part of the book contains seven interconnected essays, all of which hover around the challenge posed by what Kendall called the "Liberal Revolution." The second part consists of a selection of his book reviews. Not only do the reviews put some of his larger ideas "into action," but the review form, since it is necessarily short, frees Kendall from his dialectical style and allows him to employ more humor, irony, and—his special forte—textual analysis. Running throughout the book is Kendall's magnificent style. His serpentine sentences, stretching out and coiling back on themselves, with their multiple parentheses (often containing disclaimers he termed "verbal parachutes") and exhortations to the reader, are easily comprehended and convey the sense of a mind which is taking everything into account. Kendall's irrepressible persona is always present; he is the teacher taking his students on a guided tour. But far from being didactic, Kendall's style is warm and inviting. His diction modulates between the cultured language of a man immersed in European culture, and the laconic, storefront wisdom of his Oklahoma hometown. As one friendly critic put it, Kendall's language is "one part Edmund Spenser, one part Will Rogers." Kendall's style reflects the complexity of his thought and the contradictions of his character, but it is always coherent.

To some critics, however, Kendall's complexity and contradictions are incomprehensible: Kendall is a majoritarian who cherished "aristocratic" impediments to the popular will, an individualist who celebrated community, a dissenter who proclaimed the need for orthodoxy. Kendall was aware of the tensions in his analysis, but he asserted that they were *valid* tensions. One of the least noted aspects of Kendall's thought is his insistence that the perennial truths are paradoxical. In Chapter 6, "A Conservative Statement on Christian Pacifism," Kendall writes:

The mark of a mind civilized by our primarily Christian inheritance, and therefore pervaded through and through by *civility*—a term I take from Dr. Johnson—is its ability to entertain intellectually and experience emotionally a complex of propositions whose unity consists, difficult as the idea may be for some persons to grasp, in the very *tension* among them.

In one of the book reviews included in this volume Kendall deplores the liberal's "refusal to let the dilemmas [of American politics] drive him to those deeper levels of discourse on which contradictions are translated, as in the American political system so many contradictions are, into the tensions of meaningful paradox." If the mark of orthodoxy is the tension of opposites fusing into a wholeness, the heretic is one who wrenches part of the truth from its context and who will fanatically seek to impose his version of truth on others. In the terms of modern politics, the heretic is the ideologue.

The Conservative Affirmation upholds the American political tradition against the two enemies of society, the heretics and the barbarians. Kendall had no doubts as to the identity of the barbarians, those who threaten society from without: they are the agents of "World Communism." This was a plain fact to Kendall, learned from bitter experience and confirmed by reflection. The Liberal heretics, undermining society from within, were not representative of the American people, whom Kendall believed carried their tradition "in their hips"; they came from the ranks of the intellectuals, the "egg-heads" as he liked to call them (they are now known as the "New Class"). Kendall knew that it was the academics whose modernist premises gave the Liberal Revolution its intellectual gloss and respectability.

Imposing their spurious reading of the American heritage on a living tradition, denying the existence of public truth and hence sanctioning those who would destroy the institutions of a free people, these academics were part of an unprecedented *trahison des clercs*—the treason of the intellectuals. Put bluntly, the American people were being betrayed. Kendall saw the Conservatives as a counter-revolutionary force.

What was Kendall's conception of Conservatism? *The Conservative Affirmation* was published at a time when American conservatives were trying to establish their identity, and Kendall, with his passion for distinctions and clarity, was bent on providing his own definition. In doing so, he occasionally indulges in a bit of posturing, twitting Russell Kirk, M. Stanton Evans, or Frank Meyer—for not being Willmoore Kendall. But the criteria he sets down for a relevant, non-ideological conservatism remain sound. The true conservative must defend his own political order; in this country, he must be an *American* conservative first, loyal to the political system constructed at the "Philadelphia Convention." The danger of "literary" conservatism is that it can become a paper tradition, extolling nostalgically some old order, but having little direct relevance to the raging battle that imperils American society. While Kendall doubted the importance of Edmund Burke for American conservatives on these grounds, in practice he admitted that Burke's understanding of the nature of social change and the ideological problems posed by the French Revolution, was the touchstone of conservatism. He insisted that a conservative could not be a "doctrinaire," committed to some abstract idea of individual "rights," the free market, or even limited government. Such abstractions could not be the foundation of a philosophical conservatism because they are too narrow and tend toward creating their own ideology. Kendall himself remained remarkably free from ideology.

The Liberal Revolution made its first inroads as early as the 1860s and 1870s, according to Kendall, but Conservatives have only slowly and fitfully become aware of the assault on the American tradition. Above all, the Liberal Revolution is based on the *egalitarian* principle which is not satisfied with equality of opportunity in a society governed by just laws, but must *make* people equal, levelling all natural differences. Like all modern ideological revolutions, it must be a "perpetual" revolution, since it cannot rest until a utopian equality is achieved. The only instrument capable of bringing about the Liberal Revolution, Kendall concludes, is the omnipotent state.

It is over the nature of the American political system that the Liberals have been concentrating their attack, Kendall believes, since their egalitarian program has been frustrated by the "deadlock" brought on by a recalcitrant Congress. Impatient to enact their agenda, the Liberals have favored a strong, activist Executive branch (president and bureaucracy), and have sought to abolish such "aristocratic" and "anti-democratic" institutions as the filibuster, the seniority system in congressional committees, and the electoral college. In making presidential elections "the central ritual of American politics," Liberals have tried to bypass a legislative body composed of men who are more focused on the concrete needs and expectations of their constituents. Kendall's chapter on "The Two Majorities in American Politics" is a magisterial defense of the "Madisonian system," that bulwark against the growth of demagogic "majority factions." The presidential majority, Kendall notes, has been engrafted onto the system set up by the Framers, and it tends to seek a "mandate" for an ideological program. Presidential candidates "talk about nothing" since they pour out vague and "pleasant-sounding maxims," while Congressmen must be responsive to "structured communities . . . involving numberless, highly complex face-to-face hierarchical relations among individuals." Kendall also counselled resistance against the recurrent pleas for making the parties more ideologically distinct: traditionally, the Congressman comes to Washington without a program, seeking that "deliberate sense of the community" which is guided by a devotion to the common good.

In the light of recent events, Kendall's confidence in the innate conservatism of Congress may seem misplaced. Paying little attention to economics, Kendall was not aware that the redistributionist welfare state has created innumerable special interest groups— Madison would have called them "factions"—dividing every constituency into blocks of voters, many of whom will press for government programs favorable to themselves, while at the same time deploring the ballooning federal bureaucracy. Ironically, the election of Ronald Reagan may signify the reversal of the system as Kendall saw it: since Congressmen perpetually "buy" votes from special interests, the American public chose a president who could "rise above" such considerations and make the hard decisions needed to curb the size of government. Nonetheless, Kendall's essential argument retains its analytical power. The "aristocratic" institutions are fully intact (Liberals are even finding a use for the filibuster), and are under less challenge now than they were twenty years ago. The presidential elections have indeed become the "central ritual of American politics," and have generated head-shaking over their shallow, Madison Avenue-style campaign tactics. And the Congress, despite its incontinence when it comes to the welfare state, has not pursued directly socialist policies; proposals for a nationalized health service, for instance, have gone nowhere.

Yet if Liberal programs have suffered a loss of credibility, the prevailing climate of ideas is still permeated by the egalitarian ethos which Kendall identified as the source of the Liberal Revolution. The engine that drives political egalitarianism is ultimately a radical skepticism about man's capacity to know truth. The core of Liberalism is thus the idea of the "Open Society," where "all questions are open questions." In his chapter on the "Social Contract," Kendall traces the roots of Liberalism to the modern rejection of a higher law which can be known by human reason; society thus becomes governed by laws and regulations which have no other basis than in the fact that they are willed. But the "Open Society" can only end as a totalitarian state where the ideologues impose "their" truth upon others. Kendall sees the Liberal Revolution as an attack against the foundations of political order. In what may be the central passage of *The Conservative Affirmation*, Kendall writes:

> All political societies, all peoples, but especially I like to think our political society, this *"people of the United States,"* is founded upon what political philosophers call a *consensus*; that is, a hard core of shared beliefs. Those beliefs that the people share are what defines its character as a political society, what, above all perhaps, expresses its understanding of itself as a political society, of its role and responsibility in history, of its very destiny . . .
> "We," cries the people of the United States at the very moment

of its birth . . . "hold these *truths*." That is, "we" believe there is such a thing as Truth, believe that the particular truths of which Truth is made up are discoverable by man's reason and thus by our reason, recognize *these* truths as those to which our reason and that of our forebears have led us, and agree with one another to *hold* these truths—that is, to cherish them as ours, to hand them down in their integrity to our descendants, to defend them against being crushed out of existence by enemies from without or corrupted out of all recognition by the acids of skepticism and disbelief working from within.

The modern champion of the "Open Society" is John Stuart Mill, and it is no coincidence that Mill's brand of "classical liberalism" evolved into the egalitarian liberalism of the twentieth century.

In "Conservatism and the 'Open Society,' " Kendall forces Mill's premises to their horrifying logical conclusion and indicates that the Supreme Court has in recent decades gone a long way toward making that state of affairs a reality. By twisting the "establishment" and speech clauses of the First Amendment out of the context intended by the Framers (who, Kendall says, were not well disposed towards adopting the Bill of Rights in the first place and, anyway, left the states free to curb speech or establish religion at their discretion), the Court has denied any public truth, in effect revoking the American people's understanding of their tradition. Kendall is thus the great enemy of "pluralism," insofar as that catch-all word has come to mean the inadmissibility of recognizing our national identity as that of a Christian, self-governing people. Kendall dared to believe that the people, operating through their elected representatives, had the right to declare some group or action "un-American," and remained one of the few articulate defenders of that much-maligned body, the House Un-American Activities Committee.

It was the question of the right of the United States government to exclude and punish Communists and others dedicated to subverting the American political order that caused the near civil war over the efforts of Senator Joseph McCarthy, Kendall avers. The anger and hysteria which surrounded and continues to surround the Senator from Wisconsin stems not from disagreement over his tactics or character, the nature of the Communist threat, or even the struggle between Executive and Legislative branches: it originated when Liberals and Conservatives clashed over the question of whether heretics can be excommunicated—that is, literally barred from political communion. Kendall considers it a national tragedy that the Liberals shifted the debate onto the "clear and present danger" test; it obscures the more fundamental problem of political orthodoxy.

Kendall was profoundly troubled about the future of a society which could no longer generate a loyalty to its basic traditions, traditions that men would fight and die for. In "A Conservative Statement on Christian Pacifism," an essay replete with significance for the current "peace" movement, with its high moral (and often overtly Christian) rhetoric, Kendall uses the paradox of Christian love to show that we must be willing to stand up to our enemies. An entity, whether a human being or a society, cannot will its own destruction: that is the heresy of suicide. You cannot will the ends of a political society— including its right to maintain itself in existence—without granting it the means to defend itself. Resistance against evil is a duty, as even most liberals will admit in the case of Hitler, when they see evil for what it is. Kendall boldly proclaims the paradox: we must fight our enemies in order to love them. He writes:

> Peace is something waged for, fought for; and the reason our world today may well find itself forced to wage war again is not that it cannot rise to pacifist love of peace, but that it loves peace really, and knows it to be inseparable from the obligation to maintain order.

For the West in our time the major force of evil stems from World Communism, as it is driven by the Soviet war machine. Without the will to resist the agents of disorder, a will which can only arise from an affirmation of a just moral and political order, the West will bring about its own extinction.

Willmoore Kendall made that affirmation, without apology, at a time when his fellow intellectuals abandoned themselves to a solipsistic fantasy world which affirmed nothing. In a book review included in this volume, Kendall contended that the intellectuals who see the crisis of the West and yet refuse to make an affirmation inevitably end by telling themselves, and the American people, comfortable lies. The lies may not be deliberate, but their effect is real, and entails "the resultant rejection of the role of the intelligent and courageous man in history—that is, the careful and responsible weighing of the goods and evils among which man is free to choose. For to reject that role is to refuse to be free." Willmoore Kendall possessed the courage of a free man.

Gregory Wolfe
Intercollegiate Studies Institute
April, 1985

Preface

The business of this book is rather to identify the "Conservative affirmation" than to affirm it, rather to situate it on the map of American politics than to defend it, rather to render it intelligible than to win converts for it.

The writer does, to be sure, affirm Conservatism. He spends a good deal of his time (on debate platforms, in the editorial columns of a certain magazine, anywhere *except* in the college or university classroom in which he earns his keep) defending it; he wishes there *were* a book that would start sinners down the sawdust trail that leads to the Conservative affirmation, and may, someday, try to write such a book. But this is not that book. The reader will find passages and arguments in it which, if they struck home, might well move him to the "Right" in our politics. But those passages and those arguments are not there for that purpose. They are there because, as I believe, they further the book's central purpose, which (I repeat) is to identify the Conservative affirmation, situate it, and render it intelligible.

This book is, in consequence, quite different from those with which it is destined to rub Dewey-decimal shoulders (because they also, in one way or another, answer the question "What is Conservatism?"). And a few words are perhaps in order, here at the beginning, as to how and why it is different:

A. This book, unlike at least the other academic (that is, non-senatorial) books I have in mind, avoids or tries to avoid the charge: "Sir, your procedure appears to be the following: You start out from the fact that you *feel* yourself a Conservative; your Conservatives are merely the people you find saying or writing things in response to which your own heart goes pit-a-pat; your Conservative creed is merely *your* creed; your Conservatives are, so to speak, a club, in which you admit or blackball members according as they can or cannot reproduce your pronunciation of 'shibboleth.' " (The procedure, let us note in passing, can and has been reversed—by identifying as "Conservative" those with whom you are in deepest disagreement.) I, by contrast, begin my search for Conservatives where my greatest teachers have taught me that a political inquiry ought to begin, namely, down in the political market-place—where Americans are disputing the issues that *they* deem decisive as regards the future character and destiny of our political society. My Conservatives are, I like to think, "given" to me by the realities of American politics; my own agreement or disagreement with them is not in point. If I do happen to agree with them, that is because of a choice I have made among alternatives that I am not myself in a position to affect. To put it otherwise, I assume in this book that rightful ownership of the label "Conservative" has been, and will continue to be, decided in another place and independently of any mere book writer's personal preferences (and—dare I add?—idiosyncrasies and unbought graces of life). In a pinch, indeed, I'll just give up on the word "Conservative," and say to some of my friends, "You can have it, to fight over as you like." But the realities of American politics will remain just what they were before that gesture of humility and renunciation on my part.

B. The "definition" of Conservatism implicit in this book is, in consequence, somewhat less literary than that to be found in those other books; people can, in fact most people do, join my Conservatives without writing a book, or even an article, at all. My Conservatives are men who have taken a *stand*, on issues that are a) important, and b) relevant—that is "up." Indeed, not the least of my quarrels with those other books I have in mind is that they are so preoccupied with what writing-men have written that they overlook, or give wide berth to, the issues that are "up"—are in the process of actually being decided in a way that will affect events—and tacitly suggest that Conservatism does or conceivably could do likewise.

C. This book is written, as those books clearly were not, in the belief that it is idle to speak of Conservatism without at least tacit adjectival reference to a particular time and place (wherefore *this* writer would always write "American Conservatism," *not* "Conservatism in America," and "The Anglo-American Conservative Mind 1750(?)-1950(?)," and *not* "The Conservative Mind"). I do this out of the conviction that in any given time and place Conservatives are those who are defending an established order against those who seek to undermine or transform it; and that, *in the absence of urgent and express reasons to the contrary*, the words "Conservatism" and "Conservative" should not be used in any other meaning. I make no sense, that is to say, of calling "Conservative" the man who takes a dim view of his country's established institutions, feels something less than at home with its way of life as it actually lives it, finds it difficult to identify himself with the political and moral principles on which it has acted through its history, dislikes or views with contempt the generality of the kind of people his society produces, and—above all perhaps —dissociates himself from its Founders, or at least holds them at arms' length. Such a man may be the better or nobler or wiser for all this dim-viewing and the yearning-away-from; he may be right as rain. But I fail to see where you can get by calling him a Conservative (or where he gets by calling himself one). The Conservatism of this book is, then, Conservative in the sense just indicated; we may discern some amount of continuity or overlap, as regards stands on issues, between it and other "Conservat*isms*," but that is something we establish only by documenting the relationship, and not in any other way. Such continuity or overlap is an interesting fact to take note of (and we can indeed learn much about any particular "Conservatism" by noting its continuity with other "Conservatisms") but it is not the continuity or overlap that makes the "Conservatism" of a given time and place "Conservative."

D. The American Conservatism of this book, unlike that of those other books, has accordingly no axe to grind for "aristocracy," no quarrel (any more than had the authors of the *Federalist*) with America's commitment to "democracy," no flirtation with the idea that the way to have a government of laws is to somehow get men out of the picture. It views the pre-1789 John Adams with suspicion not reverence, shies off of vast reaches of the argument of Burke's *Reflections on the Revolution in France,* and deplores the pre-*Federalist* writings of even Alexander Hamilton. With Madison and Hamilton, and with the subsequent American political tradition as a whole, it shares the conviction that the United States, because of the qualities of its people, must and should be governed by the "deliberate sense of the community." Indeed, its objection to Liberal proposals for the "reform" of our political system is precisely this: Those proposals would (by eliminating deliberation) render impossible the expression of that deliberate sense—or, for that matter, any sense that would be, properly speaking, that of the community. And, *pace* James Burnham, the Conservatism of the book can—and for these same reasons—do no business with Calhoun. Or Babbitt. Or More. Its highest political loyalty, in fine, is to the institutions and way of life bequeathed to us by the Philadelphia Convention.

E. This book, unlike those other books, does not, I like to think, trip itself up over the frequently-alleged preoccupation of Conservatives with preventing "change"—that is "change" as such. Its Conservatism distinguishes between "change" directed at the *development and perfection* of our heritage as *that which it is,* and "change" calculated to transform that heritage into *that which it is not;* and far from opposing the former, stands forth as its champion. To put the point otherwise (I shall require a further book in order to drive it home), this book's Conservatism opposes not "change" but "change" in certain *directions* that it condemns on grounds of inherited principle—inherited principle, however, which it values not merely or even primarily because it is inherited, but because it is the product of rational deliberation moving from sound political and moral premises.

F. This book, accordingly, fixes a kind of attention upon the *flat opposition* between American Conservatism and contemporary American Liberalism that, as I believe, is entirely missing from most of those other books. This is to say that the issues that are important for Conservatives are those that have been forced upon them by Liberals demanding certain "changes" that would involve the substitution of novel principles for inherited principles—relativism for (if you like) "absolutism"; government-imposed egalitarianism for (as I put it in Chapter One) equality; the "open society" for the kind of society that we in America (acting upon our interpretation of the First Amendment and not Mr. Justice Hugo Black's) have in fact always maintained. (That is, a society seen as embodying a public truth, which it defends against barbarians outside its confines and heretics within them.) And the fact that these are not the issues that figure prominently in those other books (insofar as they project themselves in terms of issues at all), has a quite simple explanation—namely that those other books are wrong.

G. This book, unlike those other books, accepts without protest or complaint the fact that American Conservatism, though principled, is not (*pace* Frank Meyer, upon whom the distinction seems sometimes to be lost) doctrinaire and, in the absence of some sea-change in the American mind and the American spirit, is not going to become doctrinaire. It has sworn no vow of absolute fidelity either to free enterprise á la von Mises, or to a certain list of "rights" á la John Chamberlain, or to a certain holy trinity of government functions á la (I must mention him again, for he is a great though lovable sinner) Frank Meyer, or to revolving-door mistrust of political authority as such á la Frank Chodorov.

H. This book, written as it is by a practicing political scientist whose field is political theory, and larded as it is with theses that have seen exposure in professional journals, invites judgment by harsher standards than most, at least, of the other books: its approach is avowedly theoretical, and as and where it blunders it should *not* be let off lightly—on, e.g., the grounds that one must not expect too much from, say, a historian doubling in brass (like Russell Kirk); or from a young man, even a very brilliant young man, having his first go at these matters (like Stanton Evans); or from a popularizer (like Clinton Rossiter). This goes especially for the book's subordinating itself, or failing to subordinate itself, to the norms that, since the early days in Greece, have been understood to govern political discourse projected on the level of theory:

do not suppress evidence, do not place reliance on rhetoric in lieu of demonstration, do not stack the cards, do anticipate and attempt to deal with at least obvious objections to a given line of argument, do use terms univocally, do take your opponents' case at its strongest and, preferably, as it is put by its most distinguished defender. And, since duties do carry with them correlative rights, the author has claimed unabashedly the right of working the reader a bit harder than do the authors of those other books.

I. This book, unlike those other books, treats the relation between American Conservatism and "religion" as *problematic;* and in doing so it merely imitates American Conservatism itself. The problem, put briefly, is this: the United States is—has been down to now anyhow—a Christian society governed, or rather self-governed, under a secular Constitution; nothing, short of the sea-change I mentioned a moment ago, is likely to deprive Judaeo-Christian religious beliefs of the special status, approximating that of a public truth, that they enjoy within it. But, also, nothing short of such a sea-change is likely, in the forseeable future, to gain for them a *more* privileged status than they now enjoy. Attempts to resolve the religious-society-secular-Constitution tension in the United States, in either the one direction or the other, are not only divisive, but contrary to the American tradition itself. They do a poor service *both* to America and American Conservatism who say and write things that tend to read out of the ranks of Conservatives men in whose hearts Judaeo-Christian religious teachings evoke no response; as, also, do those who say and write things that suggest that religious men must somehow divest themselves of, or abstract from, their deepest commitments in order to make sense as Conservatives. This, also, is an area in which doctrinairism is an un-American activity.

J. This book, unlike those other books, is open to the charge that it wrongly attributes to American Conservatism some special mission with respect to World Communism, a peculiar point of view from which to observe and cognize the World Communist movement, perhaps even a "monopoly" of "tough" anti-Communism. Such a charge might well come from either of two directions —from, on the one hand, those who pick quarrels with "my" Conservatives on the grounds that they are not anti-Communist enough, and, on the other hand, those who exaggerate the incidence of meaningful and determined anti-Communism among Liberals (and so deny that there is any issue between Conservatives and Liberals in this area). My reply to both—a reply that the reader of this book will learn to expect from me—is: *Keep an eye on the Congress of the United States,* with regard first to its continuing harassment of the Executive on behalf of more vigorous policies and commitments in the struggle against Communism, and with regard second to the Congress' manifest restlessness over the years about "containment" and "coexistence," and with regard third to the divisions *within* Congress on such points—which divisions, with rare exceptions, follow Conservative-Liberal lines. In any case, one does not write a book entitled *Conservatism in America,* as Clinton Rossiter managed to do, without noticing a relation between Conservatism and anti-Communism that wants talking about.

The plan of the book is as follows: There is an initial block of chapters that might well have been isolated in a "Part One: The Conservative Affirmation in the American Market-Place." They deal, respectively, with egalitarianism and political reform as issues between contemporary American Conservatives and Liberals (Chapter One); the continuing issues between Congress and the Executive as issues between Conservatives and Liberals (Chapter Two); "McCarthyism" as an issue between Conservatives and Liberals (Chapter Three); and, as a sort of bridge to what follows and without, at that stage, explicit reference to the struggle between Conservatives and Liberals, with the issue of freedom of expression in the United States (Chapter Four).

There is then a chapter (Chapter Five) that I should like the reader to think of as standing by itself: as, in the terminology of my greatest teacher, the "center" of the book. It deals (on as I like to think the level of the Great Debate in political philosophy and with little specific reference to the *American* Conservative affirmation) with that one of the issues previously touched upon about which American Conservatives are least likely to be sure of the case for their position. (And least likely, in consequence, to under-stand themselves, and so least likely to be understood by their opponents.) Namely, the crucial issue of the "open society."

Then there is a brace of chapters (Chapters Six and Seven) which deal with two issues (pacifism, and the role of "consent" in politics) with respect to which American Conservatism is con-spicuously continuous and overlapping with the great tradition of the West.

In the final chapter (not I hope too presumptuously) I have brought together some thirty of the reviews I have written in re-cent years, including them on the assumption that one good way to understand the Conservative affirmation is to watch it in the give-and-take of political controversy among egg-heads.

WILLMOORE KENDALL

Los Angeles
February 3, 1963

Chapter 1

What Is Conservatism?

What, I ask, is Conservatism? Or, more concretely—since I write with an eye to present-day politics in the United States—what, to begin with, is contemporary, American Conservatism? [1]

The question, make no mistake about it, is "up"; people, American undergraduates especially, are wondering about it, as wonder they well may. Contemporary political journalism finds the terms "conservative" and "liberal" somehow indispensable, so that people encounter them now twenty times a day: [2] The coalition of Republicans and Democrats that struck down most of Mr. Kennedy's legislative program in the last session of Congress is a "conservative" coalition. Senator Byrd and Senator Goldwater are "conservatives," just as Senator Humphrey and Senator Douglas are "liberals." *National Review* is a "conservative" magazine, the *New Republic* a "liberal" magazine. Moreover, the journalists who employ the terms in question now do so unapologetically, and with what seems an easy confidence that their readers will understand by them what they mean by them.

[1] Note the two-fold implication that (a) Conservatism in contemporary America has something in common with "conservatism in general," but (b) is by no means necessarily the same thing as "conservatism in general." Again more concretely: we should expect a certain overlap between contemporary American Conservative principles and, say, Burke's principles—as also between Burke's principles and, say, those of the natural-law philosophers of the Middle Ages. But it is not easy to say how much or what kind of overlap, and the whole question has, in this writer's opinion, been a booby-trap for writers on contemporary American Conservatism —e.g., Russell Kirk, *The Conservative Mind* (Chicago: Henry Regnery, 1953) and Clinton Rossiter, *Conservatism in America* (New York: 2d ed. rev. 1962, Knopf).

[2] Not so, I think, in my own undergraduate days, when there were, quite simply, "radicals" and, so to speak, the rest of us. The present chapter should help make clear why new adjectives have become necessary in the interim.

That meaning, however, is certainly not to be found in any dictionary or encyclopedia;[3] nor, we may safely guess, could the writers who spend the terms as common coinage (or the readers who accept them) come up with definitions that they themselves would consider even marginally satisfactory. Nor can anyone with an ear for these things long remain unaware that there are difficulties about the terms, and that people, who generally tend to be very wise about the language they speak, sense those difficulties, especially what I believe to be the major difficulty. That is to say, Yes, Senator Goldwater is a "conservative" and Senator Humphrey, who does seem to disagree with Senator Goldwater pretty much all the time, is a "liberal"; that is easy, presumptively without difficulties, if only because these are the terms that these distinguished statesmen apply to themselves. And Yes, *National Review* is "conservative" and *New Republic* "liberal"; that also is easy, again because each of them applies the relevant term to itself but also because—for that seems to help—they so identify each other. But what, most people still have to ask, am I? What is *The New York Times,* which *National Review* excoriates as the *fons et origo* of the "Liberal propaganda line," and which Professor Rossiter, apparently without a bat of an eyelash, describes as a "great conservative newspaper"? What is Senator Thomas Dodd, who is said to owe his seat in the Senate to the labor (i.e., Liberal) vote in Connecticut and yet, when he speaks on foreign policy, receives "hero-treatment" in the editorial columns of *National Review?* What of the average newspaper reader, who can only say to himself that he seems to agree with the "conservatives" about some things and with the "liberals" about others?

All this adds up to a "major difficulty," as I see it, for the following reason: Current usage of the terms "conservative" and "liberal" clearly implies (a) that there is a *line,* on one side of which we may fairly expect to find conservatives who are consistently "conservative," standing over against, on the other side,

---

[3] Edition after edition of the *Encyclopaedia Britannica* appears with no article on "Conservatism," though the present writer has documentary evidence that four persons have been invited to write such articles in the past decade and a half.

Liberals who are consistently "liberal," and therefore (b) that the line exists, and falls where it does fall, for *good reason.* It is, in consequence, an intelligible line and makes sense as a line (the words as currently used don't make sense unless that line makes sense). Yet one runs across no one who seems able to say where the line is and why and how it does make sense. So, I repeat, people are wondering, and, paradoxically, the more not the less because they feel fairly certain they can say, and say with assurance, which side of the line *some* things belong on. And my purpose in the present chapter can best be stated in just that context: I am going to try to say where in contemporary America that line is, and why and how it makes sense, as I confidently believe it does. And I believe it does because I believe the people who are being called "conservatives" do have something in common that can be put into words, as also do the people who are being called "liberals." (The Senator Dodd case, the case of the man who really does agree with the "conservatives" about some things and with the "liberals" about others, is of course a spurious difficulty. We do not despair of drawing a line between, e.g., Catholicism and Protestantism because there are persons who agree with the Catholics about everything except remarriage-after-divorce and birth-control. We merely note that they are all mixed up, and get on with the job.)

The present writer is not, of course, the first to notice that current usage of the terms "conservative" and "liberal" presupposes a "line," and so poses the question, "Where exactly is it?" Indeed, one could assemble quite an anthology of recent comments whose authors attempt, in one way or another, to dispel the attendant mystery. I have before me, for example, one from Gettysburg's most renowned Gentleman Farmer, the burden of which is that Yes, current usage does presuppose a line, but that line is in fact nonexistent and we should, therefore, abandon the usage: "We should discard such shopworn terms as 'liberal' and 'conservative' . . . I have never yet found anyone who could convincingly explain his own definition of these political classifications." I have another from Mr. Frank Meyer, the burden of which is that Yes, the usage presupposes a line, that such a line

3

does in fact exist, and that it is religious in character. "The Christian understanding of the nature and destiny of man," he writes, "is always and everywhere what Conservatives strive to conserve." And still another, with that same burden, from a colleague of Mr. Meyer's: "The Conservative believes ours is a God-centered universe; that man's purpose is to shape his life to the patterns of order proceeding from the Divine Center of Life." [4]

I have several—from Professor Ludwig von Mises, for instance, or adepts of his like Mr. Murray Rothbard or Miss Ayn Rand—the burden of which is Yes, there *is* a line, and it divides the sheep from the goats, the virtuous from the wicked, but in economics (or, in Miss Rand's remarkable variant of the position, in morals). On the one hand we have those who put their faith in the free market, in free enterprise, in individualism; on the other are those who put their faith in interventionism, in welfarism, in collectivism, in statism. Or, as Miss Rand put it on television some months ago, on the one hand those who believe in competition, in self-reliance, in each for himself and the devil take the hindmost, and on the other, those who believe in the "slave morality" of altruism, in rewarding the weak and the shiftless at the expense of the strong and the industrious. Or, as any of this school might be found stating it, on the one hand those who believe in freedom, on the other those who merely pretend to, that is, pay lipservice to freedom but forward the purposes of unfreedom, of "our enemy the state."

I have yet others from those—Professor Clinton Rossiter, for instance, in one of his many moods—who take the position: Yes, there is a line, but it is, let's face it, faint and zigzaggy. The "conservative" is to a large extent a "liberal," the "liberal" to a large extent a "conservative"; the "conservative" is "pessimistic" about reforms calculated to improve the lot of men, tends to think such reforms won't work, while the "liberal" is "optimistic" about such reforms, thinks they will work. "Conservatives," however, differ in the degree of their pessimism, and liberals differ in the degree of their optimism, so that, Rossiter adds in his ingeni-

---

[4] For both quotations see the exchange in *National Review*, "Do-It-Yourself Conservatism," Vol. XII, No. 4, pp. 57-59.

ously confusing way, the line between them is occupied simultaneously by the most optimistic of the pessimists, and the most pessimistic of the optimists—both of whom, one gathers, might very well, and with strict accuracy, be called *either* a "conservative" or "liberal." [5] I have yet others from those—again Professor Rossiter for instance, but in another of his many moods—who take the position: Yes, there is a line, and it separates those who believe in keeping things as they are, in the old ways, in the wisdom of the fathers, on the one hand, and those who want to change things, to pick and choose among the old ways, to subordinate the wisdom of the fathers to the wisdom of the present generation.[6]

I have a great many—from, for example, speakers at the 1962 Rally of the Young Americans for Freedom—that at least *seem* to take the position: Yes, there is a line, and it separates the tough and genuine anti-Communists from the supporters of postwar American foreign policy. It separates those who want to liberate the world from Communism by utterly destroying Communism, from those who want to contain Communism or coexist with it. It separates those who are willing to risk nuclear warfare rather than permit further advance by the World Communist Empire, and those who are determined that no such risk shall be incurred. I have a great many, too, from spokesmen of those millions of Americans who take the position (Alas! for their task is a veritable task of Sisyphus): There *must* be a line, and it *must* be the line that divides Republicans from Democrats, and we are going to find it at whatever cost, let the Heavens fall!

If, then, people are wondering, they have good reason to wonder, since even those supposedly "in the know" about such matters—I have included in my rundown of the various positions an ex-President, the leading academic authority on Conservatism and several persons whom the *Times* would describe, not inaccurately, as outstanding Conservative spokesmen—come up with mutually exclusive specifications of the supposed line. Not only cannot all of them be right, no *two* of them can be right. And,

[5] Rossiter, *op. cit.*, p. 13.
[6] Rossiter, *op. cit.*, p. 9.

worse still, if we leave aside the Republican-Democratic specification (which we may fairly dismiss as silly) and fix attention on
the other specifications, we may well feel that each of them,
though perhaps partially right, or right as far as it goes, leaves
a good deal unexplained.

Take, for example, the notion that the Conservative is the man
who believes in a God-centered universe, which we get from a
writer who is by general consent a leading spokesman of contemporary American Conservatism. Yet we know, as he must
know too, (a) that at least some leading spokesmen of contemporary American Conservatism happen to be unbelievers, and (b)
that many *anti*-Conservatives, that is Liberals, are deeply convinced Christians; and we wish he had explained how, on his
showing, that can be. Or take the notion that Conservatism is
one and the same thing with tough anti-Communism—what,
then, do we do with Professor Sidney Hook, among the toughest,
surely, of tough anti-Communists, but surely also a leading American Liberal. We could, if we had time, show the inadequacy of
each of the other there-is-a-line positions, and with equal ease;
and we are obliged to conclude that each of them must be, in
Plato's sense, a *vulgar* opinion. That is, an unreflective opinion,
even though it may come from a very highly-situated mouth.
Each of them, like Plato's *doxoi*, is demonstrably an oversimpli-
fication, which is to say that the correct opinion, when we find
it, must take into account a more complex and inclusive set of
facts. We do not have to conclude, however, that we have been
wasting our time. For that same Plato, who remains our greatest
teacher in this area, teaches us that the first step toward clarity,
on *any* topic, is to get the vulgar opinions in front of you, and
start out from them in an attempt somehow to seize on the heart
of the matter. And that you are likely to get yourself pointed
toward the heart of the matter by seizing upon something fairly
obvious that all the vulgar opinions, or most of them, overlook.
That, I feel sure, is the case with the topic before us. For all our
market-place commentators, except Professor Rossiter, seem to
forget that the line in question is a *line of battle,* a line of battle moreover *in contemporary American politics* and a line of

battle between two sets of *combatants,* each fighting to *defeat* the other—which, read out in a little more detail, is what the current usage (remember my warning that people generally are wise about their language) clearly implies. Moreover, current usage implies (as we have already begun to notice in an earlier paragraph) that there is a *battle in progress,* even a *war in progress,* one that is about something sufficiently intelligible to all the combatants to seem worth fighting over. Drawing the line, then, if we are willing to be really attentive to our metaphor (which even Rossiter is not) is a matter not merely of locating some point on the line at which the battle is raging, but also of locating the line *in its entire extension.* And furthermore it is a matter not merely of locating the line, but of understanding it —and that includes finding out how the war got started, and what actually will have been decided when the war is over and one side has won.

And we begin, properly instructed by the metaphor, to see what is the matter with (Rossiter apart) our other unreflectives. They are fixing attention on a single sector of a line that they do not treat seriously as a line; they can at most help us see the battle-line as it looks when you are on the ground, on one side —where you may mistake the skirmish over Hill 16 for this week's entire engagement, or this week's engagement for the whole war. What you need, the metaphor implies, is dependable intelligence reports from *all along the line*—reports, preferably, with some historical depth to them plus, if possible, some projection into the future (and, I repeat, some attention at least to the war aim or aims of the respective opponents). Rossiter is the exception; he does embrace the full metaphor, but only, in one mood, to explain the line away, and, in the other mood, to give us what is certainly a phoney war issue. For Conservatism as we shall see cannot be mere opposition to change. If that were so, we should never find Conservatives proposing change—as, according to my intelligence reports, they are doing today in some sectors of the line of battle.

My thesis, then, is that the line we are looking for is a battle-line, and that that line stretches from the bottom of the chart of American politics all the way to the top, passing through pretty much every issue that enters into our politics. My further thesis is that the battle-line is a battle-line in a war actually in progress, between *Liberal* troops on the *left* of the line (note that the usage on which we are depending is very clear that the line divides a Left from a Right)—and *Conservative* troops on the *right* of the line. My further thesis, based on what I have called intelligence data with historical depth, is that the war began as a war of aggression, launched from positions that for good reason are not visible on the chart, by the Liberals (or, more accurately, by little unrelated bands of Liberals which did not, to begin with, have a name and certainly not *that* name), who began, at some moment, to make inroads into territory to which the people we now see on the right of the line had held undisputed title for a century or more. My further thesis is that the attacking forces, after driving a big salient into the victims' territory in the 1860's and 1870's (emancipation of the slaves in the name of equality, the post-Civil War "equality" amendments to the Constitution), rolled pretty much to a stop at a certain moment—whether because they ran out of steam, or because they ran out of supplies, or because they ran into stubborn resistance, it is not easy to say. All we can say is that there were subsequent offensives by different and unrelated bands of aggressors (e.g., the various movements for expanding the suffrage, and for "democratizing" the political system in the name of "political equality"), who until a fairly recent date did not think of themselves as an army properly speaking, and certainly did not think of themselves as engaged in a war properly speaking (indeed that kind of thinking, even on the American Left, is no older than the second decade of this century). While the attacks did continue, and did drive new salients at various points from bottom to top of the chart, I am saying, even the brightest and most knowledgeable military observers did not think of the attackers as, even potentially, an army—or of their small conquests as other than shall we say landgrabs, analogous to taking land from the Indians for homesteading purposes. Never was the war thought of as analogous to—so the Liberals now think of themselves—a wave of the future, powered by something called high principle. Bringing the small bands together into a disciplined army, an army conscious of itself as staging a general advance along an extensive front, with a common service of supply and a common general staff, has been, even on the Left, a matter of concern for only the last ten to twenty-five or thirty years.

As for the forces on the Right, their history, for reasons that you would now for the most part easily guess for yourselves, roughly parallels that of the attackers—though always with a very considerable time-lag. (Many of them, it seems, actually supported that earliest aggression—government-enforced emancipation of the slaves—back in the 1860's; many others appear to have been indifferent or what we fashionably call apathetic; only a handful, the Southerners, put up a genuine resistance, and they, as far as that original salient was concerned, were easily not to say ignominiously overcome.) For many decades, it seems safe to say, the men on the Right could not get it through their heads that any major attack was shaping up. Each enemy thrust from off the chart met stubborn resistance to be sure, so that many were completely repelled and even the most successful (e.g., woman's suffrage) had to inch its way to its most advanced position. But the resisters were so-to-speak irregulars, self-recruited, self-armed, and far far too busy *resisting*, in their respective localities, to be concerning themselves with events elsewhere on the chart. That, even as recently as ten years ago, was in strict accuracy still the state of affairs on the Right. The Rightists were engaging the enemy in numerous sectors. They were, sector by sector, for the most part preventing him from making any significant advance, and forcing him, in any case, to expend energies out of all proportion to his gains. But even the Rightists' most experienced and far-seeing commanders (Senator Byrd, Senator McCarran, and Senator McCarthy, for example) were confining their attention to the attackers in their particular sector, conducting you might say their own little local wars against them, and thought of them also as conducting their own little local wars. If, therefore, an advance threatened or occurred at some point further along the line (which, for that matter, they were

9

not thinking of as a line) it was, each could say to himself, none of his business. Even today, moreover, the forces on the Right constitute an army only in the loosest sense of the word. All we can speak of is an increasing realization among them that they are indeed engaged in a general war, against a disciplined and battle-wise enemy, with crystal clear war-aims and a grim determination to win. On the Right there are as yet no war aims; there is merely *resistance*. Against what? I weigh my words: Against a full-scale revolution, which most Rightists continue to mistake for a series of local rebellions, or, to repeat my earlier phrase, local landgrabs; they continue to mistake it for that although the enemy now makes no secret of the revolutionary and integrated character of his enterprise. He does, clearly, have a general staff that concerns itself with all the engagements being fought, and does show profound awareness of what the war, when it is over, will have decided—that is, what exactly the war is about. What is it about? I say, about the question, Is the destiny of America the Liberal Revolution, or is it the destiny envisaged for it by the Founders of our Republic? Just that.

Let me now drop my metaphor, and spell out what I have been saying in terms of the political market-place, in terms of what actually is and has been going on in recent years in American politics. We stand, I am saying, in the presence of a Liberal *Revolution;* that revolution is a revolution *sensu stricto,* and one that means business. Its purpose is to establish in America, in Machiavelli's phrase, *new modes and orders.* Conservatism, I am saying, is first and foremost the *resistance* to that revolution. And the line that divides Conservatism from Liberalism, the line that is implied in current usage of the terms "conservative" and "liberal," is the line that passes through all the battles and skirmishes about this or that issue of public policy, that the resisters are today fighting to prevent further advances by the Revolution. To put it in slightly different terms: The Liberals are the supporters of the Liberal Revolution, the Conservatives are its opponents— not necessarily its conscious opponents, but still its opponents: those who, for whatever reason articulate or inarticulate, do things that block the Revolution, or that frustrate and harass its leaders, and say to it, "Thus far perhaps but no further," or say to it, as, I repeat, in some cases I believe the resisters *are* beginning to say to it (e.g., with respect to Liberal domination of the universities), "This advance on your part we intend to reverse; here on the line we intend not merely to resist but to drive you back." That I believe to be the correct answer to the question "What is Conservatism in contemporary America?"—which besides being correct, both justifies current usage of our two key terms, *and* makes ample room for the partial answers put forward by our unreflectives.[7] They speak as they do because they tend to concentrate upon a single issue, while the war, which the current usage recognizes, is being fought over many issues.

I know, I think, what the reader must be thinking by now. That my metaphor—with its armies that don't know they are armies, its attackers and resisters, its salients and penetrations—has turned into a riddle, and that it's high time I got started reading him the riddle instead of milking the metaphor. He must be thinking, too, that while he has heard of Liberals he never before heard of a Liberal Revolution, and has his doubts whether any such thing exists. Or again, that while he has heard of Liberals, and perhaps even known some Liberals, he has never thought of them as particularly warlike or bloodthirsty, or as particularly bent upon invading and occupying territory to which other people hold clear title, or as particularly under orders from a general staff somewhere. On the contrary, he must be thinking, the Liberals are notorious for their love of Peace, for their concern for the lot of their fellow men, for their desire for everyone to be happy and well-fed and well-educated and, above all, *free*—to say nothing of their devotion to what everyone agrees to be the *highest* "values" of the American community, namely, "liberty" and "equality." And all that apart, he must be thinking, why all this talk about the so-called line of battle being 'way over to the Left of that chart, with the so-called resisters still occupying pretty much all their original territory? Has the au-

---

[7] Except Rossiter, who is so to speak beyond justifying.

thor never heard of the New Deal and its social gains (note, however, the military sound of that word "gains"), of the Fair Deal, of the New Frontier and of how popular our young and handsome President is (and of all the things he would do if only it weren't for the obstructions thrown temporarily in his way by that "rural-dominated" Congress of ours—which obstructions he will, of course, ultimately find a way to circumvent, so that there will be yet further "gains" for the Left). It would be surprising, indeed, if the reader were at this point thinking anything else since, let me concede it at once, my war has been poorly reported to date—not only in those newspapers and journals and books that we should expect to try to conceal the continuous and cumulative defeat of the Left in American politics, but also in those from which we should expect a tendency in the opposite direction. (It is, indeed, hardly too much to say that the great obstacle to clear thinking about the progress of the war to date is by no means the deliberate misrepresentation of the array of forces by publicists on the Left, but rather the now-habitual mood of defeatism among publicists on the Right.) My answer to the reader is, in any case: stay with me until I have read my riddle, and let him then decide what he thinks.

Let me begin to read the riddle by identifying some of those sectors where, on my showing about these matters, the battle between attackers and resisters is now raging.

Take, for example, our long-established immigration policy, with its old-fashioned concept of immigration quotas based on present shares of population. (We let in more British immigrants every year than, say, Albanians, because a great many of us are of British descent, and very few of us of Albanian descent, so that—yes, let's swallow hard and admit it—we largely exclude certain types of immigrants that some of us regard as undesirable.) Now the Liberals, so it says anyhow in *my* copy of *The New York Times,* are forever mounting, or fighting, or finishing a new attack in that sector, intended to overthrow the "old way" [8] of han-

---

[8] I now and then hear the objection at this point: the quotas are in fact of relatively recent date, and are not an "old way." But that is to overlook two very important points: (a) That quotas or no quotas, the bulk of our immigration, down

dling immigration and substitute for it a new one—to be based on the findings of modern science which, we are told, forbid discrimination on grounds of race. Look around every couple of years and you can see them—the attackers (the sociologists, the anthropologists, the psychologists and biologists from the nation's far-flung universities, the *professors*)—exulting in the applause from the nation's Liberal-dominated press, demanding a stop to all that quota nonsense. Then, after a while, the smoke clears, and you see that the professors have gone home, to resume the indoctrination of their students, and all you have left is the resisters—Mr. Francis Walter and the members of his sub-committee, bloodstained but victorious, with an unchanged immigration statute in their hands.

Take, for another example, the successive Liberal attempts to close the loopholes in the income-tax laws that would have to be closed in order for the progressive income-tax to have the effects the Liberals intend it to have. (These loopholes, according to a recent article in the *Reporter,* enable the very rich to get away with paying a mere 40% or less of their income instead of the 92% they would otherwise pay.) Here again, loud applause from the press, especially from those organs of virtue: the *New Republic,* the *Nation, America,* and *Commonweal.* Yet when Congress goes home, biennium after biennium, the loopholes remain open —so that in the United States it is still possible, as in England for example it is not, for a man to get smacking rich and even, incredible as it may seem in so advanced an age as ours, to will considerable sums to his grandchildren. Here also, it would seem, the resisters always do dusk the day, and the attackers always eat the dust.

Or take MVA, TVA's little sister who was only a twinkle in TVA's father's eye when TVA was born. When, a quarter of a century ago, the attackers forced TVA's passage—in the name of

---

to a fairly recent date, "behaved" more or less as it would have had there been quotas, because, as is well known, brother followed brother, cousin followed cousin, parents followed sons and daughters (in part, of course, because the followers were financed from the beachhead in America). (b) The quotas, though generally supposed to be quite indefensible on grounds of principle, emerge in this context as entirely consistent with the principled Conservative bias in favor of the family.

publicly-owned power, of welfarism in the stricken Tennessee Valley, of justice for the nation's depressed farmers in the form of government-produced fertilizers, and other such noble slogans —everyone expected, Liberals and Conservatives alike, that MVA, like her big sister, would as a matter of course happen along after the two-year period of gestation appropriate to that species of animal. But twenty-five years have passed, and we still do not have an MVA, or even hear of one very often. Again, the resisters have won every time the attack has been renewed. The line never budges, nor could anything be so dead in America today as the socialism for which, in the silent depths of his heart, the Liberal constantly yearns.

Or take the continuing Liberal attack on the House Committee on Un-American Activities, and its predecessors. Abolish the Committee! they are forever crying. Down with its outmoded notion that all opinions are *not* created equal, and so do *not* have an equal right to toleration! And away with its further outmoded notion that the people of the United States, through their representatives, have a right to keep an eye on and expose the machinations of those who prefer World Communism to our free society. In this sector, more conspicuously perhaps than in any other, the attackers have been fought off, month after month, for upwards of *thirty* years, and the Committee is—well, still there, so that only a few months ago I had the honor to co-author a book about it.[9]

Or take each biennium's proposals that would lead to further inflation of the dollar (what matters, say the Liberals, is full employment, not sound fiscal policy). Or to a further increase in the national debt (we owe it to ourselves, cry the Liberals, so what difference does it make?). Or to a public housing program that would actually build houses for a significant number of people instead of just talking about it (why, ask the Liberals, should people be expected to save money out of their *own* income to buy themselves houses to live in?). Or to federal aid to education,

[9] William F. Buckley, Jr., and the Editors of *National Review, The Committee and Its Critics* (New York: Putnam, 1962; now republished, Chicago: Henry Regnery, 1963). For an account of HUAC's predecessors, see Chapter 4.

14

which is going to provide equality of educational opportunity everywhere (why, ask the Liberals, should the education a person receives depend on the accident—accident, mind you—of birth?). In each of these sectors, I say, the attackers are always attacking and the resisters always resisting and—the big piece of news of which, to my great surprise, I find myself to be the prime and original bearer—resisting for the most part successfully!

Or take the ten thousand comparable but far more drastic proposals, for this, that, and the other new forward steps toward the omnipotent and omnicompetent welfare state—the ten thousand comparable but more drastic proposals cooking away in ten thousand bureaucratic heads in Washington that the attackers do not dare even to embody in a bill, do not dare even to mention, because the proposals would not stand a Chinaman's chance. These also are part of the Liberal Revolution, its future war plans, and at the same time the most eloquent testimony we have to the formidability of the resistance to the Revolution.[10]

But, the reader may protest, "Revolution" seems a pretty strong word to apply to the Liberal programs you mention. You are playing games with a word that does not lend itself to games —and this regardless of which of the great revolutions, the Industrial Revolution or the French Revolution, you are using as your analogy. The changes we lump together under the heading "Industrial Revolution" all had something in common—namely, the shift to a new principle for organizing production—and the Liberal "attacks" you speak of do *not* involve a common principle. Similarly, if your analogy is the French Revolution, the obvious reply is that there is no question here of an attempt to overthrow an established order, or regime, or form of government. The "attacks" you speak of are merely attempts, tardy attempts for the most part, to remove irrationalities from a social order that we *all* want to maintain and improve. They are exactly the kind of thing our Constitution, in its Preamble, clearly calls for: proposals looking to the ends of justice—that is, liberty and equality —and to the general welfare. Your so-called "resisters," therefore,

---

[10] For further discussion of this point, see below, Chapter 2, "The Two Majorities."

do not deserve the respectable name of Conservatives; they are, rather, obstructionists, defenders of sordid vested interests that ought to have no defenders. Most of us prefer to think of Conservatives as, at the very least, men of principle, and your resisters are not that at all. So, the reader may conclude, come off it. It is, I concede, a good, sharp protest that, for the rest, I have clearly invited—one, therefore, that calls for a good sharp answer. Which is the kind of answer I am going to make as I read the rest of my riddle.

My analogy in using the word "revolution" is, let us be clear at once, both the French Revolution *and* the Industrial Revolution. I claim there is both a "common principle" involved in the Liberal attacks, and, partly for that reason and partly for another, an intention, hardly concealed any more, "to overthrow an established and traditional social and political order." I am, therefore, using the word "revolution" in the full sweep of its meaning, as witness the following considerations:

First, nothing can be more certain than that the Founders of our Republic bequeathed to us a form of government that was *purely* representative—a form of government in which there was no room, in which moreover there is *to this day* no room, for policy decisions by the electorate—that is, for electoral "mandates" emanating from popular majorities. Or rather there is one thing more certain: namely, that the Liberals intend to overthrow that traditional form of government, have a carefully-worked-out program for overthrowing it, and labor diligently, year-in-year-out, to seize the strategic points they must seize in order to accomplish its overthrow. The only reason that this is not more generally understood, indeed, is that the Liberal proposals in this area are so seldom brought together and looked at as an integrated design. Put an end, the Liberals insist, to "rural overrepresentation" in the lower house of Congress and in the state legislatures—bringing them in line with the principle one-man one-equal-vote. And that principle, once adopted (it is French political philosophy, not American), must call finally for abolition even of the U. S. Senate as a check on majorities, and would in any case make the House the creature of numerical majorities at the polls. Abolish the electoral college, the Liberals insist further, and so make the President also the direct agent of the popular majority. Reform the party system, the Liberals insist still further, so that each of our parties shall be programmatic, ideological—like those of the "real" democracies in Europe—and that the two parties together shall submit, at election time, a genuine choice to the electorate. Abolish the filibuster—so runs the next point in the program—because it frustrates, serves no other function except to frustrate, the will of the majority. Rescind the seniority-principle in congressional committees, the program continues; it also obstructs the will of the majority. Now give the Liberal attackers their way on all these points, and the form of government explicated in the *Federalist Papers* will be no more. In at least this area, then, the question "Is Liberalism a Revolution?" can have only one answer. Since it seeks a change of regime, the replacement of one regime by another, of a different type altogether, it is, quite simply, revolutionary. And it is in this area above all others, we may note in passing, that my resisters are most conscious of themselves, both as opponents of a revolution and as principled—yes, principled—defenders of a tradition.

Second, Liberal proposals do involve a common principle—one moreover which, once you grasp it clearly, appears on the face of it as revolutionary because it looks to the overthrow of an established social order. The principle in question is the *egalitarian* principle—not the equality principle of the Declaration of Independence, which "holds" merely that all men are created equal. That is, as I understand it, are created with an equal claim to be treated as persons (though by no means necessarily as equal persons), with an equal right to justice, and an equal right to live under a government limited by law (and constitutionally excluded from concern with certain major spheres of human endeavor). The egalitarian principle stands over against the equality principle in a relation like that of a caricature to a portrait, or a parody to a poem.[11] It says that men are not merely created

11 See Harry V. Jaffa, *The Crisis of the House Divided* (New York: Doubleday, 1959), *passim*, which traces, and traces precisely as an attempt on the part of Abraham Lincoln to re-do the allegedly inadequate work of the Framers, the birth of the egalitarian principle.

equal, are indeed not created equal at all, but rather ought, that is have a right, to be *made* equal. That is to say equalized, and equalized precisely by governmental action, so that if they end up other than actually equal—in political power, in wealth, in income, in education, in living conditions—no one shall ever be able to say that government has spared any effort that might conceivably have made them equal. The equality of the Declaration is the equality to which, say, Abraham Lincoln was born—an equality that conferred upon him merely an equal right to compete with his fellow-men in the race, as we run it here in America, for whatever prize he in his equality chose to go after. Not so the egalitarianism of the Liberals. It must pick Lincoln up at dawn in a yellow bus with flashing lights, so saving him shoe-leather, whisk him off to a remote consolidated school (financed, in all probability, by inflationary bonds), feed him a free lunch, educate him for democracy, protect him from so-called concentrations of social and economic power, eke out his income by soaking the rich, doctor him, hospitalize him, and, finally, social-work him—if, as he probably will now, he turns into a juvenile delinquent. Equality, by offering him the rewards of self-reliance, encourages him to become, above all—self-reliant; egalitarianism encourages him to learn to play the angles. Revolutionary? Yes indeed, and in a three-fold sense: revolutionary, because give the Liberals their way and the American social order will not bear even a cousinly resemblance to that which is traditional among us; revolutionary, because the revolution must go on and on forever, since if you are in the business of making people equal there is and can be no stopping-place; revolutionary, finally, because the job cannot be done by a government of limited powers —any more, to use James Burnham's phrase, than you can use an automobile to dig potatoes.

Third, it is in general true that my resisters make no great showing, to date, on the level of articulate grand principle. The noises they make do, I concede, seldom seem to echo a vital and combat-ready Conservative philosophy, capable of matching the militant moralism of the Liberals. For the most part the Senator

Byrds, the Senator Russells, the Senator Hruskas do not seem even to be trying to explain themselves. In a sense, therefore, they invite the allegation that their motives are sordid and selfish. But it would be rash to conclude from this that they are not men of principle at all, and foolhardy to conclude from it that no respectable case can be made out, in political and moral philosophy, for what they do. Such a case is, I should say rather, ready-to-hand for them, the moment they need it—in the great documents that lie at the root of the American political tradition: the Declaration of Independence, the deliberations of the Philadelphia convention, the Constitution itself, the Bill of Rights, and, above all, the *Federalist*. For my resisters do not, I contend, act otherwise than they would if they had made the *Federalist* their political Bible, and lived with it, steeped themselves in it, modeled themselves upon it—as Liberals appear to do with Mill's *Essay*. And the principles of the *Federalist*, make no mistake about it, are high principles—wrong principles perhaps, wrong principles certainly if Liberal principles are right principles. They are, that is to say, principles projected on a very high level of moral aspiration and discursive circumspection.

The case is ready, I say, the moment it is needed. Ah! the reader may well ask, but when is that going to be? And I can only answer: if and when the Conservative *movement* now shaping up in the United States becomes sufficiently conscious of itself to require an overall doctrine and an overall strategy. Ah! the reader may ask further, when and how would that come about? And I can only answer: when the pools of Conservative resistance I have described above have become fully aware of one another; when they have become ready, instead of going it alone, to make common cause; and when they will have made it their business to establish, back and forth among themselves, the channels of communication without which large-scale warfare is impossible. Or, again, when the Conservative egg-heads, as we know them in *National Review* and *Modern Age,* have learned, which they have not yet done—they also are not much shakes when it comes to philosophy—to make conscious common cause with the resisters in Congress. That moment, to be sure, is not yet. But things have moved very rapidly in the directions indicated during the past ten years, and there is reason to believe they will move still more rapidly in the years just ahead.

If they do—well, American politics are going to get mighty exciting.

Chapter 2

The Two Majorities in
American Politics

My point of departure is the tension between Executive and Legislature on the federal level of the American political system. My preliminary thesis is that the character and meaning of that tension, as also its role in the formation of American policy, has been too little examined during the period in which the tension has been at its highest; that the explanations of the tension that are, so to speak, "in the air," do not in fact explain it, but rather tend to lead us away from a correct explanation (and, by the same token, away from a correct understanding of our recent political history); that the entire matter, once we have the elements of a correct explanation in hand, opens up a rich field for investigation by our "behaviorists," hitherto unexplored because (in part at least) of the latter's lack of interest in what politics is really about.[1]

First, then, as to the character of the tension:

A. The tension between our "national" Executive and our "national" Legislature, though as suggested above it varies in "height" from time to time and at one moment seemed to have

---

[1] This is almost, but not quite, the same point as that involved in the frequently-repeated charge that the behaviorists spend their time (and a great deal of money) studying the trivial and the obvious, a charge too often put forward by writers who are something less than ready with an answer to the question, "What *is* important?" My point is less that the reader of our behavioral literature finds himself asking "So what?" (though indeed he does), than that he finds himself asking (to quote Arnold Rogow) "What happened to the great issues?" The behaviorists go on and on as if the latter did not exist.

disappeared altogether, has in recent decades been a character-istic feature of our politics.

B. The tension typically arises in the context of an attempt or expressed wish on the part of the Executive to "do" something that a majority of one or both houses is inclined to oppose. Typi-cally, that is to say, we have an Executive proposal which—now successfully, now unsuccessfully—a large number of legislators seeks to disallow, either as a whole or in part.[2]

C. The tension is peculiarly associated with certain readily identifiable areas of public policy, and in these areas it is both continuing and predictable.[3] Those that come most readily to mind (we shall ask later what they may have in common) are:

1. The Legislature tends to be "nervous" about internal se-curity. The Executive tends to become active on behalf of in-ternal security only under insistent pressure from Congress; it (the bureaucracy probably more than the President and his offi-cial family) here tends to reflect what is regarded as enlightened opinion [4] in the universities and among the nation's intellectuals in general.

2. The Congress adheres unabashedly to the "pork barrel" practices for which it is so often denounced. It tends to equate the national interest, at least where domestic economic policies are concerned, with the totality of the interests of our four-hun-dred-odd congressional districts.[5] The Executive regards "pork

---

[2] A distinction that is indispensable for a clear grasp of the problem. We may call it the distinction between "whether to?" and "how much?" And failure to keep it in mind often results, as I shall argue below, in our seeing Executive "victories" where there are in fact Executive defeats.

[3] We shall have something to say below about what we might call the "latent but always present tension" in certain other areas of public policy, where the Ex-ecutive would like to do such and such, but because of Professor Friedrich's "law of anticipated reactions" does not dare even to formulate a proposal. Much of what we hear about the so-called "decline" or "eclipse" or "fall" of Congress becomes less convincing when we take into account the matters in which Congress always gets its way because the Executive, much as it would like to do such and such, is not sufficiently romantic even to attempt it.

[4] No implication is intended, at this point at least, as to whether the opinion *is* enlightened, as that question is inappropriate to our immediate purposes.

[5] Cf., *The Federalist*, ed. Edward Mead Earle ("The Modern Library" [New York: Random House, n.d.]), *No. 64:* ". . . the government must be a weak one indeed if it should forget that the good of the whole can only be promoted by advancing the good of each of the parts or members which compose the whole." All subsequent citations to *The Federalist* are by number of the relevant paper.

barrel" measures as "selfish" and "particular," and does what it can, through pressure and maneuver, to forestall them. It appeals frequently to a national interest that is allegedly different from and superior to the interests of the constituencies.

3. The Legislature *tends* to be "protectionist" as regards external trade policy. The Executive, again reflecting what is regarded as enlightened opinion among intellectuals, tends to favor ever greater steps in the direction of "free trade," and acceptance by the United States of a general responsibility for the good health of the world economy.

4. The Legislature (again a similar but not identical point) tends to "drag its feet" on foreign aid programs, unless these promise a demonstrable military "pay-off." The Executive seems to be deeply committed to the idea of foreign aid programs as the appropriate means for gaining American objectives that are not exclusively, or even primarily, military.[6]

5. The Congress (though we must speak here with greater caution than has been necessary above because the relevant tension expresses itself in a different and less readily visible way) does not, by its actions at least, reflect what is regarded as enlightened opinion among intellectuals on the complex of issues related to the integration of the southern schools, withholding all action that might ease the Executive's path in the matter. The Executive stands ready to enforce the ruling in the *Brown* case, and seems unconcerned about the difficulty of pointing to any sort of popular mandate for it.

6. The Legislature insists upon perpetuating the general type of immigration policy we have had in recent decades. The Executive would apparently like to bring our immigration legislation under, so to speak, the all-men-are-created-equal clause of the Declaration of Independence.

7. The Legislature is, in general, jealous concerning the level of the national debt, and thus about government spending; it clings, in principle at least, to traditional notions about sound government finance. The Executive, at least the vast majority of

---

[6] It perhaps gives to "military objectives" a wider and looser meaning than the congressmen are willing to accept.

the permanent civil servants (who are, as is well known, in position to bring notable pressures to bear even upon a President who would like, on this or that, to side with Congress), appears to have moved to what we may call a Keynesian position about the national debt and year-to-year spending.

8. The Legislature tends to be "bullish" about the size of the United States Air Force and, in general, about military expenditure as opposed to expenditures for "welfare." The Executive, though no simple statement is in order about its policies, continuously resists congressional pressure on both points.

9. The Legislature tends to be "nationalistic," that is, to be oriented to the "conscience" of its constituents rather than the "conscience of mankind." The Executive tends to be "internationally minded," that is, to subordinate its policies in many areas to certain "principles" concerning the maintenance of a certain kind of international order.

10. The Legislature appears to have little quarrel with Right-wing dictatorships; it tends to favor policies with respect to them based rather upon expediency than upon ideological commitment to democratic forms of government. The Executive, despite the tendencious charges we often hear to the contrary, is disposed to hold governments not based upon free elections at arm's length.

11. The Executive [7] tends to favor each and every component of the current program (the product of what is generally regarded as enlightened opinion among political scientists at our universities) for transforming the American political system into a *plebiscitary* political system, capable of producing and carrying through *popular mandates*. These components, so well known as to require only the briefest mention, are: Remake our major political parties in such fashion that their programs, when laid before the American people in presidential elections, will present them with "genuine" "choices" concerning policy, and that candidates for office within each party will stand committed to their party's program. (The major public spokesmen for such a reform

---

[7] For the sake of simplicity of exposition, I here reverse the previous order, and speak first of the Executive.

are the chairmen of the national committees, one of whom is of course the appointee of the President.) Get rid of the Senate filibuster, as also of the seniority principle in congressional committees (which do indeed make it possible for little bands of willful men to "frustrate" alleged majority mandates). Iron out inequalities of representation in Congress, since these, theoretically at least, are capable of substituting the will of a minority for that of the majority. (Although it is perhaps difficult to attribute any policy on the latter two components to the White House itself, anyone who has himself been a permanent civil servant knows that in the executive departments the animosity against the filibuster, the seniority principle, and the alleged "over-representation" of rural folk and white southerners is both intense and deeply-rooted.) Further, assure equal representation and thus genuine majority mandates, by enacting ever stronger "civil rights" legislation calculated to prevent the white southerners from disfranchising or intimidating potential Negro voters, and by putting the Department of Justice permanently into the business of enforcing the "strengthened" civil rights. (The extreme "proposals" here do normally originate with senators and congressmen, but it will hardly be disputed that the White House is consistently on the side of the proponents, and consistently disappointed by Congress' final reply from session to session, to the question, "How much?") "Streamline" the executive branch of government, so as to transform it into a ready and homogeneous instrument that the President, backed up by his "disciplined" majority in Congress, can use effectively in carrying out his mandate, and so as to "concentrate" power and make it more "responsible" (by getting rid of the independent agencies, and eliminating the duplication and competition between agencies that perform the same or very similar tasks). Finally, glorify and enhance the office of President, and try to make of presidential elections the central ritual of American politics—so that, even if the desired reform of the party system cannot be achieved at once, a newly-elected President with a popular majority will be able to plead, against a recalcitrant Congress, that *his* mandate must prevail.

Congress seldom shows itself available to any such line of argument, and off-year congresses like to remind presidents, in the most forceful manner possible, that the system has rituals other than that of the presidential election. For the rest, it resists the entire program with cool determination. With respect to the party system, it is clearly wedded to our traditional system of decentralized parties of a non-"ideological" and non-programmatic character. With respect to mandates, it clearly continues to regard the American system as that which, as I contend below, its Framers intended it to be—that is, one in which the final decisions upon at least the important determinations of policy are hammered out, in accordance with "the republican principle," in a deliberative assembly made up of *uninstructed* representatives, chosen by their neighbors because they are the "virtuous" men. That is, a system which has no place for mandates. As for the filibuster and the committee chairmen, Congress clearly regards as their peculiar virtue that which the Executive and its aggrandizers within the bureaucracy and out among the nation's intellectuals regard as their peculiar vice, namely, that they *are* capable of frustrating an alleged majority mandate. With respect to "streamlining" the executive branch of government, Congress appears to yield to proposals in this sense only when it has convinced itself that further resistance is an invasion of presidential prerogatives rooted in the same constitution from which it derives its own. It clearly clings to the traditional view, again that of the Framers themselves, that power should *not* be concentrated, but rather (since a most efficient Executive might well turn out to be most efficient against the liberties of the people) shared out in such fashion that ambition may counter ambition. With respect to civil liberties, Congress clearly cherishes the notion that the Tenth Amendment has not been repealed, and that, accordingly, there is room in the American system for differences in civil liberties from state to state and even, within a state, for differences in civil liberties from differently situated person to differently situated person. With respect to the aggrandizement of the office of president and the glorification of presidential elections, it again takes its stand with the tradition and the Framers:

26

there is no room in the American system for a presidential office so aggrandized as to be able itself to determine how much farther the aggrandizement shall go. The ultimate decisions on that point, Congress holds, must be made not by the President but by itself, in the course of the continuing dialectic between its members and their constituents: plebiscitary presidential elections cannot become the central ritual of our system without destroying the system.

II

What general statements—of a sort that might throw light on their meaning in the American political system—may we venture to make about these areas of tension? [8]

At least, I believe, these:

A. They all involve matters of policy which, by comparison with those involved in areas where tension is not evident and predictable, bear very nearly indeed upon the central destiny of the United States—on the kind of society it is going to become ("open" or relatively "closed," egalitarian and redistributive or shot through and through with great differences in reward and privilege, a "welfare state" society or a "capitalist" society); on the form of government the United States is to have (much the same as that intended by the Framers, or one tailored to the specifications of egalitarian ideology); or on our relatedness to the outside world on points that, we are often told, nearly affect the central destiny of mankind itself. They are all areas, therefore, in which we should expect disagreement and thus tension

[8] I do not forget that the areas of tension are also areas of tension *within* both houses of Congress, where the Executive always, when the big issues are "up," has considerable support, and sometimes "wins" (or at least seems to). It would be interesting, though not relevant to the purposes of the present chapter, to study the incidence of the tensions within Congress (as revealed, e.g., in voting, about which we have a rich and growing literature), particularly with a view to discovering whether there is a discernible "trend" in this regard. As also whether there is any relation, of the kind my analysis below would lead us to expect, between the character of an M.C.'s constituency and the "side" he takes in these matters. One imagines that the tensions are also repeated within the bosom of the Executive. But we must not get in the habit of permitting our sophistication about such matters to obscure for us the fact that "Congress" acts finally as an institution, whose "behavior" as an institution can and for some purposes must be observed without regard to its internal divisions.

in a heterogeneous society like ours (though by no means necessarily, I hasten to add, tension between its Legislature and its
Executive—not, at least, for any reason that leaps readily to the
eye).

B. They are areas in which the Executive (as I have already
intimated) is able, with good show of reason, to put itself forward on any particular issue as the spokesman for either "lofty
and enlightened principle" or still undiffused professional *expertise,* or both. The Executive tends, that is to say, to have the
nation's ministers and publicists with it on "peace," the nation's
professors and moralizers with it on desegregation, the nation's
economists with it on fiscal policy and redistribution, the nation's
political scientists with it on political reform and civil rights,
etc. To put it otherwise, Congress at least *appears,* in all the areas
in question, to be holding out for either the repudiation or eva-
sion of the moral imperatives that the nation's "proper teachers"
urge upon us, or the assertion of an invincibly ignorant "lay-
man's" opinion on topics that are demonstrably "professional"
or "expert" in character, or both. The Executive is for world government, for the outlawing of war, for unselfishness in our relations with the outside world, for the brotherhood of man, for
majority-rule, for progress, for generosity toward the weak and
lowly, for freedom of thought and speech, for equality, for the
spreading of the benefits of modern civilization to "underdeveloped" lands, for science and the "scientific outlook," for civil
rights. And apparently it is its being for these things that somehow runs it afoul of Congress in the areas in question, so that it
is difficult to avoid the impression that Congress is somehow
against the things mentioned, and against them because wedded
to bigotry, to selfishness both at home and abroad, to oppression,
to the use of force, to minority rule, to outmoded notions in science. Because the Executive so clearly represents "high principle
and knowledge," the conclusion is well nigh irresistible that Congress represents low principle (or, worse still, no principle at all),
reaction, and unintelligence, and does so in full knowledge that
the President (both he and his opponent having, in the latest election, asserted the same high principles and the same generally

enlightened outlook)[9] has not merely a majority mandate but a virtually unanimous mandate to go ahead and act upon high principle.

C. They are areas that, for the most part, do not lend themselves to what is fashionably called "polyarchal bargaining." For example, the internal security policies that Congress has in recent years imposed upon the Executive have been in no sense the result of protracted negotiations among "groups," conducted with an eye to leaving no group too unhappy; so too, with the policy that it imposes (by inaction) with regard to the desegregation of the southern schools, and that which it imposes (by action) concerning immigration and the armed forces. To put it otherwise, the policy problems involved are by their very nature problems about which everybody can't have a little bit of his way, because we move in either this direction (which some of us want to do) or in that direction (which others of us want to do). The line Congress takes with respect to them seems to be determined much as before, the now fashionable "group interpretation" of our politics took shape, we supposed all policy lines to be determined—that is, by the judgment of individuals obliged to choose between more or less clearly understood alternatives, and obliged ultimately to choose in terms of such notions as they may have of justice and the public weal.

D. They are areas—though we come now to a more delicate kind of point—in which, little as we may like to think so and however infrequently we may admit it to ourselves, Congress pretty consistently gets its way. Indeed the widespread impression to the contrary seems to me the strangest optical illusion of our politics, and worth dwelling upon for a moment. The question actually at issue becomes, quite simply, whether in recent decades (since, say, 1933) the Liberals—for, as intimated repeatedly above, the tension between Executive and Legislature is normally a Liberal-Conservative tension—have or have not been "winning." I contend that the reason both Liberals and Conservatives tend (as they do) to answer that question in the affirma-

[9] See below, pp. 47-49.

tive is that we are all in the habit of leaving out of account two
dimensions of the problem that are indispensable to clear thinking about it.

First, we cannot answer the question without somehow "ranking" political issues in order of "importance"—without, for example, distinguishing at least between those issues that are most
important, those that are important but not most important,
those that are relatively unimportant, and those that are not important at all—meaning here by "important" and "unimportant"
merely that which the Liberals and Conservatives themselves
deem important or unimportant. In the context of such a ranking
we readily see that "winning" in our politics is a matter of getting
your way on the matters that are most important to you, not getting defeated too often on those that are merely important to you,
and taking your big defeats on those that are relatively unimportant to you or not important at all. Take for instance that
Liberal "victory" of the period in question that comes most
readily to mind: the creation and maintenance of the Tennessee
Valley Authority. Everyone familiar with the politics of the
period knows that the TVA enthusiasts intended TVA to be the
first of a *series* of "authorities," which would have the effect of
shifting the entire American economy away from "capitalism"
and "free private enterprise." That was what the Liberals wanted,
and that was what the Conservatives, if they meant business, had
to prevent. That was what was "most important," against the
background of which the creation and maintenance of a single
TVA (one, moreover, that men could support out of no animus
whatever against private enterprise) was at most "unimportant."
And, once we put the question "Who won?" in those terms, and
remind ourselves where the White House and the bureaucracy
stood, we are obliged to give an answer quite different from that
which we are in the habit of giving: The Executive got its TVA
in particular, but Congress put a stop to TVA's in general (nor
—a point worth making again and again—is there any issue so dead
in America today as that of "Socialism").

Secondly, there is the dimension we have mentioned briefly
above, that of the things that the Executive would like to pro-

pose but has the good sense not to because of its certain fore-knowledge of the impossibility of getting the proposals through Congress—it being here that Congress most consistently gets its way, and without anyone's noticing it.[10] James Burnham is quite right in arguing that the capacity to say "No" to the Executive is the essence of congressional power; [11] but he exaggerates the infrequency with which Congress does say "No," partly by ignoring the "No's" that Congress does not have to say for the reason just given, and partly by failing to distinguish between the "No's" that are "most important" to the Congress itself and those that are not.

To summarize: The areas of tension are typically "most important" areas in which this or that application of high principle desired by the Executive gets short shrift from enough congressmen and senators to prevent it, or at least to prevent it on anything like the *scale* desired by the Executive. And in these areas the Congress normally "wins," "high principle" seemingly going by the board. Nor would it be easy to show—and this brings us to the nub of the matter—that the tensions are less acute, or produce a notably different result, during the two-year periods that precede presidential elections than during the two-year periods that follow them. The latter, if it were true, might enable us to argue that the tensions arise because of shifts of opinion in the electorate, or that they relate particularly to the two-thirds of the senators who, after any biennial election, are "holdovers." And, that being the case, we are obliged, as I have already intimated, to confront an unexplained mystery of our politics: the fact that *one and the same electorate maintains in Washington, year after year, a President devoted to high principle and en-*

10 Let anyone who doubts the point (a) poll his Liberal acquaintances on the question, Is it proper for non-believers in America to be taxed for the support of churches and synagogues (which they certainly are so long as churches and synagogues are exempted from taxation)? and, (b) ask himself what would happen in Congress if the Treasury Department were to propose removal of the exemption. There is no greater symbol of Executive-Legislative tension than the fact that the sessions of both houses open with prayer, whereas we cannot imagine a prayer at the beginning of a meeting of, say, an interdepartmental committee of bureaucrats.

11 Cf., James Burnham, *Congress and the American Tradition* (Chicago: Henry Regnery, 1959), p. 278.

lightenment, and a Congress that gives short shrift to both; that, even at one and the same election, they elect to the White House a man devoted to the application of high principle to most important problems of national policy, and to the Hill men who consistently frustrate him. More concretely: the voters give an apparent majority mandate to the President to apply principles "x, y, and z," and a simultaneous (demonstrable) majority-mandate[12] to the Congress to keep him from applying them. And the question arises, Why, at the end of a newly-elected President's first two years, do the voters not "punish" the congressmen? Are the voters simply "irrational"? Our political science has, it seems to me, no adequate or convincing answer to these (and many kindred) questions.

III

What is "in the air" in American political science (to return now to the hint thrown out above) because of which my statement of the problem of executive-legislative tension sounds unfamiliar—not to say "against the grain"? Not, I think, any doctrines that clash head-on with such a statement on the ground that it appears to move in a direction that might be "pro-Congress"; that would be true only if contemporary American political science were "anti-Congress," which I, for one, do not believe to be the case[13] (besides which the statement is not, up to this point, "pro-Congress"). Not either, I think, any specific doctrine or doctrines concerning executive-legislative tensions as such; for though contemporary American political science is certainly not unaware of the tensions (it might, at most, be accused of sweeping them now and then under the rug, contrary to the rules of tidy housekeeping), it seems safe to say that there is no prevailing "theory" of the problem. The answer to our question lies rather, I believe, in this: there are overtones in the statement, perhaps even implications, that simply do not "fit in" with

---

[12] Unless we want to argue that Congress does not have a majority mandate. See below my reasons for thinking such a position untenable, pp. 41-43.

[13] There is, of course, an "anti-Congress" literature, but there is also an enormous literature that is friendly to Congress.

what we are accustomed these days to say or assume—not about executive-legislative tensions, but about some very different matters; namely, elections, majority rule, and the comparative "representativeness," from the standpoint of "democratic theory," of the Executive and the Legislature. And perhaps the best way to bring the relevant issues out into the open is to fix attention on what we *are* accustomed to hear said and assumed about these matters.

I propose to use for this purpose Robert A. Dahl's celebrated Walgreen lectures,[14] which precisely because they are not "anti-Congress" (are, rather, the handiwork of one of our major and most dispassionate experts on Congress) have the more to teach us about the problem in hand. The lectures seem to me to show that we are accustomed now to assume (if not to say) that when we speak of "democratic theory," of majority rule in the United States, we can for the most part simply ignore Congress and congressional elections. This is nowhere asserted in the *Preface,* but I submit to anyone familiar with it *both* that such a tacit premise is present throughout its argument—which goes on and on as if our presidential elections were not merely the central ritual of our politics but also the sole ritual—and that Dahl's tacit premise seems, in the present atmosphere, perfectly natural.

But let us think for a moment about that premise, and the resultant tacit exclusion of executive-legislative tension as a problem for democratic theory (Dahl, I think I am safe in saying, nowhere in the *Preface* refers to it).[15] To put the premise a little differently, the majority-rule problem in America is the problem of the presidential elections; either the majority rules through the presidential elections (which Dahl thinks it does not), or it does not rule at all. A book about majority rule in America does not, in consequence, any longer need to concern itself at any point with the possibility that fascinated the authors of *The Fed-*

---

14 Robert A. Dahl, *Preface to Democratic Theory* (Chicago: University of Chicago Press, 1956).

15 The function of his Congress, in the *Preface* anyhow, is that of "legitimizing basic decisions by some process of *assent*" (italics added), and of registering pressures in the process he likes to call "polyarchal bargaining." See respectively pp. 136, 145.

eralist, namely, that of the "republican principle" as working precisely through the election of members to the two houses of Congress. And the effect of that premise, whether intended or not, is to deny legitimacy, from the standpoint of "democratic theory," alike to Congress as a formulator of policy, and to the elections that produce Congress as expressions of majority "preferences." That is, to deny the relevance of those elections to the problem to which the authors of *The Federalist* regarded them as most relevant, i.e., the problem of majority rule in America.[16] Nor is the reason for the premise difficult to discover: for Dahl, and for the atmosphere of which his book may fairly be regarded as an accurate distillation, Congress, especially the lower house, is a stronghold of entrenched minorities [17]—and in any case is, and was always intended to be, a barrier to majority rule, not an instrument of majority rule.[18] It is bicameral; its members are chosen in elections deliberately staggered to prevent waves of popular enthusiasm from transmitting themselves directly to its floors. It "overrepresents" rural and agricultural areas and interests; many of its members are elected in constituencies where civil liberties, including even the liberty to vote, are poorly protected, so that the fortunate candidate can often speak only for a minority of his constituents. And as the decades have passed it has developed internal procedures—especially the filibuster and the seniority principle in the choice of committee chairmen—that frequently operate to defeat the will of the majority even of its own members.[19] It reflects, in a word, the anti-democratic, anti-majority-rule bias of the Framers, who notoriously distrusted

[16] Cf., *The Federalist, No. 54:* "Under the proposed Constitution, the federal acts . . . will depend merely on the majority of votes in the federal legislature. . . ." Cf., *No. 21:* "The natural cure of an ill-administration, in a popular or representative constitution, is a change of men"—through, of course, elections. Cf. also *No. 44:* If Congress were to ". . . misconstrue or enlarge any . . . power vested in them . . . in the last resort a remedy must be obtained from the people, who can, by the election [in elections where the candidate who gets the largest number of votes wins?] of more faithful representatives, annul the acts of the usurpers."

[17] Dahl, *op. cit.,* p. 142.

[18] *Ibid.,* p. 14.

[19] *Ibid.,* p. 15. I am sure Professor Dahl will not object to my mentioning that the point about civil liberties, although not present in his book, he has pressed upon me in private conversation.

human nature (because of their commitment to certain "psychological axioms").[20]

Now the doctrine just summarized is so deeply imbedded in our literature that it may seem an act of perversity to try, at this late moment, to call it into question (as the overtones and implications of my discussion in I and II certainly do). The present writer is convinced, however, that a whole series of misunderstandings [21]—partly about the Framers and partly about majority rule—have crept into our thinking about the matter, and that these have disposed us to beg a number of questions that it is high time we reopened. The Framers, we are being told, distrusted the "people," cherished a profound animus against majority rule, and were careful to write "barriers" to majority rule into their constitution. But here, as it seems to me, the following peculiar thing has happened. Taught as we are by decades of political theory whose creators have been increasingly committed to the idea of majority mandates arising out of plebiscitary elections, we tend to forget that that alternative, not having been invented yet, was not in the mind of the Framers at all. Which is to say, we end up accusing the Framers of trying to prevent something they had never even heard of,[22] and so cut ourselves off from the possibility of understanding their intention. Above all we forget that what the Framers (let us follow the fashion and accept *The Federalist* as a good enough place to go to find out what they thought) were primarily concerned to prevent was the states' going their separate ways—their becoming an "infinity of little, jealous, clashing, tumultuous commonwealths" [23]—so that there would *be* no union in which the question of majority rule could arise. The "majority rule" they feared was the unlimited majority rule *within the several states* that would, they thought, result from disintegration of the union; and we are misreading most of the relevant passages if we read them in any other

[20] *Ibid.*, p. 8.
[21] To which I must plead myself guilty of having contributed, particularly in my *John Locke and the Doctrine of Majority-Rule* (Urbana: University of Illinois Press, 1941).
[22] This is not to deny that the "barriers" do, as it turns out, operate to prevent a plebiscitary system. My point is they were not, and could not, have been intended to, but also that a plebiscitary system is not the only possible majority-rule system.
[23] *The Federalist, No. 9.*

sense. We take an even greater liberty, moreover, when we sire off on the Framers the (largely uncriticized) premise that the proper remedy for the evils of some form of majority rule is as a matter of course non-majoritarian. No one knew better than they that the claim of the majority to have its way in a "republican" (or "free") government cannot be successfully denied; [24] indeed what most amazes one upon rereading *The Federalist,* in the context of the literature with which we have been deluged since J. Allen Smith, is precisely the degree of their commitment to the majority principle,[25] and their respect and affection for the "people" whose political problem they were attempting to "solve." [26] Their concern, throughout, is that of achieving popular control over government, not that of preventing it.[27] That they thought to do by leaving the "people" of the new nation organized in a particular way,[28] in constituencies

[24] Cf., *ibid., No. 58:* ". . . the fundamental principle of free government would be reversed. It would no longer be the majority that would rule. . . ." Cf., *No. 22,* with its reference to the fundamental maxim of republican government as being: that the "sense of the majority shall prevail." Cf., *ibid.:* ". . . two thirds of the people of America could not long be persuaded . . . to submit their interests to the management and disposal of one third." Compare Dahl, *op. cit.,* pp. 34, 35, where after citing various strong pro-majority-rule statements from political philosophers, he concludes that they are all "clearly at odds with the Madisonian view." Note that one of the statements, curiously, is from Jefferson, whom Dahl immediately describes as a "Madisonian."

[25] See preceding note. The point has been obscured by our habit of reading the numerous passages that insist on ultimate control by the "people" on the assumption, impossible in my opinion to document, that the authors of *The Federalist* thought they had discovered some way to have matters decided by the people in elections, *without* having them decided by a majority of the people. See following note.

[26] Cf., *ibid., No. 14:* "I submit to you, my fellow-citizens, these considerations, in full confidence that the good sense which has so often marked your decisions will allow them due weight and effect. . . . Hearken not to the unnatural voice which tells you that the people of America . . . can no longer continue the mutual guardians of their mutual happiness. . . . Is it not the glory of the people of America [that they have heeded] . . . the suggestions of their own good sense, the knowledge of their own situation, and the lessons of their own experience?" Such passages abound in *The Federalist.*

[27] Cf., *ibid., No. 40:* ". . . the Constitution . . . ought . . . to be embraced, if it be calculated to accomplish the views and happiness of the people of America." Cf., *No. 46:* ". . . the ultimate authority . . . resides in the people alone. . . ."

[28] Cf., *ibid., No. 39:* "Were the people regarded . . . as forming one nation, the will of the *majority of the whole people* . . . would bind the minority . . . and the will of the majority must be determined either by a comparison of the individual votes, or by considering the will of the majority of the States. . . . Neither of these rules has been adopted" (italics added).

which would return senators and congressmen, and by inculcating in that people a constitutional morality that would make of the relevant elections a quest for the "virtuous" men [29]—the latter to come to the capital, normally, without "instructions" (in the sense of that term—not the only possible sense—that we are most familiar with). These virtuous men were to *deliberate* about such problems as seemed to them to require attention and, off at the end, make decisions by majority vote; and, as *The Federalist* necessarily conceived it, the majority votes so arrived at would, because each of the virtuous men would have behind him a majority vote back in his constituency, represent a popular majority. (My guess, based on long meditation about the relevant passages, is that they hoped the deliberation would be of such character that the votes would seldom be "close," so that the popular majority represented would be overwhelming.) That, with one exception, is the only federal popular majority of which Madison and Hamilton were thinking—the exception being the popular majority bent on taking steps adverse to natural rights,[30] that is, to justice. What they seem to have been thinking of here, however, and took measures (though not drastic ones) [31] to prevent, was precisely *not* an electoral majority acting through a plebiscitarily-chosen president, but rather a demagogically-led movement that might sweep through the constituencies and bring pressure to bear upon the congressmen. Nor must we permit our own emancipation, because of which we know that the difference between unjust steps and just ones is merely a matter of opinion, to blind us to the implied distinction between a popular majority as such and a popular majority determined to commit an injustice. Madison and Hamilton not only thought they knew what they meant, but did know what they meant when they used

29 Cf., *ibid., No. 57:* The chosen are to be those "whose merit may recommend [them] to . . . esteem and confidence. . . ." Cf., *No. 64*, with its reference to assemblies made up of "the most enlightened and respectable citizens" who will elect people "distinguished by their abilities and virtue. . . ."

30 *I.e.*, a majority "faction." See *ibid., No. 10, passim.*

31 Indeed, Madison clearly believed (*ibid.*) that nothing could be done *constitutionally* to block a majority "faction."

such language; [32] and we err greatly when we confuse their animus against the popular majority bent on injustice with an animus against the popular majority, the majority of the people, as such.

Ah, someone will object, but you have conceded that the measures they took operate equally against both; the Framers, that is to say, made it just as difficult for a popular majority as such, even a popular majority bent upon *just* measures, to capture the Congress and use it for its purposes, as for an "unjust" majority. But here again we must hold things in their proper perspective —by keeping ourselves reminded that Madison did not think the measures we have in mind (staggered elections and bicameralism in particular) would constitute much of a barrier to either. As Dahl himself points out, Madison placed his sole reliance against the popular movement that snowballs through the constituencies in the hope that the constituencies would, because of the growth and development of the nation, become so numerous, so widely flung, and so diverse as to make it impossible to bring people together into the kind of popular movement he feared. But there are several other dimensions to the thought implicit in *The Federalist* on this matter. There is, first, the constitutional morality suggested in the doctrine concerning the virtuous men; these being, by definition, men bent upon justice, constituency elections turning upon the identification of virtuous men would on the face of them constitute a major barrier to a popular movement bent upon injustice,[33] *but not to a widespread popular movement demanding something just*.[34] Second, there is the fact that the Constitution, being a constitution that limits govern-

---

[32] That is, when they distinguished between just and unjust, and measures adverse to the rights of others and measures not adverse to them. Cf., *ibid.*: ". . . measures are too often decided, not according to the rules of justice and the rights of the minor party, but by the force of an interested and overbearing majority." Cf., Dahl, *op. cit.*, p. 29, where he illustrates the gulf between himself and the Madisonians by writing "good" and "bad," the implication being, I take it, that the distinction is operationally meaningless.

[33] Cf., *ibid.*, No. 51: ". . . a coalition of a majority . . . could seldom take place [except on] principles . . . of justice and the general good."

[34] Cf., *ibid.*, No. 57, where it is argued that a political constitution should aim at obtaining for "rulers men who possess most wisdom to discern, and most virtue to pursue, the common good of the society"—and taking the "most effectual precautions for keeping them virtuous. . . ."

mental power, might fairly be expected to bear more heavily upon the prospects of an unjust movement, which as Madison must have known is of the two the more likely to run afoul of the relevant limitations, than on a just one. And there is, thirdly, the fact that so long as the system works as Madison intended it to, bicameralism and staggered elections themselves might be expected to bear more heavily upon an unjust movement than upon a just one. They constitute a "barrier," as far as Congress is concerned, only to the extent that the hold-over senators and the congressmen from constituencies not yet captured by the spreading popular movement *resist* the relevant popular pressures—which they are most likely to do by debate in the course of deliberation, and can do most effectively precisely when they are able to wrap themselves in the mantle of justice (which by definition they cannot do if the popular movement is itself bent upon justice). In fine, once we grant the distinction between a popular majority in the constituencies bent upon injustice and a popular movement bent upon something just, grant it with all the literalness with which it was intended, there remains no reason to attribute to Madison, or to the Constitution he defended, any animus against popular majorities (as such) having their way. He simply wanted, I repeat, the majority to be articulated and counted in a certain way, and had confidence that so long as it was it would produce just results. And we must, if we are to bring the whole problem into proper focus, recognize that the Madisonian majority, articulated through and counted within the constituencies, is still present in the American political system. Which is to say that we must learn to think in terms of what we may call *two* popular majorities, the congressional and the presidential. And we must accept, as an unavoidable problem for American political theory, the problem of the respective merits of the two (and must not, like Professor Dahl, talk as if one of them did not exist). What is at stake when there is tension between Congress and President is not the majority principle (the "Rule," Dahl calls it), but rather the question of where and how we are to apply it.

IV

What we are always dealing with in the American system is, on the present showing, Two Majorities, two *numerical* majorities,[35] each of which can, by pointing to the Rule, claim what Dahl calls the "last say," and each of which merits the attention of that part of "democratic theory" that deals with the problem of majority rule. The moment this is conceded, moreover, the problem of executive-legislative tensions begins to appear in the light in which it is presented above.

As for the merits of the respective claims of the two majorities, I content myself here with the following observations:

A. One of the two majorities, the presidential, has (as I have intimated) been *engrafted* onto our political system: it was not intended by the Framers, not even present to their minds as something to be "frustrated" and have "barriers" put in its way. It is, in other words (insofar as we can satisfy ourselves that it exists *qua* majority and eventuates in "mandates"), something new in our politics; something therefore whose appropriateness to the spirit and machinery of our system may fairly be regarded as still open to question. (I hope I shall not be understood to mean that its newness necessarily establishes a presumption against it.)

B. Professor Dahl, for all his fascination with presidential elections, is himself the author of the most brilliant demonstration we have (or could ask for) that nothing properly describable as a majority mandate, sanctioned by the Rule, emerges from a presidential election.[36] Indeed, one way of stating the question concerning the merits of the respective claims of the two majorities is: Is the congressional majority open to the same objections, from the standpoint of the Rule, that Dahl brings so tellingly against the presidential? If not, we should be obliged to view with suspicion Dahl's contention that, there *being* no majority in

[35] But cf., Burnham, *op. cit.*, p. 316 (and the preceding discussion) for a different view of the two majorities. Burnham, of course, follows Calhoun.
[36] Dahl, *op. cit.*, pp. 124-131.

America, the majority cannot rule (so that we can stop worrying about majority tyranny).[37]

C. It is interesting to notice that some of the claims that Madison (were we, like Professor Dahl, to go, so to speak, to his assistance) might be imagined as making for *his* majority "mandate," cannot, as Dahl demonstrates, be made for the side that gets the most votes in a presidential election:

1. Madison's majority mandate does not stand or fall with the possibility of proving that the voters who are its ultimate sanction voted for the same man because they endorse the same policies; the other kind of majority mandate, as Dahl admirably shows, does.[38] Madison's is *heterogeneous* by definition—is supposed to be and was intended to be heterogeneous. Indeed, without its being heterogeneous, it cannot accomplish its intended purpose, which is the ultimate arriving at policy decisions through a process of deliberation among virtuous men representing potentially conflicting and in any case different "values" and interests.

2. It is at least potentially *continuous* in its relation to the voters, whereas, as Dahl shows, the presidential sanction is *discontinuous*[39] (his majority speaks, insofar as it speaks at all, then promptly disappears), and because continuous not sporadic, potentially simultaneous with policy decisions even when they do not coincide with an election. Indeed, the major difference between Madison and Dahl as theorists of majority rule is precisely that Dahl clearly cannot, or at least does not, imagine a popular majority-rule system as working through any process other than that of elections, which, as he himself sees, are in the nature of the case discontinuous and prior to actual policy decisions. Madison, on the other hand, is not in the first place all that preoccupied with elections, and ends up describing a majority-rule

---

[37] *Ibid.*, p. 25, and Chap. V, *passim*. It might be pointed out that Dahl has difficulty deciding just how to phrase the point; "rarely, if ever," does not say the same thing as "rarely," and "ruling on matters of specific policy" does not say the same thing as "ruling."

[38] *Ibid.*, pp. 127-129.

[39] *Ibid.*, p. 130.

process rich in possibilities (as we all know) for what we may, with Burnham, call a continuing dialectical relationship between the virtuous men and their constituents. However, this relationship by no means necessarily takes the form of the member of Congress "keeping his ear to the ground" and seeking to carry out automatically the "will" of a majority of his constituents; he is himself a part *of* his constituency, potentially "representative" in the special sense of reacting to policy problems just as his constituents *would* were they present, and he also is informed (which, of course, they often are not). The dialectic, moreover, as Madison could hardly have failed to realize, may take the form of the representative's actually *thinking with* his constituents, whether by communication back and forth or in the course of visits back home.[40] Finally, as again Madison certainly knew, the member of Congress will, if normally ambitious, wish to be re-elected, and will not willingly become a party to policy decisions that, when they come to the attention of his constituents, will seem to them foolish or outrageous; which means that he must ask himself continuously how at least his general course of behavior is ultimately going to go down at home.

3. In two senses, Madison's majority mandate does not need to be, and Madison did not expect it to be, "positive" in the way that a writer like Dahl assumes a mandate must be if it is to be really a mandate.[41] First, it is as likely to express itself in prohibitions and "vetoes" as in imperatives. And second, the popular command involved is basically, as Madison conceived it, a command to help produce *just* policy decisions in a certain manner, and normally does not presuppose a positive mandatory relation with respect to particular matters.

4. Madison's is a mandate that emerges from a process that was always intended to emphasize specifically moral considerations, e.g., the kind of considerations involved in deciding who are the virtuous men. To put the point otherwise: it is a process that

---

[40] The essence of *Federalist* thought here is that of a "deliberate sense of the community" (meaning by community, surely, not less than a majority?) formed as problems arise and get themselves discussed in the Congress and out over the nation, and by no means necessarily expressing itself always through elections.

[41] *Ibid.*, pp. 129, 131.

was originally conceived in terms of a moral theory of politics, while the theorists of the presidential mandate tend, to say the least, to a certain relativism about morals (which is why they can end up insisting that this and this must be done because the majority demands it *tout court*). Its emphasis, therefore, is on the ability of the people (i.e., at least a majority of the people) to make sound judgments regarding the virtue of their neighbors, not on their ability to deliberate on matters of policy. (Dahl leaves us in no doubt about their inability to do the latter.)

V

The above considerations seem to me not only to throw light on the respective claims of the Two Majorities, but also to show why (assuming that the older of the two continues to function much as Madison intended it to, which I do believe to be the case) we have no cause to be astonished at the fact of executive-legislative tension in our system. There is no reason *a priori* to expect the virtuous men to be attracted as a matter of course to the proposals put forward by the Executive (with whatever claim to a "majority mandate" for them); at least, that is to say, we see how such tension might occur. But there are some further considerations that seem to me to show why it *must* occur, and at the same time to throw light on how each of us should go about making up his mind as to which of the two to support. These are:

A. The essentially aristocratic character of the electoral process that produces the older of the majorities as over against the essentially democratic character of the electoral process that produces the newer (despite the fact that the electors are in the two cases the same men and women). A moment's reflection will reveal at least one reason for that aristocratic character: although the constituencies and states differ greatly in this regard, they all nevertheless approximate, in a way in which the national constituency cannot do, to structured communities, involving numberless, highly complex face-to-face hierarchical relations among individuals—of superordination and subordination, of capacity to influence or subject to pressure and susceptibility to being influenced or subjected to pressure, of authority and obedience, of economic power and economic dependence, of prestige enjoyed and respect tendered, etc., all of which are patently relevant to the choice of a congressman or senator in a way that they are not relevant to the choice of a president. In the election of the member of Congress, a community faithful to the constitutional morality of *The Federalist* makes a decision about whom to send forward as its most virtuous man, a decision which is the more important, and which it accordingly takes the more seriously, because the community knows that it can have little effect on a presidential election (i.e., its most direct means of defending its own interests and "values" is by sending the right senator or representative to Washington, and sending the right one becomes therefore a matter of sending a man who will represent the hierarchical relations in which those interests and values are articulated). In the congressional election, therefore, the "heat" can and will go on if there is a powerful community "value" or interest at stake in the choice among available candidates; so that although the voters vote as nominal "equals" (one man, one vote) they do so under pressures that are quite unlikely to be brought to bear on their "equal" voting for President (especially as the powerful and influential in the community are normally unable to estimate accurately, for reasons we shall notice below, the probable impact of the presidential candidates upon their interests and "values," whereas they can do so with the candidates for the legislature). This state of affairs is reflected in the notorious fact that congressmen and senators, when they phone home to consult, are more likely, other things being equal, to phone bank presidents than plumbers, bishops than deacons, editors than rank-and-file newspaper readers, school superintendents than schoolmarms—and would be very foolish if they were not more likely to. And the unavoidable result is that the men chosen are likely to be far more Conservative, far more dedicated to the "status quo," than the candidate whom the same community on the same day helps elect President (or, to anticipate, than the candidate whom the same community on the same day helps defeat for President). And the chances of their disagreeing with that candidate a few months later on "most important" and "important" questions are, on the face of it, excellent—so that we have at least one built-in reason for expecting executive-legislative tension.

B. The difference in the discussion process as we see it go forward in the constituencies, and the discussion process as we see it go forward in the national forum. This is partly a matter of the point just made (that the constituency is to a far greater extent a structured community), and partly a matter (not quite the same thing) of the sheer difference in size between the local constituency and the nation—or, as I should prefer to put it, of the kind of considerations that led that remarkable "empirical" political theorist, J.-J. Rousseau, to declare, at a crucial point in *Du contrat social,* that there is more wisdom in small bands of Swiss peasants gathered around oak trees to conduct their affairs than, so to speak, in all the governments of Europe. One of the questions that that sentence necessarily poses, when we examine it carefully (and that which leads on to what I believe to be a correct interpretation of it), is whether it intends a tribute (which the attribution of wisdom certainly was for Rousseau), (1) to the Swiss, or (2) to peasants, or (3) to peasants who are also Swiss, or (4) to small groups of persons caught up in a certain kind of discussion situation. The context, I suggest, leaves no doubt that the correct answer here is (4): Rousseau certainly thought highly of the Swiss, but not so highly as to claim any sort of monopoly of wisdom for them. He also thought highly of peasants, because of their simplicity of life (if you like—which I don't—because of their closer approximation to the "noble savage"), but precisely *not* because of their native wisdom in the sense intended here, which evidently has to do with wise decisions concerning public affairs. By the same token, as we know from the *Julie,* he thought highly of Swiss peasants in particular, but not so highly as to permit himself the claim that the small bands, merely because made up of Swiss peasants, are the repositories of wisdom. The emphasis, in other words, is upon the "small bands," the fact that each embraces only a small number of individuals, and on the fact of that small number being gathered to dispatch the public business of a small community—the Swiss peasants and

The Two Majorities in American Politics

the oak tree being simply the symbol, the example, that comes most readily to Rousseau's mind. So we are led on to ask, what difference or differences does Rousseau think he sees between their "deliberation" and other kinds of deliberation? We can, I think, answer with some confidence. First, there is a presumption that each small band is talking about something, not nothing. Second, there is a presumption, because of each band's relatedness to the community whose affairs it is dispatching, that its members are reasonably well-informed about the something they are talking about—the implication being (it is caught up and developed in the *Government of Poland*) that, as a discussion group increases in number and a constituency in size, there is greater and greater danger that the persons concerned will find themselves talking about nothing, not something, and will also find themselves talking about situations and problems that are too large, too complicated, for them to understand. Wise deliberation—the point recurs again and again in Rousseau's political writings—occurs only where people are discussing problems that they can, so to speak, "get outside of," and where the participants in the discussion are not so numerous as to give scope to the gifts of the orator and the rhetorician.

Now: evidently a congressional or senatorial constituency is not a small band gathered around an oak tree; but also nothing can be more certain than that the *national* constituency in America long ago became so large and complex that, even were there candidates who themselves understood it (which is doubtful), the audiences to which they must address themselves do not understand it, cannot even visualize it. Yet we have engrafted upon our constitution an additional electoral process that forces discussion of "national" problems in the national constituency; that obliges candidates to "go to the people" and court votes; and that, for the reason just mentioned, makes it necessary for them to avoid talking about something and leaves them no alternative but to talk about nothing—that is (for this is always the most convenient way of talking about nothing), to talk about high (or at least high-sounding) principle, without application to any concrete situation or problem. Add to this the fact that

46

the candidates, hard put to it to produce in a few weeks enough speeches to see them through the campaign, must enlist the assistance of speech-writers, who come as a matter of course from the intellectual community we have frequently mentioned above, and things—*inter alia,* the sheer impossibility of saying, after a presidential election, what "issues" it has decided—begin to fall into place. There are no issues, because both candidates for the most part merely repeat, as they swing from whistle-stop to whistle-stop and television studio to television studio, the policy platitudes that constitute the table-talk in our faculty clubs. No one, not even the most skilled textual analyst, can tease out of the speeches any dependable clue as to what difference it will actually make which of the two is elected. It seems probable, indeed, that the candidates themselves, unless one of them be a White House incumbent, do not know what use they would make of the vast powers of the presidency. And the inevitable result, as intimated above, is that what you get out of the presidential election is what amounts to a *unanimous* mandate for the principles *both* candidates have been enunciating, which is to say: the presidential election not only permits the electorate, but virtually obliges it, to overestimate its dedication to the pleasant-sounding maxims that have been poured into its ears. Even did the electorate not deceive itself on this point, moreover, it has no way to arrest the process: it must vote for one of the two candidates, and tacitly commit itself, whether it likes it or not, to what they have both been saying.

We now stand in the presence, I believe, of the decisive explanation of executive-legislative tension in the American political system, and the decisive clue to its meaning. Elections for congressmen, and up to now at least most elections for senator, do not and cannot follow the pattern just outlined. With rare exceptions, for one thing, the relevant campaigns are not running debates between the candidates, and thus do not offer them the temptation to raise each other's ante in the matter of principle. For another thing, principle is for the most part *not* what gets talked about, but rather realities, problems, the potential benefits and potential costs (and for whom) of doing this rather than that—all in a context where the principles that are applied are those (very different we may be sure from those of the presidential candidates) upon which the constituents are actually accustomed to act. The talk generated by the campaign, much of it at least, is in small groups made up of persons involved in the actual face-to-face situations we spoke of earlier, and is, therefore, not wholly dissimilar to that of those peasants under the oak tree. So that, insofar as the presidential election encourages the electorate to overestimate its dedication to moral principle, the congressional election encourages them, nay, obliges them, to take a more realistic view of themselves, and to send forth a candidate who will represent, and act in terms of, that more realistic view. By remaining pretty much what the Framers intended them to be, in other words, the congressional elections, in the context of the engrafted presidential election, provide a highly necessary corrective against the bias toward quixotism inherent in our presidential elections. They add the indispensable ingredient of Sancho Panzism, of not liking to be tossed up in a blanket even for high principle, and of liking to see a meal or two ahead even if the crusade for justice has to bide a little. And it is well they do; the alternative would be national policies based upon a wholly false picture of the sacrifices the electorate are prepared to make for the lofty objectives held up to them by presidential aspirants. And executive-legislative tension is the means by which the corrective works itself out.

If the foregoing analysis is correct, the tension between Executive and Legislative has a deeper meaning—one which, however, begins to emerge only when we challenge the notion that the "high principle" represented by the President and the bureaucracy is indeed high principle, and that the long run task is to somehow "educate" the congressmen, and out beyond the congressmen the electorate, to acceptance of it. That meaning has to do with the dangerous gap that yawns between high principle as it is understood in the intellectual community (which makes its influence felt through the President and the bureaucracy) and high principle as it is understood by the remainder of the population (which makes its influence felt through the Congress). To put it differently, the deeper meaning emerges when we abandon the fiction (which I have employed above for purposes of exposition) that we have on the one hand an Executive devoted to high principle and a Legislature whose majority simply refuse to live up to it, and confront the possibility that what we have is in fact two *conceptions* of high principle about which reasonable men may legitimately differ. Whilst we maintain the fiction, the task we must perform is indeed that of "educating" the congressmen, and, off beyond them, the electorate, "up" to acceptance of high principle. Once we abandon it, the task *might* become that of helping the congressmen to "educate" the intellectual community "up" to acceptance of the principles that underlie congressional resistance to executive proposals. In the one case (whilst we maintain the fiction), discussion is unnecessary; in the other case (where we recognize that what we stand over against is two sharply differing conceptions of the destiny and perfection of America and of mankind, each of which conceivably has something to be said for it), discussion is indispensable. And in order to decide, as individuals, whom to support when executive-legislative tension arises, we must reopen (that is, cease to treat as closed), reopen in a context of mutual good faith and respect, the deepest issues between American Conservatism and American Liberalism. Reopen them, and, I repeat, discuss them; which we are much out of the habit of doing.

Chapter 3

McCarthyism: The Pons Asinorum of Contemporary Conservatism

My purpose in this chapter is neither to bury Joseph R. Mc-Carthy, nor to praise him. As for burying him, that was done many years ago by more competent, and far more eager, hands than mine. As for praising him, that, like damning him, seems to me to have entered upon a phase in which everybody merely spins his wheels. The basic claims put forward on both sides— we should bless McCarthy's memory, we should rue the day he was born—no longer change; the claimants do not listen to, or even hear, one another, would not understand one another even if they did listen. They are likely, from now on, to persuade only themselves, and those who already agree with them. My purpose, I say, is neither to bury McCarthy nor to praise him but rather, starting out with one simple, non-controversial statement about the McCarthy episode (perhaps the only non-controversial statement that can be made about it), to raise and try to answer one simple question, which statement and which question I propose to put as follows: There were "McCarthyites," and there were "anti-McCarthyites," and they got mad at each other, very mad, and stayed mad at one another—if anything, got madder and madder at one another—through a period of several years.[1] And

[1] Note the implication, which I believe to be correct, that at some point the two camps stopped being mad at each other, or at least *that* mad—a point to which I return *in extenso* below. I am not unaware, of course, that McCarthyism remains, especially in "intellectual" circles, a "touchy" subject, so that the hostess in those circles who likes everything to go nicely all evening keeps an ear cocked for Mc-Carthy's name, remains constantly poised to intervene (even at the far end of the

the question arises: What exactly was everybody so mad about? What was the issue?

Or, to expand the statement a little, there was a fight, if not a war at least a long, sustained battle; heavy artillery was brought into play on both sides; men fought in that battle with the kind of bitterness and acrimony that human beings appear to reserve for those occasions on which brother fights brother,[2] cousin fights cousin, Damon—yes, it was often so, as I can testify from personal experience—fights Pythias. For a long while smoke hung thick over the field of battle, so that visibility was poor and there was great confusion on the part of the observing public, not merely as to how, at any given moment, the battle was going, but even as to what precisely the fighting was about—as to what exactly was getting decided, as to what actually the victor, once he emerged triumphant, would have won. Moreover, so thick was the smoke that the combatants themselves often became hazy in their minds, even differed among themselves, as to who was whose enemy and as to the sense in which this or that "enemy," if he was an enemy, was an enemy. At the time, therefore (and even for a long while afterwards), the question I raise here— What was everybody so mad about?—probably could not have been answered in a satisfactory manner. There had to be time first for the smoke to clear, and then for McCarthy to be buried, and, finally, for McCarthy to be praised and damned to such a point that no single laudatory or vituperative word that could be said about him remained still to be said.

By now, however—so at least I like to think—it should be otherwise; not only has the smoke lifted, but we have a whole generation amongst us who know of the battle only by hearsay; if we cannot answer the question now, we never shall be able to answer

table) with if not the weather then something more adroit like, "Steve, did you read Arthur Krock's column yesterday?", and heaves a silent sigh of relief if the ploy works. But things have cooled down very considerably.

[2] See William F. Buckley, Jr., and L. Brent Bozell, *McCarthy and His Enemies* (Chicago: Henry Regnery, 1954 and 1962), *passim*. This remains the only serious book we have about the battle—as, to this day, it continues to await an intellectually responsible reply from those who disagree with its conclusions. Richard Rovere's *McCarthy* (New York: Harcourt, Brace & Co., 1959), is, by comparison, contemptible, especially as no one can plead in its defense that its author, one of the two most gifted Left-wing publicists of our day, is capable of nothing better.

it. And it would, I submit, be sickening to have to conclude, as conclude we must if we cannot answer my question, that the fight was over nothing you can put your finger on; that the energies and heartaches that went into it were wasted energies and wasted heartaches; that, most horrible of all to contemplate, nobody won, nothing got decided, and it was all sound and fury, signifying nothing. My question, though simple, is also a grave question: either the McCarthyites and anti-McCarthyites got that mad at each other for some good and intelligible reason, or we all (for all of us of a certain age were, I suppose, one or the other, McCarthyites or anti-McCarthyites) made colossal fools of ourselves; and if we did we had best now face up to it, lest tomorrow we go make fools of ourselves again.[3]

Now let us, for the moment, postpone my question and, fixing attention on the statement itself, pause to say several things about it that need to be said in order to place it in its proper context:

First, that this sort of "getting-mad" is not usual in American politics. Our politics, as Professor Clinton Rossiter has observed at length in a recent book,[4] tend to be "low-key" politics, politics that precisely do not divide men on issues that are mad-making. And I have myself argued, in a book I wrote several years ago with a collaborator,[5] that the *genius* of our political system lies in the sloughing-off of genuinely controversial issues—sloughing them off in order for them either to be handled outside the system itself (or better still, to be handled not at all, that is, suppressed or [6] as sometimes happens, repressed—into the deep re-

---

[3] Note, in anticipation of my subsequent argument, that the question "Were they mad at each other for some good and intelligible reason?" and the question, "Did anything get decided, did anybody win?" are different questions—so that the answer to the first could be "Yes" and that to the second "No," or if not "No" then "What got decided was to postpone a decision on the big issue."

[4] See Clinton Rossiter, *Parties and Politics in America* (Ithaca: Cornell University Press, 1960), *passim*.

[5] See Austin Ranney and Willmoore Kendall, *Democracy and the American Party System* (New York: Harcourt, Brace & Co., 1955).

[6] The classic case, perhaps, arose from an article by J. B. Matthews on the penetration of the Protestant churches by Communism. When, many months after its publication, the article became the topic of angry controversy, Dwight Eisenhower restored peace by proclaiming that the Protestant churches are among our basic institutions, and therefore could not be penetrated by Communism. The issue—I do not exaggerate—promptly disappeared.

cesses of our collective unconscious, where, providentially, we can forget all about them). The McCarthy phase, or episode, or set-to—call it what you like—was then something presumptively special in our political history, something that we must not expect to explain to ourselves with everyday concepts and everyday tools of analysis. It was no mere quarrel, for example, over allocation of the contents of the porkbarrel or whether a businessman from Kansas City is to be confirmed as Ambassador to Ghana.

Secondly (that is, the second thing that needs to be said about how mad everybody got), we must not take for granted that the real issue ever, at the time, actually got put into words, ever actually thrust itself into the consciousness of the actors in the drama. To assume that the real issue was what got talked about —so we are assured by, variously, marriage counselors and trade-dispute arbitrators, all of whom are in debt here to the greatest of female political scientists in America, Mary Follett—to assume such a thing, they say, is to show ignorance of the way quarrels among human beings generate and develop. John and Mary may *think* they are quarreling about whether to send Jo-Ann to Mount Holyoke or Chicago, and end up getting very mad at each other about it, and staying mad weeks on end. But not so, says the marriage counselor; the issue must be one that goes to the very depths of the marriage relation between John and Mary. What is really being fought about is Mary's feeling that John somehow does not treat her as an equal, or if not that then some far-reaching sexual maladjustment that neither John nor Mary would dream of articulating and may not even be aware of, or John and Mary's shared but inarticulate feeling that John has turned out to be a second-rater in his profession. The quarrel, according to Miss Follett and her followers, must go on and on about this basically irrelevant issue or that one, go on and on and get worse and worse, either until it is repressed or until the real issue is somehow brought out into the open and, with or without the help of an outsider, dealt with on its merits.

Thirdly—a similar but not quite the same point—the chances are that the real issue, once out in the open, will prove to be far more "important" and difficult than the issue over which the quarrelers think they have been quarreling; that, concretely, it will prove to involve the meaning and quality and above all the destiny of the relatedness of the quarrelers. He who delves into the depths of a quarrel, an honest-to-goodness, bitter, and sustained quarrel, must not expect to come up with peanuts, or any known equivalent of peanuts.

Two other small points of that kind and we shall have done with preliminaries:

A. The McCarthyites were mad at the anti-McCarthyites, and the anti-McCarthyites were mad at the McCarthyites, which, I am saying, is unusual in our low-key politics. But to that I must now add (not, as I am tempted to do, that the anti-McCarthyites were madder than the McCarthyites—angrier, more bitter, more ready to paste someone in the nose—because that would perhaps slosh over into the controversial) that what is most unusual, and a different matter altogether, is that the anti-McCarthyites got mad at all. For the anti-McCarthyites were the Liberals; and the Liberals, as I understand them, have some built-in reasons for not getting mad that the McCarthyites, the anti-Liberals, do not have—built-in reasons connected, as I understand the matter, with the whole metaphysical and epistemological stance of contemporary American Liberalism. That is to say, the Liberals are usually the Tentative Ones of contemporary politics: they believe that everyone is entitled to his point of view, that in general one man's opinion is as good as another's, that, as I like to put it, all questions are open questions. Officially, therefore, they don't get mad—have, in point of fact, got really "fightin' " mad only twice within the memory of living man—once, of course, at Adolf Hitler, then a few years later and on their own principles equally unaccountably, at Joe McCarthy. Let us be quite clear about this. When A gets mad at B and sets out to defeat him cost what it may, A, whatever his metaphysics and whatever his epistemology, ends up saying, and saying in the most eloquent manner possible, which is by his actions: B is *wrong* about the issue over which we have fallen out, and *I* am *right*. Now A's metaphysical and epistemological commitments may or may not admit of his making any such assertion; if A is a Liberal, they certainly do not admit of it, because the Master, John Stuart Mill,[7] taught above all that one does not assert one's "infallibility." In asserting it, A postpones until later (perhaps, as in the two cases mentioned, until the Greek kalends) a day of reckoning that, properly speaking, he has no right to sidestep (and along with it, the day on which he will get back to normal, which is to say: not be mad at Stalin, not be mad at World Communism, not be mad at Khrushchev—because who can say, after all, who is right and who is wrong in politics?). Yet, I am saying, A the Liberal did get mad at Joe McCarthy, did set out to defeat him *coûte que coûte,* did proclaim to the four winds that McCarthy was wrong and he was right. And this, I suggest, forces upon us a slightly revised but still more fascinating version of my original statement, namely that everybody got mad, including the professional Tentative Ones, the professional Don't-get-madders. At the same time, it lends color to our suspicion that the issue actually at stake went very deep, and never got itself stated in satisfactory terms. (As for the McCarthyites, they, unlike the Liberals, have built-in reasons for getting mad; they are the Non-tentative Ones of our politics, the Absolutists, the people who couldn't care less if they get caught assuming their own "infallibility." We have, therefore, less reason to be surprised at their getting mad. They are on the point of getting mad, and for good reason, all the time.) [8]

B. We might profitably, though without making too big a thing of it, remind ourselves of the other issues about which Americans, despite their low-key politics, have had big quarrels in the past. Mercifully, there have been very few of them; and conspicuously absent from among them, mercifully again, have been the Constitution, the Bill of Rights, and, surprisingly perhaps, the Amendments to the Constitution posterior to the Bill of Rights. Let us, by way of background, tick them off: During the years 1776-1779 there was the issue of *Loyalism,* which resulted in our driving the Loyalists into Canada. In the early

---

[7] See below, Chapter Six.
[8] See below, pp. 69-76.

years of the Republic there arose the issue of the Alien and Sedition Acts—which resulted in the silencing, nay, the persecution, of the alleged seditionists. During the years just before and during the Civil War, there was the issue of slavery. All three, I say, are cases where Americans got very mad at one another. They stayed mad for a long time, and were determined not to compromise, or let the matter drop, but to *win*—either to repudiate or perpetuate the authority of the King in Parliament, either to enforce or get rid of the Alien and Sedition Acts, either to abolish slavery or to save it as the South's "peculiar institution." And all three, as we can see in retrospect, involved an issue that bore, in the deepest and most direct manner possible to imagine, on the very destiny of the American people. All three involved, that is to say, a question that the American people must answer in order to know themselves as the kind of people they are, in order to achieve clarity as to their identity as a people, their mission in history, their responsibility under God—so, at least in those days, they would have put it—for the kind of political and social *order* they were to create and maintain in history. All three, let us note finally, are cases in which people kept on being mad until somebody won, and was understood by both sides to have won, and so made good its point about the destiny of America.

So much for preliminaries. I turn now to my question, and I propose to work my way toward an answer to it by taking up, then rejecting, in good Socratic manner, some "easy" answers that for one reason or another (as I hope to show) simply will not do. They are, as the reader will guess from my reference to Socratic method, the answers you will get if you go button-holing people down in the market place, putting the question to them, and listening attentively to what they come up with. I got mine by bringing the question up one evening in the Spring of 1962, at a "stag" dinner party made up of professors of political science at a well-known East Coast university. I shall, for convenience' sake, assign numbers to them, and devote a section of the present chapter to each.

ANSWER NUMBER ONE

The issue was Joe McCarthy himself. McCarthy was rude, ruthless, fanatical. He lacked, as the good Mr. Welch [9] put it, all "sense of decency." He was a master of demagogy, of, to quote the Federalist Papers, those "vicious arts, by which elections are too often carried." He reflected a mood of "hysteria" amongst the electorate, was himself hysterical, generated hysteria in others. He did not play politics according to the rules of the game as we understand them here in America. His conduct, as a Senate majority finally got around to putting it, was unbecoming a Senator and a gentleman. He browbeat witnesses. He took advantage of his senatorial immunity in order to blacken the reputations and assassinate the character of innocent persons; like Fr. Coughlin, like Gerald L. K. Smith, like Fritz Kuhn himself, he was a hater, a know-nothing, a man who knew and spoke no language other than that of hatred. He represented, in any case, a tendency that had to be nipped in the bud—lest it develop into an American version of that which it most resembled, namely, Nazism. He was, finally, a fraud; he never uncovered a single Communist. All you had to do was *see* him, on television, in order to realize that here was a man who must be struck down. What more natural, then, than that he should divide the country into two fanatically warring groups, namely, (a) those who like and go in for that kind of thing—of whom there are always only too many, all only too ready to respond with fury to any who resist them—and (b) the rest of us, who cling to at least minimum standards of civility?

That, I think, is a fair summary of the "case" against McCarthy as, say, a *Washington Post* editorial might have put it in 1952, or as a deeply convinced anti-McCarthyite (with, of course, a longer memory than most anti-McCarthyites have) would put it today.

Now, the McCarthyites among my readers would, no doubt, like me to linger over the charges, one by one, and refute them— as, for the most part anyhow, they have been refuted in The Book

[9] Counsel for the Government in the "famous" televised hearings.

No Liberal Reads, Buckley and Bozell (see Note 2, above). I propose, however, to do nothing of the kind, since one of the advantages of my simple question—as compared to the questions on which discussion in this area has turned in recent years—is this: It frees us from the necessity of conducting the argument on that plane and enables us to take what we may, I think, fairly call higher ground. It enables us even to enter a demurrer—not, of course, to plead McCarthy guilty as charged, but to plead that the facts, even if they were as alleged, do not support the claim with which we are concerned, namely, that we have before us an answer to my simple question. The facts, as alleged, can at best illuminate only a small part of our problem, and for the following easy-to-document reason: The McCarthyites and anti-McCarthyites were mad at each other, "fightin' " mad at each other, before ever McCarthy appeared on the scene, and long, long before he became Chairman of the Committee on Government Operations. Which is to say, those who offer the answer before us are, quite simply, talking bad history and exaggerating out of all proportion the importance of McCarthy in the development of what I, at least, have no objection to calling McCarthyism. They are answering at most only a tiny part of our question, when what we want, what we must demand, is an answer to the whole question. McCarthy, like Achilles after the death of Patroclus, stepped into a battle that was already raging, one in which the lines were already drawn, one whose outcome he could and did still affect, but *not* one in which he could possibly become the issue being fought over. Never mind that the battle-waging armies ended up with new names—McCarthyites, anti-McCarthyites—because of his entry into the fray. Never mind, either, that the anti-McCarthyites do seem, as a matter of history, to have promptly got a lot madder at the McCarthyites than they had been before. Never mind, finally, that both armies increased considerably in size between the famous speech at Wheeling and the famous censure motion in the United States Senate. We are not asking why people got madder off at the end, or even why at some point the anger suddenly spread in ever-widening circles (as it did), but rather, What were people mad about to begin with?

*What, for example, what were they mad about at the (earlier)
time of the Hiss case?* What was the *real* issue? And the real issue was not, could not have been, McCarthy himself.

ANSWER NUMBER TWO

The issue was an issue between two conflicting views of World
Communism and the World Communist movement, between—
I shall try here, as I did with Answer Number One, to put the
thing from the side of the anti-McCarthyites, lest I be accused
of stacking the cards in favor of the position with which, for
good or ill, my own name is associated—those who are running
scared in the presence of the so-called Communist threat, and
those who are keeping their heads. Between those who would
seek a false security by attempting to use against Communism
the Communists' own weapons, and those who are prepared to
settle for that degree of security that is possible, who believe that
security can be achieved with an arsenal limited to democracy's
normal weapons, which are those of negotiation and persuasion.
Between those who think that by striking out at the Communist
danger in all directions at once we can somehow eliminate it,
somehow conjure it out of existence, and those who have got it
through their heads that Communism, the Communist Empire
on the world scene, the Communist minority at home, is something you have to learn to live with and ought to learn to live
with because it is, after all, something that *we*, by our shortcomings, have brought upon ourselves. Between those who believe
that the correct answer to Communism is military force internationally and coercive thought-control domestically, and those
who know that these are not answers at all, that the struggle
against Communism is a struggle over men's minds and hearts
and souls, is in any case a battle that you win, if you win at all,
by eliminating the poverty, the discrimination, the injustice, the
inequality, that make Communism attractive and give the Communists their strategic opportunities. Between those who see the
Communist danger as imposing upon us a choice between liberty
and security, and would unhesitatingly sacrifice the former to
the latter, and those of us who know for one thing that Com-

munism is not that kind of danger, and know for another thing that the battle against Communism is not worth winning if, in winning it, we must lose our freedom. Between those who attribute to the Communists supernatural, nay, miraculous powers of seduction, of deceit, of winning against even the most unfavorable odds, and those who know that the Communists are mere men like ourselves, no more able to infiltrate our councils, our institutions, our high places, than we are to infiltrate theirs. Between those who have somehow convinced themselves that the Communists never sleep, and those of us who know that Communists, like other people, need their eight hours in the sack. Between those who think the Communists actually believe in their so-called ideology: Marxism, the inevitability of Communist victory, etc., and those of us sufficiently knowledgeable to take that sort of thing with a grain of salt, to realize that what we are up against is not something new and different properly called the Communist Empire, but something old and familiar properly called Russian nationalism. Between those who think that a Communist dictatorship can keep on being Communist and keep on being a dictatorship for ever and ever, and those of us who know that dictatorships, including Communist dictatorships, mellow and go soft as they get old, and that revolutionaries, even the wildest of revolutionaries, grow conservative and cautious as they become habituated to power. Between those who think the Communists will stop at nothing, not even totally destructive universal war, in their bid for world empire, and those of us who know that the Communists, the Russian government and the Russian people alike, want, above all, peace. Between those so addled in their wits by Communism that they think that even their next door neighbor may well be a Communist, and so see a Communist stripling behind every sapling, and those of us who remember, in the teeth of the Communist threat, that America is built upon trust among neighbors, that Americans do not sow the seeds of suspicion in each other's back yards. Between those who think the Communists really have found a way to repress, and hold in check, the forces that make for freedom in any society, and those of us who know that man's desire for freedom must in the end triumph over all obstacles. Between those who think the Communists mean it when they say they will "bury" us, and those of us who know that all that is just Communist "talk" and blustering. Between those who cling stubbornly to the notion that there are deep and irreconcilable differences between our so-called free society and the so-called slave society of the Soviet Union, and so take no cognizance of the political and economic and social change that goes forward within the Communist Empire, and those, better-informed, unencumbered by dogmatic preconceptions, who realize that with each passing day American society and Soviet society become "more alike"—become, each of them, a closer approximation to the universal society of the future, which will of course combine in beneficent union the better features of them both.

Answer Two is, clearly, a better answer than Answer One. It is, for one thing, better history. Through the period that we ought to have in mind when we speak of these matters, there have indeed been current among us two views of the nature and meaning of World Communism, two views of which, as I like to think anyhow, the little rundown I have just given provides a not inaccurate summary; two views and, in general, two groups of "those who's," respectively committed to the one or the other; two groups, moreover, whose stand on a whole series of issues in public policy that arose through the period tended to reflect the one or the other of the two views. No harm is done, furthermore, by calling the one of the two views the McCarthyite view and the other the anti-McCarthyite view—*provided*, however, that we remember, here as before, that both views had crystalized, and attracted numerous adherents, long before McCarthy appeared upon the scene; that the McCarthyite view was not invented by McCarthy; that it had, indeed, through the years in question, both more knowledgeable and more vigorous exponents than McCarthy; that, in a word, *it had best be thought of as having itself produced McCarthy rather than McCarthy it.* Insofar as it is correct, then, Answer Two has the further advantage of being correct for the whole period and not, like Number One, only for the years immediately following the Wheeling speech.

One easily sees, moreover, why those who entertained the Mc-Carthyite view tended to get mad at those who entertained the anti-McCarthyite view. At least one of the two views, possibly perhaps both of them but at least one of them, must be wrong, intellectually incorrect, which is to say they cannot both be correct. Each of the two views, pretty clearly moreover, is pregnant with implications about policy, both foreign policy and internal security policy, that flatly contradict the implications of the other, so that any time a policy decision has to be made in either of those two areas the two groups are likely, other things being equal, to array themselves on opposite sides. Nor is that all. Since each view, from the standpoint of the other, would commit the nation to policies certain to turn out to be suicidal, we readily understand how and why the two groups did get mad at each other early in the period, and got madder and madder at each other as the period progressed. For each, in the eyes of the other, was guilty of an error of judgment so great as to seem unforgivable.

Indeed, Answer Two makes so much sense that we are tempted to adopt it out of hand as the correct answer to our question, and let it go at that. Our question is answered, and we can all settle back in our chairs and forget about it.

I suggest, nevertheless, that we take (but hold until we are sure we can do better) a rain-check on Answer Two as well as on Number One—not because Answer Two isn't correct as far as it goes (which I have conceded it is), but because, to me at least, it seems inadequate psychologically, and because its assumptions about the articulateness of American political struggles are somewhat more flattering than we deserve. Concretely, I find that Answer Two explains to me why some people got mad, but not why so many people got mad, or why anybody—to go back to my original form of words—got all *that* mad. The issue that Answer Two insists upon is (a) for the most part an issue about foreign policy, and I do not believe that Americans in general were at any time during that period that interested in foreign policy, and (b) an intellectual issue, where the ultimate crime the alleged criminals are being accused of is merely stupidity, and I do not believe we had yet reached the day when intellectual issues, issues ultimately capable of being talked out or, failing that, capable of being resolved by sound scholarship, arouse in us the kind of passions that were displayed in the clash between McCarthyism and anti-McCarthyism.[10] Millions of the persons who rallied around McCarthy, I should guess, and hundreds of thousands (for I do not believe there were millions) of the persons who rallied against him, entertained no view whatever on the nature of Communism, and, in any case, were not about to be moving in the direction of civil war against those who entertained a view different from their own. In other words, our correct and inclusive answer, if and when we find it, will tap a dimension that Answer Two conspicuously avoids, namely—for they were not a slip on my part, those words "civil war"—the civil war dimension, the dimension, if you like, of mutual accusations of heresy. And having said that, I can venture the following thesis: The ultimate crime of which McCarthyites and anti-McCarthyites were accusing one another was, make no mistake about it, that of heresy; the passions generated were, make again no mistake about it, passions appropriate not to an intellectual debate but to a heresy-hunt, and we shall not understand them, ever, unless we bear that in mind.

To which let me add, before passing on to Answer Number Three: if Answer Two were correct, people would evidently be madder today than they were in 1953, which in point of fact, as I have intimated above, they certainly are not. For the differences among us as to the nature and meaning of Communism are no less deep, no less unresolved, than in 1952; nor, I feel safe in saying further, have the stakes, which I repeat involve the very survival of the United States, got any lower. The correct answer to our question, then, must be able to explain why the clash between McCarthyites and anti-McCarthyites seems not only not to have become sharper, but to be less sharp today than it did nine years ago; and Answer Two cannot explain that for us. The cor-

---

[10] Not that intellectual issues never arouse passions. They do, but exactly in the quarters where we are taught least to expect them, namely, those of the so-called "exact" physical scientists. On the latter point, see Michael Polanyi, *Personal Knowledge: Towards a Post-Critical Philosophy* (Chicago: University of Chicago, 1958), *passim*.

rect explanation, in short, must explain not only the storm, but also the apparent ensuing calm.

ANSWER NUMBER THREE

The clash between McCarthy and his enemies was merely another chapter in the history of the separation and balancing of power within the American political system. What was at issue was neither differing views of Communism as such (the clash might equally well have occurred over some other topic), nor, to go back to Answer One, McCarthy himself as such (although, say the proponents of this view, McCarthy had personal qualities that made the dispute angrier than it would otherwise have been, perhaps even innate tendencies of character that disposed him to play the role of hysteria-monger), since the forces operating through McCarthy might equally have expressed themselves through some other leader. The issue was, rather, that of legislative encroachment on the constitutional powers of the Executive. For one thing McCarthy pressed the prerogatives of congressional investigating committees to hitherto-unheard-of-lengths—as witness, for example, his apparent belief that those prerogatives extended even within the sacred precincts of the nation's universities. For another, even if we were to grant that Congress was acting within its constitutional powers when it put the Internal Security program on the statute books (even if we were, *per impossible,* to grant that the program did not violate the freedom of speech clause of the First Amendment), still enforcement of the relevant laws was the proper business of the President and his subordinates in the executive branch of government—with, of course, appeals where appeals might be required to the courts of law. McCarthy's attempts to intervene in the dispatch of individual cases, his explicit claim that the Committee on Government Operations was entitled to watch over and criticize the detail of internal security administration, therefore represented congressional self-aggrandizement in its most blatant and dangerous form. Nor is that all. McCarthy undermined discipline in the Executive Branch by openly inviting civil servants with tales to bear to break the chain of command and come directly to him; he would right all wrongs, punish all iniquities. Nor is even that all. The day came when foreign service officers were obliged to falsify their reports lest McCarthy haul them before his committee and, with his usual techniques of insinuation and innuendo, his usual willingness to assume a man guilty until proven innocent, crucify them for their alleged pro-Communist bias. Nay, still more. The day came when the foreign service could no longer attract able recruits because no young man in his senses would expose himself to the risks McCarthy had injected into the career of the foreign service officer; considerations alike of decency and of self-interest sent men of talent into other careers. Even McCarthy's "working capital," for that matter, the scraps of so-called "information" that he "held in his hand" and that enabled him to move in on his victims, came to him through violations of security regulations; his very possession of them was legislative encroachment. McCarthy, in short McCarthy every time he opened his mouth, upset the separation of powers equilibrium that is central and sacred in the American political tradition. He upset it, moreover (if we abstract from his having been a Senator not a member of the House of Representatives), in precisely the manner contemplated by the Founders of the Republic, namely, through the workings of a demagogically-led popular movement, adverse to natural rights and to the public interest, which sweeps through the country, establishes itself in Congress, finds itself unable to accomplish its objectives because of the defensive weapons the Constitution entrusts to the two other co-equal and coordinate branches of government—and must, willy-nilly, seek to concentrate all power in its own hands. The McCarthy movement did just that, and, naturally enough, all in America who love constitutional government, that is, limited government, saw in him a threat to all that they most value in the American political tradition, responded to him with righteous anger, struck back at him as best they could. Nor, on the anti-McCarthy side at least, is any other answer needed to the question, "Why did people get so mad?"

Here, moreover, as with Answer Two though not with Answer One, the supposed issue is neat and symmetrical, that is, joined in almost identical terms from the other side: The Internal Security Program, or Loyalty Program as it was called in its early days, went onto the statute books by virtue of the exercise by Congress of powers clearly vested in it by the Constitution. The Executive Branch of government, the Department of State in particular, refused from the first moment to recognize the necessity for such legislation. It called its constitutionality into question, showed a complete lack of sympathy both with its underlying principles and its objectives, openly defied it, did everything it could to frustrate the committees—the Internal Security Committee in the Senate, the Committee on Un-American Activities in the House—Congress charged with responsibility for studying and reporting upon the Communist threat. The Executive withheld information from them (on the mostly spurious grounds of so-called "classification"), lied to them *ad libitum*, refused, even in the clearest cases, to act upon information provided by them—or, for that matter, upon information provided by their great ally within the Executive Branch itself, the F.B.I. The Executive kept in positions of high authority and honor men who obviously could not meet the loyalty-security standards set by the Congress. It moved—through the Truman Loyalty Order of 1947, which arbitrarily shifted the administrative standard in loyalty cases so as to give to the individual not the government the benefit of doubt—to emasculate the Program, starved the security offices in the great government departments, and mobilized against the Program not only the formidable opinion-making resources of its bureaucracy but also those of the newspapers and the radio and television networks. Subsequently, after McCarthy's appearance on the scene as a sub-committee chairman, it denied Congress' crystal-clear right to inquire whether its statutes were being faithfully executed. If there was encroachment, then it was clearly a matter of the Executive's encroaching upon Congress. Congress, off at the end, had no alternative but to raise up a McCarthy, and insist upon its right to exercise the investigative powers needed in order to prevent the Executive from becoming, quite simply, a law unto itself. Nor could any man capable of grasping the clear language of the Constitution hesitate as to where, in the interests of constitutional govern-

ment and of the American political system as traditionally understood, to throw his support. If McCarthy had not existed it would
have been necessary, for the sake of constitutional equilibrium,
to invent him; and, naturally enough, the people, jealous always
of the powers of that branch of government which, because closest
to them in point both of time and of distance, they regard as
peculiarly theirs, rallied around him. As for abuse of investigative powers, the Supreme Court is always there to set metes and
bounds for congressional committees, and the records contain *no*
Supreme Court decision that rules adversely to the McCarthy
Subcommittee.

The issue, I repeat, is neat and symmetrical, but as regards an
answer to our question we are back, I think, to where we were
with Answer Two. Some people no doubt got mad about legislative
encroachment in the area of internal security, and some no doubt
about executive defiance of the will of Congress. Both groups,
no doubt, got madder still because of the continuing dispute
over the nature and meaning of the World Communist movement; but also no-one ever heard of anybody with a soft view of
Communism getting worried, in those days, about *executive* encroachment, or of anybody with a tough view of Communism
getting worried about *legislative* encroachment. Once again,
therefore, the suspicion arises that we are flattering ourselves;
that is, vastly exaggerating, this time, our capacity as a people to
work ourselves up into a fury over an issue so legalistic and intellectual as separation of powers. The admittedly hard-to-read
slogan emblazoned upon the banners of the McCarthyites, whatever it proclaimed, could not have proclaimed the principle:
"All legislative powers herein granted shall be vested in a Congress of the United States. . . ." Answer Three is better than Answer Two in that it edges us over toward the kind of issue that
could breed charges of heresy not stupidity. But we do not, I
think, yet have hold of the right heresies.

TESTS FOR A CORRECT ANSWER

I have now taken up one at a time, and examined, the three
answers to our simple question that, as I put it to begin with, one
is likely to encounter in the market place of contemporary Ameri-

can political discussion. I have in each case found the answer either unconvincing or, insofar as convincing, inadequate; that is, incapable of explaining the *whole* of the phenomenon that has engaged our curiosity. I should, however, be very sorry for the reader to conclude that we have wasted our time; that is, made no progress whatever with our task. For we have, I like to think, insofar as we have reasoned together correctly, begun to apprehend certain tests that a correct answer to our question must be able to meet, namely:

First, it must point to an issue deep enough to possess what, for lack of a better term, we may call *genuine civil war potential,* an issue capable, therefore, of being mentioned in the same breath with the slavery issue, the Loyalism issue during the American Revolution, and the issue (about which, let me say, we know all too little) posed, very early in our history as a nation, by the Alien and Sedition Acts.

Second, it must be an issue that large numbers of people are capable of grasping with hooks that are not precisely those of the intellect—an issue capable, I am tempted to say, of being grasped intuitively, of being felt as well as thought. "As well as," mind you, not "rather than," for I do not wish to imply that it must be an issue not susceptible of being put into words, or an issue that wholly eludes rational discussion.

Thirdly, it must be an issue that, somewhere along the line, calls for an act, though not I should think necessarily a conscious act, of *moral choice* on the part of the man who "takes sides" on it. That is why I have stressed that one of its characteristics is that of not lending itself to resolution merely by sound scholarship, or to being just plain "talked out"—to a point where all may agree because all objections, on one side or the other, have been met and answered. That notion we may now refine a little by adding that it must be an issue that we would expect to be "talkable–outable," if I may put it so, only amongst men who move in their talk from common or at least reconcilable moral premises.

Fourthly, the issue must meet certain historical tests or requirements. We must be able to see why, as a matter of history, it might well have begun to make itself felt (again, I stress "felt," for it will not necessarily have been clearly articulated), why people began to get mad about it at such and such a period rather than earlier.

Fifthly, it must be an issue about which we can explain, not too unsatisfactorily, why it has seemed less sharp through the years since McCarthy's death than it did through the years preceding McCarthy's death.

Now I believe, as the reader will have guessed, that I know what the issue is, and I am going to try, in the next and concluding section of the present chapter, to get it into words and "justify" it over against the tests I have just enumerated.

THE CORRECT ANSWER

Let us go right to the heart of the matter. By the late 1930's, that is, by the end of the second decade after the Communist Revolution, every free nation in the world, whether it realized it or not, faced the following question: Are we or are we not going to permit the emergence, within our midst, of totalitarian movements? Every free nation, in other words, was by that time already confronted with evidence that efforts would in due course be made to call such movements into being, that such efforts would be strongly supported from the home bases of the existing totalitarian movements, and that those efforts could, to some extent at least, be encouraged or discouraged by the action of its own government. Most free nations, to be sure, chose to ignore that evidence, and did not pose to themselves the question I have named, not even in some more cautious form such as "Are we at least going to try to prevent the emergence here of the totalitarian movements we see flourishing in other countries?" Not so, however, the United States. By the mid-1940's it had on its statute-books an impressive array of legislation—the great names here, of course, are the Hatch Act, the Smith Act, and the so-called McCarran Rider—which (a) reflected a very considerable awareness that the problem of encouraging or discouraging totalitarian movements existed, and called for some kind of answer, and (b) announced in effect: We—whatever other free nations may do or not do—are going to put certain major obstacles in the way of such movements; we at least are not going to facilitate their emergence; we at least are going to take some perfectly obvious immediate steps that should make clear alike to the self-appointed leaders of such minorities, to the world in general, and to ourselves, where we stand on the matter; and we at least regard the emergence and growth of such minorities as on the face of it undesirable. Let us proceed at once, then, to exclude representatives of such minorities from the service of our governments, national, state, and local; and let us proceed also to clip the wings of such minorities by forbidding them, on pain of imprisonment, to advocate the overthrow of the government of the United States. Opinions might differ, let us be fair and concede it at once, as to the moment the question narrowed in legislators' minds from one concerning totalitarian movements in general to one concerning a Communist minority in particular. Opinions might differ, too, as to the moment at which the Communist movement burgeoned, in legislators' minds, from the status of a logical possibility to that of a clear and present danger. Opinions might differ, finally, as to the moment at which the American Liberals decided that the question as to the future of totalitarian movements in the United States came under the general constitutional rubric of so-called freedom-of-speech questions, and therefore under the rubric of actions permitted or prohibited to the Congress of the United States by the First Amendment to the Constitution. But all three of these developments did, in due course, take place; and we must, in order to approach the correct answer to my question, get them clearly in mind—first of all as background for the following (in my opinion) crucial points:

First, the motive that underlay the original internal security legislation was certainly *not* that of impairing or limiting the Communists' freedom of speech. The Communist being struck at was for the most part the Communist who precisely did not exercise his constitutional right (if any) to freedom of speech in order to advocate Communism, but rather the man who, having transferred his allegiance from the United States to World Communism, set out to systematically conceal the fact from his fellow-citizens. The "freedom" at stake in the early legislation, then, assuming there was one worthy the name, was not freedom of speech, which the First Amendment does forbid the Congress to impair, but rather, if a "freedom" we must have, freedom of thought—the freedom to entertain such and such opinions in the United States without being subjected to such and such disabilities and such and such disagreeable consequences. Freedom of *thought*, I say, about which the Constitution of the United States says nothing at all. (Never mind that the Liberals say that when the Constitution says freedom of speech it means, must mean, freedom of thought. We have only their word for it.)

Second, the authors and supporters of the original legislation do not appear to have had, in passing the legislation, any freedom of speech "inhibitions," or for that matter any notion that the legislation they were putting on the statute-books involved anything especially novel in the way of principle.

Thirdly, it was, nevertheless, not long before one began to hear, from Liberal quarters of course, rumblings about freedom of speech, about the patent unconstitutionality of all such legislation, about, finally, the incompatibility of all such legislation with traditional American concepts of—of all things!—freedom.[11] The United States could not take preventive action against the emergence of a Communist movement because, precisely, of its commitment to liberty!

Fourthly, after a certain moment in this train of events, everything, as I see it, conspired to conceal the issue actually, really and truly being fought over; everything but, as I have already intimated, two things: (a) Communism did at some moment acquire, in the eyes of Americans generally, the status of a "clear and present danger." And (b) the Liberals, at some moment, did pull in their horns, did change their public stance on anti-Communist legislation. Up to that moment (or those moments) what debate there was turned on the question, "Is the United

---

[11] The *locus classicus* remains the two-article series by Professor Thomas Emerson and David M. Helfeld, "Loyalty Amongst Government Employees," *Yale Law Journal*, Vol. 58, I and II (1948-1949).

States entitled to impose disabilities upon an emergent 'political' movement deemed undesirable even if it is not a clear and present danger?" or, variously, "Is there anything in the Constitution or in the American political tradition that prevents American government *or* American society from announcing: We intend to proscribe such and such 'political' opinions; to that end we intend to *persecute* those opinions, that is, to place the price of holding them—not expressing them, but holding them—so high that people will be forced to avoid them or, if they have already adopted them, to abandon them?" Up to that moment (or those moments) what debate there was was a matter of the legislators answering that question in the affirmative and the Liberals answering it in the negative. While after that moment (or those moments) the debate shifted to the very different question: "Is the United States entitled to strike at a body of opinion which constitutes a clear and present danger?", which question, because of the aforementioned shift on the part of the Liberals, almost everyone, the legislative majority and the Liberals alike, was suddenly answering in the affirmative. The original issue, in other words, simply disappeared, and, we may safely add, has hardly been heard of since.

Let me, so as to guard against any possible misundersanding, say that over again in a slightly different way. First we get what amounts to the proscription of the Communist movement in America on the grounds merely that such a movement is undesirable in the United States, and that the proscription of an undesirable movement is clearly within the power of Congress—clearly, and without any complications about impairment of "freedom of speech" or "clear and present danger." The Liberals oppose the proscription, on the grounds that Congress has no power to proscribe—unless, just possibly, in the presence of a clear and present danger. A debate gets under way that, had the terms not changed, would have had to be decided one way or the other, yet could not have been decided one way or the other without (as I shall argue more concretely in a moment) what each party to the debate regarded as the very gravest implications as to the nature of our constitutional system. But the terms did change, because of two developments which, though more or less simultaneous, we must keep rigorously separated in our minds. First, Communism became, in the eyes of people generally, the kind of clear and present danger in the presence of which even the Liberals might concede Congress' power to act. Second, the Liberals, pretty certainly on straight strategic grounds, suddenly decided that they not only might but would give their blessing to the proscription of the Communist movement as, or insofar as it was, a clear and present danger. The original issue, therefore, promptly disappears, since all that remains to be talked about is whether, or the extent to which, Communism *is* a clear and present danger. The first development, in the absence of the second, would presumably have resulted only in redoubled effort on behalf of a course of action already decided upon before it occurred (just as more fire-fighting equipment is called in when what has seemed a routine fire suddenly threatens to become a conflagration). The second development, in the absence of the first (in the absence, that is, of a decision that the fire was not a routine fire), would merely have signalized overwhelming Liberal defeat on the original issue—which would, accordingly, have been decided in favor of the legislators. But the second development in the context of the first could only have the effect of spiriting the original issue away. Which is what it did.

Now my thesis is that the issue that really divided the McCarthyites and the anti-McCarthyites was, precisely, that original issue; that once we see that to be true, everything falls into place; and that, to anticipate a little, the disappearance of that original issue was, any way you look at it, a major national misfortune. And it remains for me only (a) to note that that original issue is merely an alternative statement of the issue that political philosophers debate under the heading "the open society," [12] (b) to show that things do, once we recognize that as the issue at stake between the McCarthyites and the anti-McCarthyites, fall neatly into place, and (c) to make clear why I regard its eclipse as a "major national misfortune."

[12] See below, Chapter Six.

The Pons Asinorum of Contemporary Conservatism

Let me put it this way: All political societies, all peoples, but especially I like to think our political society, this *"people of the United States,"* is founded upon what political philosophers call a *consensus;* that is, a hard core of shared beliefs. Those beliefs that the people share are what defines its character as a political society, what embodies its meaning as a political society, what, above all perhaps, expresses its understanding of itself as a political society, of its role and responsibility in history, of its very destiny. I say that is true especially of our political society because in our case the coming into existence as a people, a certain kind of people with a certain conception of its meaning and responsibility, takes place right out in the open for all to see, takes place unshrouded by the mists of remote history or the hazes of possibly inaccurate legend. "We," cries the people of the United States at the very moment of its birth (and we should be grateful to John Courtney Murray for having recently reminded us of the fact [18]), "We," cries the American people at that moment, "hold these *truths.*" That is, "we" believe there is such a thing as Truth, believe that the particular truths of which Truth is made up are discoverable by man's reason and thus by our reason, recognize *these* truths as those to which our reason and that of our forebears have led us, and agree with one another to *hold* these truths—that is, to cherish them as ours, to hand them down in their integrity to our descendants, to defend them against being crushed out of existence by enemies from without or corrupted out of all recognition by the acids of skepticism and disbelief working from within.

Now, such a consensus, conceived of as a body of truths actually held by the people whose consensus it is, is incomprehensible *save as we understand it* (in Murray's phrase) *to exclude ideas and opinions contrary to itself.* Discussion there is and must be, freedom of thought and freedom of expression there are and must be, but within limits set by the basic consensus; freedom of thought and freedom of expression there are and must be, but not anarchy of thought or anarchy of expression. In such a society

[18] See especially the opening pages of his *We Hold These Truths* (New York: Sheed and Ward, 1961).

74

by no means are *all* questions open questions; some questions involve matters so basic to the consensus that the society would, in declaring them open, abolish itself, commit suicide, terminate its existence as the kind of society it has hitherto understood itself to be. And it follows from that, as August follows July, that in such a society the doctrine according to which all questions are open questions, including, for example, the question as to the merits of Communism, is itself one of the excluded beliefs—one of the beliefs that are excluded because they involve, on the face of them, denial of the consensus that defines the society and sets its tone and character. And, having said that, we can get down to cases. What the McCarthyites distrusted and disliked and got mad about in the anti-McCarthyites was the at first explicit then tacit contention: We in America can't do anything about the Communists because America is a society in which all questions are open questions, a society dedicated to the proposition that *no* truth in particular is true, a society, in Justice Jackson's phrase, in which no one can speak properly of an orthodoxy—over against which any belief, however immoral, however extravagant, can be declared heretical and thus proscribed. And what the anti-McCarthyites distrusted and disliked and got mad about in the McCarthyites was the at first explicit and then tacit contention: America is not the kind of society you describe; the First Amendment does not have that meaning; America is a society whose essence is still to be found in the phrase "We hold these truths"; it *can* therefore proscribe certain doctrines and beliefs, and in the presence of the doctrines and beliefs of the Communists it cannot hesitate: it must proscribe them, and preferably long before they have had an opportunity to become a clear and present danger. Moreover, the McCarthyites knew, instinctively if not on the level of conscious articulation, that the anti-McCarthyites had good reason (long after they had dropped their principled opposition to the internal security program) for continuing their opposition to it in the courts of law, for continuing to provide the most expensive of expensive legal talent for its so-called victims, and this quite regardless of whether or not they were so situated as to constitute a clear and present danger—had good reason because in their hearts they believed that no measures ought to be taken against the Communists at all. And the anti-McCarthyites knew that the McCarthyites, for all their willing talk of clear and present danger, had good reason for carrying the persecution of the Communists further, at every opportunity, than the clear and present danger doctrine called for; they believed in persecuting the Communists not because they were dangerous but because, from the standpoint of the consensus, their doctrines were wrong and immoral. Each group understood the other perfectly, and each was quite right in venting upon the other the fury reserved for heretics because each was, in the eyes of the other, *heretical.*

It is I repeat unfortunate for us all that the issue, once joined, did not stay joined, and that the question became so confused that each of the two groups emerged from the McCarthy period under the impression that it had won—the McCarthyites because they got the persecution of the Communists that their understanding of the American consensus demanded, the anti-McCarthyites because the persecution went forward with the incantations appropriate to the clear and present danger doctrine. Why unfortunate? Because until that issue is decided we no more understand ourselves as a nation than a schizophrenic understands himself as a person—so that, again in Murray's words, the American giant is likely to go lumbering about the world in ignorance even of who and what he is. And because—dare I say it?—next time around, people are going to get a whole lot madder.

Chapter 4

Freedom of Speech in America

I am often asked whether I am "for" or "against" freedom of speech, or what I understand to be the Conservative position on freedom of speech, or whether in my view freedom of speech is "defensible," and should be defended, "on principle." They are not "happy" questions, because I doubt whether the freedom of speech "issue," as Mill for example stated it in the *Essay*, is a genuine, non-spurious, issue. Rather, it seems to me that most arguments about freedom of speech are really arguments about some prior question, which once resolved to the satisfaction of the disputants would be the end of the matter. But if I must answer the foregoing queries, my answer would have to take the following shape:

Temperamentally, like most Conservatives, I happen to be a man who in any given situation would always favor letting everybody have his "say"—temperamentally, I repeat, which is to say, *not* on principle but partly out of a selfish wish to satisfy my curiosity about what there is *to* say on whatever question happens to be up. This is partly because of some terrible anarchic thing 'way down inside me that always puts me, instinctively, on the side of the pillow-throwers and against the umpire, on the side of the freedom-riders (even though I disagree with them) against the Mississippi sheriff, on the side of George Washington against George III—and therefore on the side of the let-'em-speak contingent against the censors and silencers. In that sense, I am "for" freedom of speech.

Again, where what is in question is freedom of speech in a

certain kind of community, where people have in some sense *con-tracted* with one another to conduct their affairs on a freedom-of-speech basis or to treat each other as equals, I am "for" free-dom of speech—in the United States or England, for instance. In such a community, I recognize, *other things being equal* (recog-nize not just "temperamentally" but, *to some extent* as a matter of principle), a *presumption* in favor of the let-'em-speak contin-gent and against the shut-'em-up contingent. But only in that kind of community. As regards communities-in-general, situa-tions-in-general, there is and can be no such presumption; and there are other kinds of communities, the present-day Dominican Republic, for instance, or contemporary Spain, where the pre-sumption for me would be very distinctly against the conduct of affairs on a freedom-of-speech basis.

I strongly feel, in other words, that the classic attempt to de-fend freedom of speech as a *compelling* principle applicable to all communities, that is, Mill's famous *Essay on Liberty,* is bad political theory (see p. 107, *et seq.*), and has done great harm—so that the less heard of any general principle of freedom of speech the better. In addition, the fact that most American intellectuals are under the contrary impression, and think that Mill settled *that* argument once and for all (so that even if they do not know Mill at first hand they yet feel sure that the day they need con-clusive arguments for freedom of speech they will have only to go to Mill and look them up) is merely a sad commentary on most American intellectuals. In short, there is no reason, in the-ory, for saying that freedom of speech is a principle that should be defended; or, perhaps I should say that if it *is* a principle that should be defended, someone should get busy and find a better defense for it than Mill was able to find.

Now, I have already said that in a certain kind of community, where people have in some sense contracted with one another to conduct their affairs by freedom-of-speech procedures, I should hold, to some extent on principle, that there is a presumption, other things being equal, in favor of freedom of speech. And I have said that for me the United States is such a community. But you will notice that I have stashed into my aircraft a great many verbal parachutes that would enable me, if and when that seemed advisable, to bail out. I stress, a "certain kind" of community, people having "in some sense" contracted to practice free speech, a "presumption" only in favor of free speech. Let me clarify all that:

The sense in which the American people have contracted together to conduct their affairs by freedom of speech procedures is this, and only this: The First Amendment to our Constitution says that Congress shall make no law impairing freedom of speech, and I do think it can be argued that that Amendment in some sense constitutes a contract among Americans to conduct their affairs according to freedom of speech procedures. *But:*

A. The First Amendment, along with the rest of the so-called Bill of Rights, was not written by the Philadelphia Convention but rather, as sort of an afterthought—like painting the front stoop after the house is built—by the First Session of the Congress, then ratified by the amendment process specified in the Philadelphia Constitution. Now, that does not make the First Amendment any the less part of the law of our Constitution, or any the less, for me at least, a contract amongst Americans. But it does perhaps create as many difficulties about freedom of speech as it solves, and for this reason. The Philadelphia Constitution was not intended to have a Bill of Rights; the most brilliant statement we have against a Bill of Rights is Alexander Hamilton's statement about freedom of the press in the Federalist Papers, where he argues in effect, What good will it do to write it into the Constitution? If Congress sees fit to violate freedom of the press it will certainly go ahead and do so; the Bill of Rights in fact changes the whole character of our constitutional system; and the authors of the Bill of Rights were, for my money, extremely careless about tidying up after painting the front stoop. Concretely, while the First Amendment forbids Congress to impair freedom of speech, the body of the Constitution seems to empower Congress to do certain things that it may feel it cannot do without impairing freedom of speech—especially if, like me and unlike the Supreme Court, you regard the Preamble to the Constitution as the essence of the contract among the American people. For the Preamble announces an intention on the part of that people to do quite a number of sweeping things—e.g., to secure the ends of justice, to promote the general welfare—and the First Amendment invites the question, Ah! What if Congress be strongly convinced that enactment *x* is needed in the interest of justice, or for the general welfare, and yet that same enactment *x* impairs freedom of speech? There is no simple answer, except to say that under our Constitution one can always argue, and argue legitimately, that this may seem to some people an impairment of freedom of speech, but it is necessary in order to accomplish the very purposes of the Constitution, and *therefore* we are going right ahead and do it because the Constitution authorizes us to. Most particularly it is not a simple answer to say, Let the Supreme Court decide. By the time it gets around to deciding, free speech will already have been impaired, and Congress, as Hamilton foresaw, will have had its way.

B. In any case, the First Amendment does not, properly speaking, require what I have called freedom of speech procedures in the United States. Still less, for all that we speak of a Bill of Rights, does it confer on anybody a "right" to freedom of speech. At most, it confers a right not to have your freedom of speech impaired by the Congress—that is, by the Federal Government. In its original form, the amendment did not even confer on anybody a right not to have his freedom of speech impaired by his state and county and municipal governments (*ut infra*). And it certainly did not confer upon anybody a right not to have his freedom of speech impaired by a whole series of non-governmental authorities—by, most especially, the persons most likely to impair it, who are one's neighbors.

C. The state of affairs I have just described, where the First Amendment leaves our state and local governments at liberty to impair freedom of speech, has been greatly complicated by a line of Supreme Court decisions which "read" the so-called Bill of Rights "into" the Fourteenth Amendment. These decisions, that is to say, seek to apply the limitations on the Federal Government involved in the first eight amendments to the states and localities, and they are so applied by the Supreme Court today. Now,

I have, I confess, never been much impressed by the constitutional logic by which that particular bit of juggling was accomplished, but that is not the main point I want to make about it. My main point is simply this: By the time we have moved away from the solid structure of the Constitution through the jerry-built lean-to of the Bill of Rights to the remote tool-shed of a mere Supreme Court decision, we may have left far behind us the kind of freedom of speech that the American people may be said to have contracted with one another not to impair. I would still be willing to say that the presumption under the Constitution is, for me, against impairment, even when the latter is by a state legislature or a city council. But the presumption now begins to wear a little thin; and I no longer feel so sure of myself, when I defend it, that I can do so on principle. That is why I speak of defending the presumption "to some extent" on principle.

D. In any case there is always one further difficulty, which I personally find rather more amusing than the all-out defenders of freedom of speech seem to find it. The place to go to learn about it, the *locus classicus,* is a very favorite book of mine that I like to call *Sam Stouffer Discovers America,* though it was published under the title *Civil Liberties, Communism, and Conformity.* Mr. Stouffer and his team of researchers asked a representative sample of Americans a number of questions calculated to find out whether they would permit (a) a Communist, or (b) an atheist, to (1) speak in their local community, or (2) teach in their local high school, or (3) be represented, by means of a book he had written, in their local public library. And consider: some two-thirds of the sample answered "Nothing doing" right straight down the line; they would not permit any of the things in question—nor was there any evidence that they would have been much disturbed to learn that the Supreme Court says that the Fourteenth Amendment says that the First Amendment says they can't do anything legally to (e.g.) prevent the Communist from speaking. Mr. Stouffer was appalled at the America he had discovered—as I am sure the Ford Foundation, or whatever foundation it was that gave him all that money to ask all those questions of all those people, must have been appalled too. Of course, anyone who had ever got off the Harvard campus long enough to visit America should have known what answers he would get, but the "of course" is not my point. My point is, quite simply, that Stouffer's statistics clearly enjoin upon us a certain caution when it comes to pressing the idea that the American people have in some sense contracted with one another to maintain freedom of speech procedures. If they have made such a contract they appear not to have heard of it; and the obligation of a contract of which the contracting parties seem not to have heard is not, perhaps, the most pressing kind of obligation one can imagine. One begins to suspect that the true American tradition is less that of our Fourth of July orations and our constitutional law textbooks, with their cluck-clucking over the so-called preferred freedoms, than, quite simply, that of riding somebody out of town on a rail.

Enough by way of explaining my verbal parachutes. Except for temperamentally, it is for me, and has got to be, a matter of "in some sense," of "other things being equal," of a "presumption," etc. But the temperamentally still stands. My own instinct would be to let (e.g.) Gus Hall speak freely pretty much anywhere— until such time as the American people have the good sense to deport him to the Soviet Union.

Chapter 5

The Social Contract:
The Ultimate Issue between
Liberalism and Conservatism

The present chapter has two purposes: First, pursuant to earlier references in this book to a sort of continuity on the part of
contemporary American Conservatism with the conservatisms of
the past (and an "overlap" between its ideas and a tradition reaching back through the entire history of the West), to show where
that continuity and that overlap are greatest, where contemporary
American Conservatism is most at one with the past. Second, to
explicate the issue at stake in the area of the overlap, an issue
not in my opinion generally understood, and carry the reader,
however sketchily, through the history of that issue. The second
of these tasks, let me warn him, will necessitate my "working"
him somewhat harder than I have done in earlier chapters; the
issue is not an easy one to grasp, and the history of it not precisely exciting—besides which the inquiry will involve my taking
him to remote times and places that he is not accustomed to think
of as having any bearing on America or on American politics.
But I perhaps have no right to do that unless I can explain to
him beforehand why he should accompany me on such an inquiry. Let me, to that end (before launching myself on the inquiry proper), get busy on the first of the two purposes.

The problem is this: We have all been brought up to believe
that the Framers of the Constitution and the Bill of Rights were

—though indeed subject to this or that other "influence"—under the spell of John Locke and of Lockean ideas; that, therefore, they believed the following: that man once lived in a "state of nature," where he was "under" a "law of nature"; that the way society and government came into existence was by man "emerging" from the state of nature to make a "compact," which could only go into effect if all men consented to it; and that the essence of that compact was that man "retained," or "held back," certain "natural rights" which the "compact" accordingly set down in black and white for all to see (these rights are, it is alleged, clearly visible in our Bill of Rights). We have been brought up to believe further, therefore, that our continuity with the past is somehow through the Framers and Locke, who was himself continuous with the past. Was he not a deeply religious man? Did he not take as his teacher the "judicious Hooker," a divine by profession? In speaking of a "law of nature" was he not following the great teachers of the centuries preceding him? Now, all that, I contend (though I shall need a second book to explain it fully) has given rise to profound misunderstandings, even on the part of American Conservatives themselves, as to what our Conservatism is committed to—what kind of "natural rights," what sort of role for "consent" in politics, and, perhaps above all, what attitude towards Locke and the "social contract."

The logic (and so the conclusion) are unexceptionable: the Framers were Lockeans; Conservatives, naturally enamored of the past, affirm the Framers and therefore must affirm Locke; and in affirming Locke they establish their continuity with the past. But the logic and conclusion are unexceptionable only because the logic involves two whopping big fibs: namely, that the Framers were Lockeans (most of them, for one thing, *opposed* a bill of rights as part of the Constitution); and that you can establish continuity with the past through Locke. The two fibs, moreover, lead on to all manner of absurdities: the mobilization of American Conservatives behind the very Bill of Rights that the Liberals are using in their attempt to undermine our social order; the over-emphasis (as with Russell Kirk, Frank Meyer, and Stanton Evans) on the role of religious belief in Conservatism; the

84

glorification by American Conservatives (especially John Chamberlain) of those late nineteenth century Supreme Court justices who sought to hammer Congress over the head with the Bill of Rights; to inhibitions about supporting Congress as Conservatives must support it if they are going to keep on winning; and near-neurosis (as with Frank Meyer, perhaps with William F. Buckley, Jr.) about governmental power and so to the cult of "weak" government.

All that, and three absurdities more:

(a) The emphasis of Locke's political theory is, ultimately, egalitarian, since if the consent of *all* is necessary for the "compact," then each man's consent is as "good" as any other man's; so that *if* you marry Locke you are ultimately without grounds for resisting current egalitarian trends—which is exactly where most of our Conservative intellectuals have ended up.

(b) The other great emphasis of Locke's political theory is on the absoluteness of the principle of consent in politics; so that *if* you marry Locke you are ultimately without grounds for resisting the things being done out over the world in the name of consent—the irresponsible liberation of colonies from their so-called oppressors, the attempt to liquidate the ruling classes in Latin America in order to enthrone the "consent" of the Latin American *peones,* and, as a final example, the enforcement of the will of the General Assembly of the United Nations because it originates in the "consent" of "all mankind." (I do not say that our Conservative intellectuals don't oppose these things; merely that until they break with Locke they have no grounds for doing so.)

(c) The belief that the Framers were Lockeans, which they were not, obscures in any mind that holds that belief *both* the nature of the Framers' continuity with the past and—what is worse, especially for Conservatives—the nature of the American political system, which it is the business of Conservatives to defend and perfect.

But I hope I have said enough now by way of justifying the remainder of this chapter—which, I repeat, deals with the history of *the* issue that separates Lockeans from non-Lockeans, attempts to situate Locke correctly in that history, and indicates, indirectly, why it is a libel on the Framers to say that they were Lockeans and believed in a "social contract" among "equals" emerging from a "state of nature."

The idea of a "social contract" is the oldest and one of the most persistent kinds of answer that political thinkers have put forward with respect to some of the basic questions of political philosophy. Namely, What is the origin of organized society? of "law"? of "justice"? of the principles of "right" and "wrong" that "justice" and "law" are said to embody? Why should the members of organized society obey its dictates? Are there limits to their duty of obedience and, if so, what are those limits? What is the "best" political regime? To all these questions, either explicitly or by implication, the exponents of the idea of social contract make replies that run in terms of *agreement* or *consent* by the individual members of organized society: Organized society came into being as a result of agreements arrived at among its members, and is, therefore, artificial, man-made. Law, justice, the principles of right and wrong, are also man-made, and are merely that which men have agreed to. Men should obey the dictates of organized society, and subordinate themselves to its principles of right and wrong, because they represent that which men have agreed to as most likely to conduce to their well-being, and because, in one way or another, they have promised or consented to do so. Their obligation to obey is accordingly limited to that which has been agreed or consented to; and the best political regime is merely that to which men have consented, or now consent.

The "social contract" philosophers do not, by any means, give identical answers to the foregoing questions. Between the idea of tacit or implied consent (which may have grown up over a long period of time) and that of a "contract" (or "compact," or "pact," or "covenant"), with specific "terms," and "concluded" at a certain place and time, there are numerous intermediate positions that one philosopher or another has made use of in offering his answers to the questions. Some have stressed far more than others the notion of an "original" or "primitive" contract. Different "social contract" philosophers have used their particular form of the contract for markedly different political purposes, ranging all the way from the support of absolute monarchy to the defense of democracy. Some appear to have meant, by insisting upon agreements or contracts, not so much that society, law, justice, principles of right and wrong, originated in *actual* agreements or contracts, but merely that we understand them best if we think of them *as if* they had originated in contracts and agreements, or as if they were contractual in character. That on which all the social contract philosophers agree, and that which sets them apart from other political philosophers, is the negative proposition that society, law, justice, principles of right and wrong, cannot be understood in terms other than those of contract and agreement, promise and consent.

We shall speak, in the following sections, of (1) the emergence of that proposition in classical antiquity, (2) its virtual disappearance from Western political philosophy from the time of Plato and Aristotle until (3) the "great age" of the social contract, which is that of Thomas Hobbes (1588-1679), John Locke (1632-1704), and J.-J. Rousseau (1712-1778), and (4) the present status of the idea of the social contract.

A word is in order as to a different possible approach to the topic in hand, and why it has been rejected for the purposes of the present chapter. *Actual* contracts, of one sort or another—from the Covenant between God and the people of Israel at the foot of Mount Sinai (Exodus, 19) to, e.g., the Charter of the United Nations signed at San Francisco following World War II—have often played a prominent role in the political history of mankind and in man's thought about politics. And it is possible, starting out from the 17th and 18th century contract philosophers, and their insistence that society is founded on "contract," to treat all such contracts, and all the ideas of philosophers about them, as part of the historical background for the ideas of Hobbes, Locke, and Rousseau; as also to deem the recurrence of such contracts, in the history of politics and political philosophy, as proper expressions of their influence. There is, indeed, a vast literature in which more or less that procedure is followed. That literature is, however, open to at least two objections, here assumed to be decisive: (1) It conceals the *revolutionary* significance of the 17th and 18th century contract philosophers, by linking their names with practices and ideas that they in fact rebelled against. (2) It distracts attention from the character and extent of the actual influence of those philosophers upon subsequent thought and subsequent events. Both objections, it may be noted, turn on the contention that the philosophers in question did not intend their appeal to contract in any such literal fashion as the procedure presupposes, and that we must in any case distinguish between contracts understood as *creating* society, justice, law, and principles of right and wrong, and contracts understood as merely *specifying* society, justice, law, and principles of right and wrong in particular situations. The Old Testament Covenant, for instance, though it appears to be understood literally as a contract, merely transforms an already-existing society or people into a new kind of society or people (a people "chosen" by God, and recognizing itself as "chosen"); the "law" and "justice" (the Ten Commandments) to which it points are not only not created by it, but are not even embodied in it. The distinction between the contract (or the idea of a contract) that *creates* and the contract that *specifies* is, for both political practice and political philosophy, fundamental. The Old Testament Covenant, as also the contract to which Socrates appeals in Plato's brief dialogue *The Crito* (see below), belong to an entirely different realm of discourse from the "contracts" of, e.g., Locke and Rousseau.

A. *Classical Antiquity.* The first genuine anticipations of the ideas of the 17th and 18th century contract philosophers are, as noted above, the first answers ever given to the major problems of political philosophy, namely, those of the early Greek "conventionalists." Many of them are unknown to us by name, Heraclitus (576-480 B.C.) being perhaps the major exception; he wrote that "men have made the supposition that some things are just and others are unjust." Most of what we know about the others we know from Plato and Aristotle, who wrote long after (though we do not know how long after) their ideas had become widely current in Greece. But we do know with certainty that the "great issues" of Greek political philosophy were the issues at stake between the conventionalist answers and the "classical" answers—those of Plato and Aristotle and their predecessors (especially Socrates); that the classical answers developed in opposition to the conventionalist answers; and that the conventionalist answers, as put forward by Plato's and Aristotle's great enemies the Sophists (chiefly in Plato's Dialogues), were still very much alive in Plato's and Aristotle's time.

Those first answers, as the term "conventionalist" clearly implies, did not, unless by implication, run in terms of anything so concrete as "contract," but merely in terms of "convention," which we may perhaps best understand by analogy with the process (which we see about us at all times) by which "language" develops. The "rules" of "grammar," the "usage" of particular words, change over the years and decades and centuries; even the youngest of us has witnessed, and to some extent participated in, the chain of events by which a new word becomes generally accepted, or an old one becomes "archaic." We know that, despite the best efforts of the authors of dictionaries and textbooks, what "governs" in the development of language is that to which, in some mysterious way, people come to "agree"—that is, "convention"; and that once "people" have agreed to "mean" and "understand" such-and-such by a given word or expression, that (for the moment at least) is what "people" are going to "mean" and "understand" by that word or expression. The power of "convention" in such matters seems, at least, to be overwhelming and indisputable; and from this it is a brief step, and an easy one, to the notion that there is no such thing as "correct" or "incorrect" in language, but merely what people happen to have "agreed" to. And from that, paradoxical though it may seem, we are led to the notion that people "ought" to use words in their agreed-upon meanings, and behave "wrongly" if they do not; that is, we begin to think of an implicit "promise," or "contract" that somehow "obliges" us not to violate the relevant conventions although we know them to be merely conventional in origin. The Greek conventionalists sought to answer the aforementioned great questions of political philosophy—once they had themselves been discovered (their discovery, since we know there was a time when the problems were unknown, was the first great achievement of political philosophy)—in comparable terms: The Greek city-state, which was the form of "society" they knew, had come into existence by "convention." The laws which any city-state, and thus all city-states, enforced upon their members, were the product of "convention"; so also were the principles of right and wrong, just and unjust, prevailing in any particular city-state. And the citizen's obligation to obey the laws, or to accept prevailing notions of justice and right and wrong, went no further than could be explained in "conventional" terms: he either obeyed because his fellow-citizens, through their "government," forced him to, or because he or his forefathers had agreed to obey them (see below).

Perhaps the fullest statement of the conventionalist position, and the most interesting for the present purpose because it uses a word ("covenant") which is closer than "convention" to the word "contract," is that which Plato places in the mouth of Glaucon in his dialogue *The Republic*. Time was, says Glaucon (whom, however, we should understand as merely repeating what he has heard from others, the Sophists in particular), when each man thought it good to inflict "injustice" upon others, and bad to suffer "injustice" at the hands of others, and when everyone behaved accordingly. In due course, however, men came to think that such a state of affairs produces great evils, and they were then ready to agree to laws and mutual covenants which would avoid those evils. Such is the origin of what men now call justice, which is that which the agreed-upon laws command, and injustice, which is that which they forbid; and men accept the new arrangement because it is in their interest to do so. There are, to be sure, two apparent additions here to the conventionalist position as stated above: First, the notion of a "state" or "condition" of mankind, "pre-social," "pre-legal," and "pre-moral," before men had entered into any agreements at all, and when, therefore, they were bound by nothing. Secondly, the notion that *self-interest* is the motivation which impels men to agree to laws and covenants. Both notions, however, are evidently implicit in the earlier conventionalism: If the history of a society and justice is the history of agreements, then there must have been, off in the past, a "first" agreement, and a state of affairs prior to that agreement. And if justice and the principles of right and wrong, which are the source of "disinterested" motivations, are created by agreement, then the first agreement can be explained only in terms of selfish motives. Some (but not all) conventionalists, moreover, advanced a third notion, namely, that of the *equality* of the interest-motivated participants in the agreements in question, which enables us to say that all the major theses of the modern "contract" philosophers were well-known in classical antiquity.

Against the conventionalist position (which as it has come down to us must be regarded as for the most part a series of flat assertions, rather than as a corpus of philosophic reasoning), the classical philosophers urged such propositions as the following: The city-state (society) is *natural* to man; its origin is to be sought in the nature of man, for whose perfection it is necessary. Justice, the principles of right and wrong, and the law are not artificial and man-made, but rather are discovered by man through the exercise of reason. Man, whose nature requires him to strive for his own perfection, has a *duty* to subordinate himself to justice, to the principles of right and wrong, to the law. The conventions and covenants into which men enter can at most give to society a particular form, or attempt to specify justice, or right and wrong, in particular situations at particular times. The justice, or rightness, of any convention or any covenant is a question to be answered by political philosophy, in the course of reasoned discussion, and one that cannot be answered in terms simply, or even primarily, of that which men have promised or consented to. Conventions and covenants are, then, to be judged by standards that men do not create, but merely discover. That is just and right which contributes to man's perfection, which we come to understand by studying man's nature, not his agreements and contracts. The best regime is that which is best for the nature of man.

The classical philosophers are not to be understood as having denied, or having been unaware of, the role of convention and covenants, or even that of self-interest (as the conventionalists understood it) in social and political life. The Socrates of *The Crito* is willing to explain his immediate obligation to Athens in "contractual" terms, and certainly regards himself as bound by that which he says he has promised. Indeed, all the classical philosophers contended that a major function of the city-state (society) is to maintain among its members, through education, fundamental agreement concerning justice and the principles of right and wrong. Their contention against the conventionalist was that conventionalism provides only a partial answer to the problems that arise when men begin to meditate about society and politics, and no answer at all to what the classical philosophers described as the "important" problems. In their view, conventionalism was an expression of a sickly and inhuman state of the soul of man, and, for that reason, a denial and repudiation of the lofty purposes that society, government, and law ought to serve: those of reason not passion, therefore those of duty not self-interest.

B. *The Interval.* During the two thousand years following Plato and Aristotle, convention and contract, consent and promise, figured prominently both in political practice and in political philosophy, but not (apart from the Epicureans) in a manner at all relevant to the present chapter. The attention of political innovators and writers on politics shifts to a new range of problems, which we briefly note, though only in order to emphasize their remoteness from those that had concerned the Greek political philosophers (and are, later, to concern Hobbes, Locke, and Rousseau). For example, What is the source of the authority of the Roman Emperor (does it, as Roman law held, derive from the consent of the people)? Is there, as St. Augustine (354-430 A.D.) held, a universal duty to obey kings? Must a king, upon pain of losing his claim to his subjects' allegiance, recognize certain "rights" on their part? Is there a tacit compact between king and people, which defines their reciprocal rights and obligations? If (as often occurred) the accession ceremonies for a new king involve a "coronation oath," in which he subordinates himself to certain "conditions" (for example, to rule justly and provide good government for all his subjects), does this create a "contract" or "pact" which he is bound to observe? Is the Pope entitled to depose an Emperor or king who misgoverns—for example, to absolve the Emperor's subjects from their allegiance to him on the ground that he has broken a contract (Manegold of Lautenbach, in his *Ad Gebehardum Liber,* answered that question in the affirmative as early as the end of the eleventh century)? All these questions, clearly, have to do with the specification (see above) of "rights" and "duties," not with the origin of the societies within which they are specified, or of the principles of justice and right and wrong. The contracts utilized or appealed to are understood merely as means of getting down in black and white rights and duties that derive ultimately from sources independent of contracts and agreements. Indeed, some commentators have distinguished, by way of emphasizing their peculiar character, between the "contracts of government" or "contracts of submission" of this period and the "social contracts" of the earlier and later periods. Such a distinction is useful, but only provided it not be permitted to obscure the general agreement (through most of the period in question) on a number of issues to which contract and agreement were not regarded as relevant at all. Namely, that monarchy, whether because willed by God or decreed by reason, is the "best regime." That not only society, justice, and principles of right and wrong but also peoples, exist prior to the establishments of particular governments. That the monarch is in any case subject to *law;* and that men do not create law, but rather *discover* it, either through *reason* or *revelation.*

The political thinkers of the period draw upon three main sources, apart from their own ingenuity and creativeness: first, the teachings of the Greek classical philosophers (insofar as they were available); second, the teachings of the Old and New Testaments; and third, increasingly over the centuries, the rapidly-developing corpus of Christian theology. And while these three sources—especially the first and the third (philosophy and theology)—by no means always point in the same direction, they are at one both in excluding, implicitly or explicitly, the social contract of the earlier and later periods and in their insistence, explicit or implicit, that social and political life serves purposes in addition to, and higher than, that of the selfish or private interest of those who participate in it. Some political thinkers seek to state those purposes in terms of a "law of nature" or "law of reason" discoverable by all men. Some seek to state them in terms of the "law of God" or "divine law." And some, insisting upon a necessary coincidence between natural and divine law, seek to state them in terms of a simultaneous appeal to both. But none seeks to state them in terms of a supposed original contract or agreement; none thinks, other than fancifully, in terms of a "pre-social," "pre-legal," or "pre-moral" condition of man; and all are agreed that exchanges of promises or consents—though useful for certain social and political purposes and, where they have occurred, binding—provide, at most, the occasion for common effort on behalf of those purposes. And there gradually takes shape, over the period, the Great Tradition of Western political philosophy which, however much its creators and custodians might disagree on other issues, speaks with a single and clear voice of the subordinate and merely-specifying role of promise and consent in man's search for, and his attempt to achieve, the true purposes of society, clearly understood to be those of justice and right.

Only toward the end of the period, only after and as a result of widespread acceptance of the idea of "contracts of government" between kings and peoples, do we begin to find writers who appear to edge over in the direction of the Greek conventionalists. Speculation arises as to the condition of men before the "first" contract between kings and people, and thus as to how the "people" that enters into that contract became a people to begin with. Some writers, of whom we may take Juan Mariana (*De Rege et Regis Institutione,* 1599) and George Buchanan (*De Jure Regni apud Scotos,* 1579) as examples, begin to toy with the notion of contracts by which peoples are "formed," by individuals who have previously lived as "free" and "solitary," and who for this or that reason, "come together" by means of "compacts." And some critics have argued that, with such writers, we stand in the presence of the "state of nature" and the "social contract" of Hobbes, Locke, and Rousseau. In point of fact, however, the emergence of speculation along these lines is worth noticing, in the present connection, precisely because it fixes attention upon the watershed that divides Hobbes, Locke, and Rousseau even from their more or less immediate predecessors. For none of the latter would have countenanced the notion that the individuals entering into the "first" contract were "free" of moral obligations, or motivated exclusively by self-interest; none of them suggests that justice and the principles of right and wrong are to be explained by the contract; all of them are carriers of the Tradition. And it cannot be overemphasized that that tradition, against which Hobbes, Locke, and Rousseau are to lead a revolution, has no necessary quarrel with the idea that particular governments come into and remain in existence by a process which involves a considerable element of promise and consent.

   C. *The "Great Age" of the Social Contract.* The names of Hobbes, Locke, and Rousseau have commonly been linked together because all three teach (1) that prior to society men lived in a "state of nature," (2) that in the "state of nature" men possessed a "natural right" or "natural rights," (3) that men emerged from the "state of nature" by concluding among themselves a "social contract" or "social compact," by means of which they "surrendered" to political society all or some of their "natural right" or "natural rights," (4) that men abandoned the "state of nature" and promised or consented to obey the government and laws of political society, because in the "state of nature" their natural right or natural rights proved, in the absence of government and laws to guarantee them, insecure, (5) that society, government, and laws therefore have as their proper function the guaranteeing of the "natural right" or "natural rights" "surrendered" by the participants, (6) that the proper authority of society, government, laws, is limited to that proper function, as laid down in the "contract" or "compact," (7) that the contract, so long as it is "kept," is binding not only upon the participants but, in one way or another, upon their descendants, and so explains "political obligation," that is, the "duty" to obey political authority, and (8) that by the same token the "duty of obedience" lapses in one way or another if the contract is "violated." A considerable body of modern political literature has seized upon this common ground among the three philosophers and, abstracting from the admittedly great differences in emphasis among them, has treated the foregoing propositions as the "contractarian" position in political philosophy, capable of being discussed and evaluated without reference to any particular philosopher. (Another considerable body of literature, of scant relevance for the purposes of this chapter, has fixed attention upon the differences among them on matters lying outside their area of agreement: the specific terms of their respective contracts; the political purposes, "authoritarian" or "democratic," to which they were dedicated; and their subsequent influence. Hobbes' contract figures in this literature as the source of modern "totalitarian" ideas, Locke's as that of modern constitutional democracy, Rousseau's as, variously, closer to that of Hobbes, closer to that of Locke, or different from both because of its insistence that democracy must be local and direct.)

D. *The Present Status of the Social Contract.* The general verdict of the literature about the "contractarian" position common to all three has, it may safely be said, been unfavorable to it in the two-fold sense that (a) objections have been urged against it to which its defenders have been unable to make any satisfactory answer, and (b) no recent political philosopher of reputation has openly adopted the position.

The objections referred to are, briefly stated, as follows: (1) There is no historical evidence that the "state of nature," which the position presupposes, ever existed. (2) If a truly "pre-social" state of nature ever had existed, the men living in it would have been incapable of conceiving of a "contract" of the kind the position presupposes, because the very idea of contract bespeaks an already-advanced stage of social development. (3) The contract, in any case, fails as an explanation of the duty or obligation to obey the laws of society, which is to say that the contract cannot itself create the obligation to fulfill its own terms; that obligation, if it exists, must therefore be explained (as Hobbes and Locke do try to explain it) in terms other than those of contract. (4) The position holds that men enter the contract, and accept its terms, because they themselves decide that it is in their interest to do so for the sake of their natural rights. At most, therefore, the position can explain why men should obey while they find it in their interest to obey; once they regard the arrangements established by the contract as disadvantageous to their natural rights, they are no longer bound by it. (5) Even if we accept the notion that the original parties to the supposed contract do have an obligation to fulfill its terms, the contractarian position cannot explain why their descendants inherit the obligation. (6) The obligation of the descendants cannot be explained (as Locke and Rousseau tried to explain it) on the grounds that they consent, and become parties, to the contract by the mere fact of remaining within the society created by the contract. Most of the persons who grow up in a society have no genuine alternative to remaining within it; their remaining is not, therefore, an expression of consent—indeed, to insist on the contract is to deprive the descendants of the original contracting parties of the very natural right or rights those original parties exercised in making the contract. (7) Since there are times when men should disobey the laws of their society, the contract proves too much. It merely confuses the problem of when men should obey and when they should not obey.

Because of these objections, numerous scholars have held, the contractarian position may fairly be regarded as "exploded," except for two important alleged truths that it embodied, namely, that all men are equal, and that government ought to be based exclusively on the consent of the governed. These truths, they argue, are separable from the other contractarian doctrines, especially that of the state of nature and that of the contract itself. And because it was the seventeenth and eighteenth century contract philosophers who gave them currency, they may be regarded as the true fathers of modern constitutional democracy as practiced in, for example, the United States and the countries of the British Commonwealth. Both the American Declaration of Independence and the Constitution of the United States are frequently pointed to as instances of their influence, especially Locke's influence, upon subsequent events.

Another, more recent, body of scholarly literature takes an entirely different view as regards both the teachings and the subsequent influence of Hobbes, Locke and Rousseau. Their genuine significance, it holds, lies in an aspect of their teachings to which the "contractarian position" is in fact incidental, namely, in their break with the idea of a law, whether natural or divine, higher than and prior to any laws originating in agreement and contract. According to the recent scholarship, that is to say, the real issue posed by the contract philosophers, and the issue in terms of which alike the validity and the influence of their teachings is to be judged, turns on the question, After we have "peeled off," in our thinking about society, justice, right and wrong, obligation, all that can possibly be explained in terms of agreement and contract, consent and promise, what do we have left? To this question the contract philosophers give the answer: Only the natural right of *self-preservation,* which is to say, only self-interest; not, as their predecessors within the Great Tradition had believed, duties. Man, in other words, was, in Rousseau's magic phrase, born "free," and without law; he can be "bound" only by his own consent; and since today we find him "bound" by society and law, his bondage is either wrongful, because not based on his consent, or it is based upon agreement and contract. The contract, in short, is for the contract philosophers a logical necessity, which must be called in to explain the fact that men who were born free can nevertheless be rightfully subject to society and its laws. Any authority which is *not* rooted in agreement, consent, is therefore wrongful. Agreement, then, is the sole creator of society, of justice, of right and wrong; and, according to the recent scholarship, we misunderstand the contract philosophers when we impute to them belief in the original contract as a historical fact. With them, as with the Greek conventionalists, the key point is not that society, government, and law are and should be founded on consent, but that they must be *rooted,* and rooted *exclusively,* in the principle of consent. The contract philosophers, from this point of view, represent therefore a return to the infancy of political philosophy; and what is being decided, in the continuing debate among political philosophers, remains essentially the question whether there is or is not a higher law, independent of agreements and contracts, among men. And the problem as to the validity of the "contractarian position" is inseparable from that of the validity of the Great Tradition.

So, too, with respect to the influence of Hobbes, Locke, and Rousseau. *Insofar as the principle of consent has been accepted, in modern political philosophy and modern political practice, as the sole principle that needs to be taken into account when we seek to arrive at judgments as to what is right and what is wrong in politics,* we stand in the presence of the influence of Hobbes, Locke, and Rousseau and, ultimately, that of the Greek conventionalists. Similarly, *insofar as it is a generally-accepted principle of modern political philosophy and modern politics that the purpose of society, government, and law is to minister to the self-interest of the members of society, rather than to the perfection of man's nature or to the attunement of human affairs to the will of God,* we again stand in the presence of the influence of the contract philosophers, and can by no means speak of their "position" as one that subsequent generations have refuted. Alike the question as to the validity of the major contention of the contract philosophers (namely, that there is no higher law), and the question as to the influence they have exerted in their attempt to discredit the Great Tradition, seem certain to remain highly controversial questions in the continuing struggles within political philosophy and political practice over the next decades.

In America, of course, these struggles are struggles between Conservatives and Liberals: Conservative affirmation and Liberal denial, Conservative faith in the growing Great Tradition (as set forth above) and Liberal relativism. The Lockeans in America, in other words, are the Liberals; and the Conservatives, who disagree and must disagree with the Liberals on all the crucial points, must learn to understand themselves as the anti-Lockeans. Then, at least, the record can be put straight.

Chapter 6

Conservatism and the "Open Society"

A little over 100 years ago John Stuart Mill wrote in his essay
On Liberty that ". . . there ought to exist the fullest liberty of
professing and discussing, as a matter of ethical conviction, any
doctrine, however immoral it may be considered." [1] The sentence
is not *obiter:* Chapter Two of the book in question is devoted to
arguments, putatively philosophical in character, which if they
were sound would warrant precisely such a conclusion,[2] and we
have therefore every reason to assume that Mill meant by the
sentence just what it says. The topic of Chapter Two is the entire
"communications" process in any civilized society ("advanced"
society, as Mill puts it) [3]—and the question he raises about it is
whether there should be limitations on that process.[4] He treats
that problem as the central problem of all civilized societies—
the one to which all other problems are subordinate because of

---

[1] Cf. J. S. Mill, *On Liberty and Considerations on Representative Government*,
ed. by R. B. McCallum (Oxford: Basil Blackwell, 1946), p. 14 fn.

[2] That is approximately how Mill himself puts it. The words preceding our
part-sentence are, "If the arguments of the present chapter are of any validity,
. . ." The chapter is entitled "Of the Liberty of Thought and Discussion."

[3] Cf. *ibid.*, p. 9, ". . . we may leave out of consideration those backward states
of society in which the race itself may be considered as in its nonage." The distinction seems to turn variously (*ibid.*) on whether "mankind have become capable
of being improved by free and equal discussion" and whether they "have attained
the capacity of being guided to their own improvement by conviction or persuasion." On the latter point he adds, perhaps a little optimistically, ". . . a
period long since reached in all nations with whom we need here concern ourselves." But cf. *ibid.*, p. 59, where he refers, astonishingly, to "the present low state
of the human mind," that being the point he needs to establish the thesis there
in question.

[4] That is, the problem as to who, in the fashionable jargon of the "communications" literature, should be permitted "to say what, and to whom?"

the consequences, good or ill, that a society must bring upon itself as it adopts this or that solution to it. And he has supreme confidence in the rightness of the solution he has to offer—of which (presumably to avoid all possible misunderstanding) he provides several alternative statements, each of which makes his intention abundantly clear, namely, that society must be so organized as to make that solution its supreme law. "Fullest," that is, absolute freedom of thought and speech, he asserts by clear implication [5] in the entire argument of the chapter, is not to be one of

[5] Those who regard "absolute" as too strong a term to be deemed a synonym of "fullest" may wish to be reminded of the following passage (*ibid.*, p. 11), ". . . the appropriate region of human liberty . . . comprises . . . liberty of conscience in the most comprehensive sense: liberty of thought and feeling; *absolute freedom of opinion and sentiment on all subjects,* practical or speculative, scientific, moral, or theological . . . [And the] liberty of expressing and publishing opinions . . . is practically inseparable from [liberty of thought] . . ." (italics added). And cf. *ibid.*, "No society . . . is completely free in which [these liberties] . . . do not exist *absolute and unqualified*" (italics added). See, in this connection, the remarkable recent line of dissenting opinions by Mr. Justice Black in such cases as *Barenblatt vs U. S.* (360 U. S. 109, 1959); *Konigsberg vs State Board of California* (6 L. ed. 2, p. 105, 1961); *In re Anastapli* (6 L. ed. 2, p. 135, 1961); *Sweezy vs New Hampshire* (354 U. S. 234, 1957); *Braden vs U. S.* (5 L. ed. 2, p. 653, 1960). The issue in these cases has been whether entities like the House Committee on Un-American Activities and the State Bar Association committees on the character and fitness of applicants, are or are not estopped by the First Amendment from asking people to answer questions regarding their present and past affiliations with possible subversive organizations. All the cases in question, be it noted, were decided five justices to four, and have gone *against* Mr. Justice Black. But be it noted also that we do not yet know which team either Mr. Justice White or Mr. Justice Goldberg will join, which is to say that the Black position may be about to become the prevailing position of the United States Supreme Court.
In the opinions mentioned, Mr. Justice Black flatly states that the freedoms of speech and press and assembly and conscience of the First Amendment are "absolute," and were intended to be that by the "Founders." (One wonders, indeed, whether Black has not taken the word "absolute" from Mill.) I should be the last to accuse Mr. Justice Black of deliberately misrepresenting the position of the Founders, but as I shall show in a book I am now writing: (a) most of the Framers of the Constitution *opposed* having a bill of rights at all; (b) the notion that there was widespread popular demand for a bill of rights at the time *the* Bill of Rights was adopted is pure myth, and (c) the "father" of the Bill of Rights, James Madison, was at most lukewarm toward it. Mr. Justice Black rests his argument mainly on the "plain language" of the First Amendment, which does indeed differ from the remaining amendments by the fact that it is stated in "absolute" terms. But "plain language" here is a very tricky business: "Freedom of speech and press" may have meant to those who supported ratification of the First merely freedom within the limits set by the existing seditious libel laws, which is why those same gentlemen felt "free" to enact the Alien and Sedition Acts. And, in any case, we must remember that the First Amendment left the *states* free to invade the freedoms in question as they saw fit. Nothing can be more certain than that the idea of an absolute freedom of speech was wholly novel to that generation, and that Mill's book, written many decades later, was the *first* theoretical defense

several competing goods society is to foster, that is, one that on occasion might reasonably be sacrificed, in part at least, to the preservation of other goods. For Mill plainly refuses to recognize any competing good in the name of which it can be limited. The silencing of dissenters from a received doctrine, from an *accepted* idea—this is an alternative statement—is never justified.[6] It can only do unwarranted hurt, alike to the person silenced, to the individual or group that silences, to the doctrine or idea in defense of which the silencing is done, and to the society in the name of which the silencers silence.[7] The quotation I started with is merely the strongest, the most intransigent, of several formulations of a general prescription Mill makes for advanced societies; and we shall do well to savor it, phrase-by-phrase, before proceeding:

"There ought to exist [ought, so that the prescription is put forward on ethical grounds] the fullest liberty [a liberty that no one—individual, group, government, even society as a whole—is entitled to interfere with] of professing and discussing [of publicly propagating] as a matter of ethical conviction any doctrine [and the word "doctrine" is not intended to exclude, since he uses the term synonymously with "idea" and "opinion"; usually, indeed, he prefers the word "opinion"] however immoral it may be considered" [where "immoral" also is used to cover what Mill considers the extreme case—where people are least likely to refrain from silencing]. He would be equally willing, as the context shows, to write "however *wrong*," that is, "however incorrect," "however dangerous," "however foolish," or even "however harmful." And of course "it may be considered" is recognizably shorthand for "it may be considered by anyone whatsoever."

---

of such an idea. See on this point Leonard W. Levy, *Legacy of Suppression* (Cambridge: Harvard University Press, 1960)—a book by a scholar who would like to believe that the Founders believed in free speech in the Black sense, but confesses that the evidence is not there.

[6] Cf., *ibid.*, p. 14, ". . . I deny the right of the people to exercise such coercion, either by themselves or their government. The power itself is illegitimate. The best government has no more title to it than the worst." The statement could hardly be more sweeping.

[7] Not to speak of "mankind." Cf., *ibid.*, pp. 14-15: ". . . the peculiar evil of silencing the expression of an opinion is, that it is robbing the human race; . . . those who dissent from the opinion, still more than those who hold it."

It is fashionable these days, in part because of a fairly recent book by the scientist-philosopher K. R. Popper,[8] to call the kind of society Mill had in mind an "open society"—by at least implied contrast with a "closed" society, that is an "hermetically sealed" society, in which Mill's grand principle is by definition not observed. And we are told, variously, by writers whom we may call (because they so call themselves) Liberals (Mr. Justice Black especially, and most eloquently), that we have an open society and ought to protect it against the machinations of those who would like to close it, or that we have a closed society and ought (heeding Mill's arguments) to turn it forthwith into an open society, or that democracy, freedom, progress—any or all of them—must stand or fall, as we maintain or inaugurate or return to an open society. Or, that all who are opposed to the idea of the open society are authoritarians, enemies of human freedom, or totalitarians.

We are told all this, however, at least in its application to civilized societies in general (as opposed to the United States in particular),[9] on grounds that have not varied perceptibly since Mill set them down in the *Essay.* Thus we are still dealing with Mill's issue; and we shall think more clearly about it, in my opinion, if we keep it stated in Mill's terms, as much as possible (no subsequent pleader for the open society has possessed either Mill's clarity or his vigor of mind). Ought there to exist in organized society—in the United States e.g.—that "fullest liberty of professing and discussing" which Mill pleads for? Are there theoretical grounds on which such liberty of professing and discussing can be defended? Is openness of the kind Mill's society would possess one of the characteristics of the *good* society?

Before attempting to deal with these questions, let me pause

---

[8] K. R. Popper, *The Open Society and Its Enemies* (London: Routledge & Kegan Paul, 1945), 2 vols. The term "open society" is of course much older (Bergson uses a distinction between "open" and "closed" society in *Les deux sources de la morale et de la religion,* though for a quite different purpose). What Popper has done is to wed the term "open society" to Mill's ideas, and the term "closed society" to those of his *bêtes noires,* Plato especially.

[9] The exception is necessary, because the American arguments are often arguments concerning the meaning of the Constitution of the United States, the First Amendment especially.

to clarify certain aspects of the open society theory in the form in which Mill proposes it:

First, Mill must not be understood to be saying, over-all, something *more* extravagant than he is actually saying. He is fully aware of the necessity for laws against libel and slander, and does not deem such laws inconsistent with his doctrine.[10] He is aware, also, of organized society's need to protect its younger members against certain forms of expression; [11] which is to say that that fullest liberty of professing and discussing that Mill would commit us to is for adults only, since he would not provide laws prohibiting, e.g., the circulation of obscene literature amongst schoolchildren, or, e.g., utterance calculated to undermine the morals of a minor (meaning by "morals" whatever the society chooses to define as morals). Nor does the doctrine outlaw sanctions against incitement to crime [12]—provided, one must hasten to add, nothing political is involved (Mill would permit punishment for incitement to, e.g., tyrannicide, only if it could be shown to have resulted in an overt act).[13] And, finally—a topic about which there is, as it seems to this writer, much confusion amongst commentators on Mill—he would permit the police to disperse a mob where a riot is clearly imminent, even if its shoutings did bear upon some political, social, or economic issue; but not, he makes abundantly clear, on grounds of any official exception to the doctrinal tendency of the shoutings. (The individuals concerned would be free to resume their agitation the following morning.) [14]

This is an important point because the passage in question, that dealing with the mob at the corn-merchant's house, has

---

10 Cf. *op. cit.*, p. 73, "Whenever, in short, there is a definite damage, or a definite risk of [definite?] damage, either to an individual or to the public, the case is taken out of the province of liberty, and placed in that of morality and law."

11 Cf. *ibid.*, p. 72, ". . . protection against themselves is confessedly due to children and persons under age . . ."

12 Cf., *ibid.*, p. 49, ". . . even opinions lose their immunity when the circumstances in which they are expressed are such as to constitute their expression a positive instigation to some mischievous act." To this writer's mind a curious concession, which Mill ought not to have made. Once it is made, a society that wishes to silence this or that form of persuasive utterance has only to declare the behavior it is calculated to produce a crime, and it may silence—with Mill's blessing!

13 Cf., *ibid.*, p. 14 fn.

14 Cf., *ibid.*, p. 49.

given Mill an undeserved reputation as an adherent of the "clear and present danger" doctrine as we know it today. That matter we may perhaps clear up best as follows: The situations covered by the clear and present danger doctrine, as applied, e.g., to the Communist "threat," and by parallel doctrines in contemporary political theory,[15] are the situations in which Mill was *most* concerned to maintain absolute liberty of discussion —those situations, namely, in which the ideas being expressed have a tendency dangerous to the established political, social, or economic order. We must not, then, suppose Mill's society to be one in which, for example, anarchists, or defenders of polygamy, could be silenced because of the likelihood of their picking up supporters and finally winning the day, since for Mill the likelihood of their picking up supporters is merely a further reason for letting them speak. All utterance with a bearing on public policy—political, social, or economic—is to be permitted, no matter what some members of society (even the majority, even an overwhelming majority, even all the members save some lonely dissenter) [16] may happen to think of it. Mill must, then, also not be understood to be saying something *less* extravagant than he is actually saying.

Second, what is at issue for Mill is not merely unlimited freedom of speech (as just defined) but, as he makes abundantly clear, unlimited freedom of thought as well, and a way of life appropriate to their maintenance. To put it otherwise, when we elevate freedom of thought and speech to the position of society's highest good, freedom of thought and speech ceases to be merely freedom of thought and speech, and becomes—with respect to a great many important matters—the society's ultimate standard of order.

[15] E.g., the doctrine that enemies of liberty must not be permitted to take advantage of "civil liberties" in order to undermine and destroy them; or the doctrine that free society is entitled to interfere with free expression in order to perpetuate its own existence. Mill would certainly not have countenanced either doctrine. Here Mr. Justice Black is certainly Mill Redivivus.

[16] Cf., *ibid.*, p. 14, "If all mankind were of one opinion, and only one person were of the contrary opinion, mankind would be no more justified in silencing that one person, than he, if he had the power, would be justified in silencing all mankind."

Mill did not dwell upon the inescapable implications of this aspect of his position, so that it has been left to his epigones, especially in the United States, to think the position on out. The open society, they never weary of telling us, must see to it that all doctrines start out equal in the market-place of ideas; for society to assign an advantaged position to these doctrines rather than those would be tantamount to suppressing those. Society can, therefore, have no orthodoxy, no public truth, no standard, upon whose validity it is entitled to insist; outside its private homes, its churches, and perhaps its non-public schools, it cannot, therefore, indoctrinate; *all* questions are for it open questions, and must publicly be treated as open. If it has public schools and universities, it will be told (and with unexceptionable logic), these also must treat all questions as open questions—otherwise what happens to the freedom of thought, and so ultimately to the freedom of speech, of the student who might have thought differently had his teachers not treated some questions as closed? Even if in their hearts and souls all the members of the open society believe in a particular religion or a particular church, each must nevertheless be careful in his public capacity to treat all religions and churches as equal, to treat dissent, when and as it occurs, as the peer of dogma, to treat the voodoo missionary from Cuba as on an equal plane with an Archbishop of his own church.[17] The open society's first duty (so the custodians of the open society will remind it, if not those at home then those abroad),[18] is to freedom, and that means that it is not free to give public status to its beliefs, its standards, and its loyalties. Mill's disciples are completely faithful to the spirit of Mill's thought when they insist that if we mean business about freedom, that is how it is going to have to be. The open society confers "freedom" upon its members; but it does so at the cost of its own freedom as a society.

Third, as we have just seen, Mill's position on freedom of

[17] Who, after all, is to say which is right? But the answer of the Founders here is crystal clear: the "deliberate sense of the community" is to say.

[18] As witness, over the years, the endless series of sermons addressed by the New York press to, for example, the Trujillo regime in the Dominican Republic.

thought conduces to a negation of the very idea of a public truth.[19] This is not wonderful, however, and neither is it wonderful that Mill's followers always end up associating freedom with precisely the absence of any public truth. For Mill's freedom of speech doctrine has its very roots in dogmatic skepticism—in, that is to say, denial of the existence, at any particular place and at any moment in time, not only of a public truth but of any truth whatever unless it be the truth of the denial itself. (Let us not press this last too far, however, lest we be accused of trying to score a mere "debater's" point; it is, of course, the Achilles' heel of all skepticisms.) Reduced to its simplest terms, the argument of the *Essay* runs as follows: Whenever and wherever men disagree about a teaching, a doctrine, an opinion, an idea, we have no way of knowing which party to the disagreement is correct. The man or group that moves to silence a teaching on the grounds that it is incorrect attributes to himself a kind of knowledge (Mill says an "infallibility") that, quite simply, no one is ever entitled to claim, short of (if then) the very case where the question is sure not to arise—that is, where there is unanimity, and so no temptation to silence to begin with. When, therefore, Mill's followers demand the elevation of skepticism to the status of a national religion, and the remaking of society in the image of that religion, they are not reading into his position something that is not there—although Mill himself, as I have intimated, preserves a discreet silence as to the detailed institutional consequences of his position. They are, rather, merely making specific applications of notions that, for Mill, are the point of departure for the entire discussion.

The basic position, in fine, is not that society must have no public truth, no orthodoxy, no preferred doctrines, because it must have freedom of speech, but that it must have no orthodoxy, no public truth, no preferred doctrines, for the same reason that it must have freedom of speech. Namely, because in any given situation, no orthodoxy, no truth, no doctrine has any proper claim to special treatment, and this in turn because any orthodoxy, any

---

[19] Except, we must keep ourselves reminded, the public truth that there is no public truth.

supposed truth, any doctrine that might be preferred may turn out to be incorrect—nay, *will* turn out to be incorrect, since each competing idea is at most a partial truth. Nor is that all. Mill's freedom of speech doctrine is not merely derivative from a preliminary assault upon truth itself; [20] it is inseparable from that assault on truth and cannot, I contend, be defended on any other ground. (Wherefore, let me say in passing, any man who thinks of himself as a religious believer ought to think not twice but many times before making the doctrine his own.)

Fourth, Mill is not saying that no man must be silenced because every man has a "right" to freedom of speech. Consistent skeptic that he is, he warns us—and from an early moment—that he disclaims any advantage that might accrue to his argument from an appeal to abstract right; he is going to justify what he has to say in terms of "utility," in terms of "the permanent interest of a man [sic] as a progressive being," [21] whatever that may mean; and he sticks scrupulously to at least the first half of the promise throughout the *Essay.* This raises interesting questions (a) as to what Mill could have meant—whether indeed he means anything at all that persons committed to the idea of abstract right might find intelligible—by such words as "ethical," "immoral," etc., (b) as to the pains Mill takes, throughout his main argument, to reduce the question, "Should some types of expression be prohibited in civilized society because the ideas they express are wicked?" to the question, "Should some types of expression be prohibited because they are intellectually incorrect?", and (c) as to the kind of moral fervor his followers have poured into the propagation of his views. Everything for Mill reduces itself to intellectual argument, where you either win or draw or lose, and in any case win or draw or lose by the sheer appeal to reason—which, for Mill, excludes *ex hypothesi* any appeal to, for example, Revelation or Authority (such appeals would merely precipitate an endless discussion as to the status, from the standpoint of reason, of Revelation and Authority).

[20] *Ibid.,* Chapter Two, *passim.*
[21] *Ibid.,* p. 9.

The notion of a "right" to freedom of speech, a capacity on the part of every man to say what he pleases that society must respect because he is entitled to it, of a right that men have to live in the kind of society that Mill projects, is a later development which occurs in different countries for different reasons and under different auspices; but, to the extent that it is intended seriously, it represents a complete break with Mill. Those who appeal to such a notion therefore have in Mill's own shrewd example a warning that they must not attempt to do so on his grounds; [22] and much current confusion about the open society would be avoided if they would but take the warning to heart. In short, if we are going to speak of a right to freedom of speech, a right to live in an open society, we are going to have to justify that right with arguments of a different character from Mill's, and so move the discussion onto a plane entirely different from that of Mill. Above all, we are going to have to subordinate what we have to say to certain rules of discourse from which Mill, by his own fiat, is happily free. For the right in question is inconceivable save as one component of a system or complex of rights. Of rights, moreover, that mutually limit and determine one another and are, in any case, meaningless save as they are deemed subject to the general proposition that we are not entitled to the exercise of any right save as we discharge the duties correlative to that right. But once we begin to argue from premises of that sort we shall begin to talk sense, not nonsense, about freedom of speech and the open society. And the essence of the sense, I hasten to add, will be found to lie in the fact that we are no longer driving the roots of our doctrine into the soil of skepticism because (as I have suggested already) once we speak of a right [23] we have already ceased to be skeptics. And nothing is more certain than that we shall come out with something quite different from Popper's conception of the open society.

Fifth, Mill was fully aware (as his epigones seem not to be)

[22] We must distinguish here between a "natural" or "ethical" "right" to freedom of expression and a mere constitutional right. The case for the latter could of course be rested upon Mill's grounds, insofar as they are valid. Mr. Justice Black, as I have pointed out, sticks to the "plain language" of the Constitution.

[23] Again, we must except the merely constitutional right.

both of the novelty and of the revolutionary character of his proposal for a society organized around the notion of freedom of speech. Just as he deliberately cuts himself off from any appeal to the notion of abstract right, so does he cut himself off from any appeal to tradition. Not only had no one before ever taught his doctrine concerning freedom of speech, no one had ever taught a doctrine even remotely like it. No one, indeed, had ever discussed such a doctrine even as a matter of speculative fancy.[24] Hardly less than Machiavelli himself, Mill is in full rebellion against both religion and philosophy, and because in full rebellion against religion and philosophy, in full rebellion also against the traditional society that embodies them.[25] Hardly less than Machiavelli, he conceives himself a "new prince in a new state," [26] obliged to destroy that which has preceded him so that he may create that which he feels stirring within him.[27] Hardly less than Machiavelli, he is a teacher of *evil:* all truths that have preceded his are (as we have noted parenthetically above) at most partial truths, and enjoy even that status only because Mill confers it upon them.[28] To reverse a famous phrase, Mill thinks of himself as standing upon the shoulders not of giants but of pygmies. He appeals to no earlier teacher,[29] identifies himself with nothing out of the past; and his doctrine of freedom of speech is, as I have intimated, the unavoidable logical consequence of the denials from which his thought moves. Not, however, because it is in fact to be the public policy of the society he will found, not because it is to govern his followers' actions with respect to the freedom of thought of others, but because it is the perfect weapon—perfect because of its alleged connection with the quest for truth—to turn upon the traditional society that he must overthrow. For he who would destroy a

[24] Plato, of course, contemplates a freedom of speech *situation* in Book IX of the *Republic;* but merely to show that it can result only in disaster.
[25] Cf., Leo Strauss, *Thoughts on Machiavelli* (Glencoe: The Free Press, 1958), ch. 4, *passim.*
[26] Cf., *ibid.*, p. 9.
[27] Cf., *ibid.*, chapter 2, *passim.*
[28] Cf., *op. cit.*, pp. 42-46.
[29] That he had broken sharply with his father and Bentham is, I take it, a commonplace.

society must first destroy the public truth it conceives itself as embodying; and Mill's doctrine of freedom of speech, to the extent that it gets itself accepted publicly, does just that. I do not, I repeat, believe it can be separated from the evil teaching that underlies it; and nothing could be more astonishing than the incidence of persons amongst us who because of their religious commitments must repudiate the evil teaching, yet continue to embrace the doctrine.

Sixth, Mill's most daring *démarche* in the *Essay* (and Popper's in *The Open Society and Its Enemies*) is that of confronting the reader with a series of false dilemmas: unlimited freedom of speech or all-out thought control; the open society or the closed society, etc. I say "false" for two reasons. First, because unlimited freedom of speech and the open society are not real alternatives at all (see below). And second, because the dilemmas as posed conceal the real choices available to us, which are always choices as to how-open-how-closed our society is to be, and thus not choices between two possibilities but choices among an infinite range of possibilities. Mill would have us choose between never silencing and declaring ourselves infallible, as Popper would have us believe that a society cannot be a little bit closed, any more than a woman can be a little bit pregnant. And we must learn, because all our knowledge of politics bids us to, not to fall into the trap Mill and Popper lay for us. Nobody on the anti-Liberal side in this matter is asking for all-out thought-control or the absolutely closed society of the Liberal false dilemmas; and no Liberal has any business accusing those on the anti-Liberal (i.e., Conservative) side of wanting them. For the real question always is, How open can a society be and still remain open at all? Or, to put it differently, is there any surer prescription for arriving—will-we, nill-we, in spite of ourselves—at the closed society than that involved in current pleas for the open society?

That brings me to the central business of this chapter, which let me put as follows: Let us adjourn any objections we may have to open society doctrines on the grounds that they are rooted in demonstrably evil teachings. Let us suppose, for argument's sake, that it would be possible, taking as our premises sound notions as to the nature of truth, the value of tradition, and the claims of Revelation and Authority, to reach a point where we feel tempted to organize society in accordance with Mill's prescriptions, and for Mill's reasons. Have we then cause to suppose, as Mill thinks, that we shall end up forwarding the interests of truth? In other words, Mill offers us a prediction, "Do such and such and you will achieve such and such a result," and we wish to know merely "What would in fact happen if we did such and such?" My contention will be that once the question is put that way,[30] we run up against some insuperable objections to Mill's prescriptions in and of themselves—objections, moreover, that remain equally valid even if one starts out, unlike Mill, from a supposed "right," whether natural or constitutional, to freedom of speech.

Mill's proposals have as one of their tacit premises a false conception of the nature of society, and are, therefore, unrealistic on the face of them. They assume that society is, so to speak, a debating-club, devoted above all to the pursuit of truth, and capable therefore of subordinating itself—and all other considerations, all other goods, all other goals—to that pursuit. Otherwise, the proposals would go no further than to urge upon society the common-sense view: that the pursuit of truth is *one* of the goods it ought to cherish (even perhaps that one which it is most likely, in the press of other matters, to fail to make at least some provision for); that it will fail to make some provision for the pursuit of truth only at its own peril (a point that could easily be demonstrated); and that, accordingly, it should give hard and careful thought to what kind of provision it can make for the pursuit of truth without interfering unduly with its pursuit of other goods. But we know that society is not a debating-club—all our experience of society drives the point home to us—and that, even if it were a debating-club, the chances of its adopting the pursuit of truth as its supreme good are negligible. Societies, alike by definition and according to the teaching of history, cherish a whole series of goods—among others, their own

---

[30] I.e., as a problem for "empirical" political theory.

self-preservation, the *living* of the truth they believe themselves
to embody already, and the communication of that truth (pretty
much intact, moreover) to future generations, their religion, etc.
—which they are likely to value as much as or more than the
pursuit of truth, and *ought* to value as much as or more than
the pursuit of truth, because these are preconditions of the pursuit of truth.

To put it a little differently, the proposals misconceive the
strategic problem, over against organized society, of those individuals who do value the pursuit of truth above all other things.
That strategic problem we may put as follows: *Fortunate* that
society that has even a small handful—a "select minority," in
Ortega y Gasset's phrase—of persons who value the pursuit of
truth in the way in which Mill imagines society's valuing it!
Fortunate that select minority in such a society—if it can prevail
upon the society to provide it with the leisure and resources with
which to engage in the pursuit of truth, or, failing that, at least
not to stand in the way of its pursuit of truth! And *wise* that
society whose decision-makers are sufficiently far-seeing and generous to provide that select minority—even in the context of
guarantees against its abusing its privileges—the leisure and the
resources it needs for the pursuit of truth! To ask more than that
of society, to ask that it give that select minority freedom to publicly treat all questions as open questions, as open not only for
itself in the course of its discharge of its own peculiar function
but for everybody, is Utopian in the worst sense of the word;
and hence certain to defeat the very purpose the asking is intended to serve. By asking for all (even assuming that all to be
desirable) we imperil our chances of getting the little we might
have got had we asked only for that little.

Let us, however, waive that objection, and pass on to another,
namely, that the proposals have as a further tacit premise a false
conception of human beings, and how human beings act in organized society. Concretely, Mill assumes that speech (the professing and discussing of any doctrine, however immoral) is incapable of doing hurt in society. (He has to assume this, since
he calls for non-interference with speech, while the overriding

principle of the *Essay* is that society is always entitled to interfere in order to prevent hurt, whether to itself or to its individual
members.) This is frightening enough (Socrates, let us remember,
taught otherwise, namely, that he who teaches my neighbor evil
does me hurt), but Mill also assumes (else again his proposal is
romantic) that people can be persuaded either to *be* indifferent
toward the possible tendency of what their neighbors are saying,
or at least to *act* as if they were indifferent. We know nothing
about people, I suggest, that disposes us to regard such an assumption as valid, once it is brought out into the open (and we
should not, I trust, think more highly of our fellow-men if we
did think it valid). Thus Mill's proposals, like all political proposals that call implicitly for the refashioning of human nature,
can be enforced only through some institutional equivalent of
the French Revolutionary Terror—through, in a word, coercion.
And I believe it to be this consideration, above all, that explains
the failure of Mill's followers, to date, to persuade any organized
society to adopt the proposals. For let us never forget that the
West has no experience of unlimited freedom of speech as Mill
defines it, of the open society as Popper defines it, unless after a
fashion and for a brief moment in Weimar Germany. And that
is an experience which, one likes to think, no organized society
will be eager to repeat.

But let us now waive that objection also, and—assuming both
a society willing to adopt the proposals and a population willing to act in the manner they require—pass on to still another.
I contend that the society will overnight become the most *intolerant* of possible societies and, above all, one in which the pursuit of truth, in the meaningful sense of the word "truth" that
we agreed to start out with, can only come to a halt. Whatever
the private convictions of the society's individual members concerning what Plato teaches us to call the important things—that
is, the things with which truth is primarily concerned—the society itself is now by definition dedicated to a national religion
of skepticism, to the idea that all questions are open questions,
to the suspension of judgment as the exercise of judgment *par
excellence*. It can, to be sure, tolerate all expression of opinion

that is predicated upon its own view of truth; but what is it to do with the man who steps forward to urge an opinion, to conduct an inquiry, not predicated on that view? What is it to do with the man who with every syllable he utters challenges the very foundations of society? What can it say to him except, "Sir, you cannot enter into our discussions, because you and we have no common premises from which discussion between us can be initiated"? What can it do but silence him, and look on helplessly as within its own bosom patterns of opinion about the important things deteriorate into an ever greater conforming dullness. Nor—unlike traditional society, which did not regard all questions as open questions—need it hesitate to silence him. The proposition that all opinions are equally and infinitely valuable, which we are told to be the unavoidable inference from the proposition that all opinions are equal, is only one—and, as we now should know, the less likely—of two possible inferences. The other tells us that all opinions are equally and infinitely without value, so what difference does it make if one, particularly one not our own, gets suppressed? [31]

This we may fairly call the central paradox of the theory of freedom of speech; and it is it that accounts for some of the most striking phenomena of our time. E.g.: The fact that the situations in American life that are dominated by Mill's disciples, that is, by Liberals not Conservatives—the federal bureaucracy, for example, and the faculties of our great institutions of higher learning—are precisely those in which we find, on the major issues

[31] Cf., Bertrand de Jouvenel, *Sovereignty* (Chicago: University of Chicago Press, 1957), p. 288, "One of the strangest intellectual illusions of the nineteenth century was the idea that toleration could be ensured by moral relativism. . . . The relativist tells us that the man professing opinion A ought to respect opinion B, because his own opinion A has no more intrinsic value than B. But in that case B has no more than A. Attempts to impose either would be attempts to impose what had no intrinsic value; but also suppression of either would be suppression of what had no intrinsic value. And in that case there is no crime . . . in the suppression of contrary opinions." On equality of opinions in Mill, see note 16 *supra*. On the progress in Mill from "equally valuable" to "equally and infinitely valuable," cf., *op. cit.*, p. 46, ". . . truth has no chance but in proportion as every side of it, every opinion which embodies any fraction of the truth, not only finds advocates, but is so advocated as to be listened to." And the presumption, he insists, is that every opinion *does* contain some fraction of the truth: ". . . it is always probable that dissentients have something worth hearing . . . and that truth would lose something by their silence" (p. 42).

of our time, a sheer monotonous conforming, a disciplined chorus of voices all saying virtually the same thing in the same accents, the like of which we encounter nowhere else. The fact that it is precisely in those situations that non-conformism is dealt with most summarily and most ruthlessly.[32] In order to practice tolerance on behalf of the pursuit of truth, you have first to value and believe in not merely the pursuit of truth *but truth itself, with all its accumulated riches to date. The all-questions-are-open-questions society cannot do that; it cannot, therefore, practice tolerance towards those who disagree with it. It must persecute—and, on its very own showing, so arrest the pursuit of truth.*

But let us waive that objection too, and assume a society willing to adopt the proposals, a population willing to live up to them, and a miracle that will somehow prevent the society from persecuting and thus arresting the pursuit of truth. I now contend that the society in question will descend ineluctably into ever-deepening *differences* of opinion, into progressive breakdown of those common premises upon which alone a society can conduct its affairs by discussion, and so into the abandonment of the discussion process and the arbitrament of public questions by violence and civil war. This is a phenomenon to which Rousseau, our greatest modern theorist of this topic, returned again and again in his writings, and identified as that of the dispersal of opinion.[33] The all-questions-are-open-questions society not only cannot arrest it (by giving preferred status to certain opinions and, at the margin, mobilizing itself internally for their defense), it by definition places a premium upon dispersion—particularly by inviting irresponsible speculation and irresponsible utterance. As time passes, moreover, the extremes of opinion will—as they

[32] Most particularly, by the gradual but relentless elimination of the non-conformists by means of personnel policy.

[33] See *Social Contract*, IV, i., as also *The Discourse on the Sciences and Arts, passim,* and Rousseau's famous letter of 1767 to the Marquis of Mirabeau. Cf., de Jouvenel, *op. cit.*, p. 286, "The whole of [Rousseau's] . . . large stock of political wisdom consists in contrasting the dispersion of feelings in a people morally disintegrated by the progress of the 'sciences and arts,' with the natural unity of a people in which dissociation has not occurred." As de Jouvenel notes (p. 287), Rousseau, though himself a Protestant, deplored the introduction of Protantism into France, and on these grounds.

did in Weimar—get further and further apart, so that (for the reason noted above) their bearers can less and less tolerate even the thought of one another, still less one another's presence in society. And again the ultimate loser is the pursuit of truth.

Let us waive even that objection, however, and suppose a further miracle: one that will somehow prevent the dispersion of opinion and the resultant civil war, and will permit the determination of issues by what the society is still fond of calling the discussion process but what is actually (and still again by definition) now a babel of voices belonging to persons upon whom Mill's proposals have conferred an unlimited freedom of speech. Again what suffers, and suffers this time the final agony since this is the last station of its cross, is that very pursuit of truth that the proposals were calculated to foster. For still another tacit premise of the proposals is the extraordinary notion that the discussion process, which *correctly* understood does indeed forward the pursuit of truth and does indeed call for *free* discussion, is one and the same thing with Mill's unlimited freedom of speech. They rest, in consequence, upon a false conception of the discussion process. What they will produce is not truth but rather, as I have indicated, sheer deafening noise and sheer demoralizing confusion. For the essence of Mill's freedom of speech is to be found in the fact that it divorces the right to speak from the duties correlative to the right, which is one point (already noted above); that for it the right to speak is a right to speak *ad nauseam*, and with impunity, which is a second point; and that it is shot through and through with the egalitarian overtones of the French Revolution, which are as different from the measured, aristocratic overtones of the pursuit of truth—the pursuit of truth by discussion, as understood by the tradition Mill was attacking—as philosophy is different from phosphorous.

Of the latter point we may sufficiently satisfy ourselves, it seems to me, by merely reminding ourselves how the discussion process works in those situations in which men who are products of the tradition organize themselves for a serious venture in the pursuit of truth—as they do in, say, a branch of scholarship, an academic discipline, and the community of truth-seekers corresponding to it.[34]

Such men demonstrably proceed on some such principles as these: (a) The pursuit of truth is indeed forwarded by the exchange of opinions and ideas among many, and helpful suggestions do indeed emerge sometimes from surprising quarters. But one does not leap from these facts to the conclusion that helpful suggestions may come from just anybody. (b) The man or woman who wishes to exercise a right to be heard has a logically and temporally prior obligation to prepare himself for participation in the exchange, and to prepare himself in the manner defined by the community. Moreover (c), from the moment he begins to participate in the exchange, he must make manifest, by his behavior, his sense of the duty to act as if the other participants had something to teach him—the duty, in a word, to see to it that the exchange goes forward in an atmosphere of courtesy and mutual self-respect. Moreover (d), the entrant must so behave as to show that he understands that scholarly investigation did not begin with his appearance on the scene, that there is a strong presumption that prior investigators have not labored entirely in vain,[35] and that the community is the custodian of—let us not sidestep the "gypsy phrase"—an *orthodoxy*, no part of which it is going to set lightly to one side. (e) That orthodoxy must be understood as concerning first and foremost the frame of reference within which the exchange of ideas and opinions is to go forward. That frame of reference is, to be sure, subject to change, but this is a matter of *meeting the arguments that led originally to its adoption, and meeting them in humble recognition that the ultimate decision as to whether or not to change it lies with the community.* (f) The entrant, insofar as he wishes to challenge the orthodoxy, must expect barriers to be placed in his way, and must not be astonished if he is punished, at least in the short term, by what are fashionably called "deprivations"; he must,

[34] A similar point might be developed as regards the difference between Mill's freedom of speech and the free discussion of the traditional American town-meeting.

[35] A point that our contemporary political behaviorists seem to forget sometimes.

indeed, recognize that the barriers and the deprivations are a necessary part of the organized procedure by which truth is pursued. (g) Access to the channels of communication that represent the community's central ritual (the learned journals, that is to say) is something that the entrant *wins*—by performing the obligation to produce at least one craftsmanlike piece of work recognized as such by, say, three of the community's elders. (h) The ultimate fate of the entrant who disagrees with the orthodoxy but cannot persuade the community to accept his point of view is, quite simply, isolation within or banishment from the community.

No suggestion is made that this is a complete statement of the rules as we see them operating about us in the scholarly disciplines, or that the particular forms of words employed are the happiest, or most accurate, that could be found. They do, however, seem to me to suggest the broad outlines of the paradigm of the free discussion process as it goes forward in an academic community, and do drive home the differences between that paradigm and that of the freedom of speech process as Mill defines it. Nor, I think, could anything be more obvious than the answer to the question, Which of the two is the more likely to forward the pursuit of truth?

But it is not only that one of the two models is more likely than the other to forward the pursuit of truth. The point about Mill's model is that by giving equal privileges to those who are in fact opposed to or ignorant of the discussion process, it constitutes as a matter of course a major onslaught against truth. The two paradigms are not only different, but incompatible.

It would not be easy, of course, to transfer rules of the discussion process as set forth above to the public forum of a society; nor is there any point in denying that the transfer would involve our openly conceding to society far greater powers, particularly as regards silencing the ill-mannered, the ignorant, the irrelevant, than it would ever enjoy under the Mill paradigm. Here, however, two things must be kept in mind. First (however reluctant we may be to admit this to ourselves), that society always has, and constantly exercises, the power to silence. And second, that no society is likely, within the foreseeable future, to remake itself in the image of either of the two paradigms. The question, always, is that of which of the two paradigms we accept as the ideal toward which we try to move. That is the real issue at stake between the proponents and opponents of the "open society." It is the issue at stake between Mr. Justice Black and the (up to now) majority of our highest court who, though they would hardly call themselves Conservatives, are adopting (on the showing of this book) a sound Conservative position. And it is the issue that—make no mistake about it—bears *most* heavily on the very destiny of America.

Chapter 7

A Conservative Statement
on Christian Pacifism

A "Conservative statement" on Christian pacifism might take either of two forms: that of an argument intended to convince the Christian pacifist himself, to "meet" his "points," to counter his Scripture with other Scripture; or the form—now unfamiliar, so accustomed are we to "debating" with the pacifist (and his omnipresent cousin the leveller)—of a review, addressed not to the pacifist but to "ourselves," that is the "rest of us," of whom we somehow know beforehand that they are not pacifists (or levellers, or relativists) and that they are not going to become pacifists, but of whom we know also that they may not be as clear in their minds as they ought to be about the grounds on which, being the kind of men they are, they should reject the extravagant proposals constantly being dinned in their ears.

In the first of the two types of argument we engage in "debate" with the energumen, the man possessed, which is what he is forever trying to trick us into doing. In the second case we turn to one another and ask, "What are we going to do about his proposals, and why?". In the first case we treat the energumen as an "equal," with a "right" equal to our own to name the terms on which the discussion shall proceed. In the second we begin by raising with ourselves the question whether we can treat him as an equal without advancing him to the status of a superior; or, if you like, by reminding ourselves that *somebody* must name the terms of the debate, and that if we do not then he will. In the first case we "play like" we might accept his proposals, and have only ourselves to blame if we find that in doing so we have delivered ourselves into his hands. In the second case we recall Burke's way of squaring off to the "proposal" of the French revolutionaries, and start out from there: "The body of the people of England have no share in it. They utterly disclaim it. They will resist the practical assertion of it with their lives and fortunes." In the first case we agree tacitly to engage in a discussion which abstracts from tradition, from the forefathers, from the pledges that the forefathers made to one another—*must* abstract from these things because they are meaningless to the energumen—and pretend, in the teeth of our knowledge that it is not true, that the decision about the proposal before us has not already been made. In the second we content ourselves with saying, as Burke does in effect throughout the *Reflections,* Since we obviously are not going to adopt this proposal—any more than our ancestors before us have adopted such proposals when they have been brought forward—let us be clear with ourselves as to why, why on our own terms, we shall not adopt it. Or, What is it that we believe, to what traditional principles do we stand committed, that exclude any save a negative answer to this proposal; and why have our minds and hearts always been carried in the direction of *these* principles rather than others? In the first case we adopt the twofold fiction that we have nothing to do but engage in a "discussion" that must go on and on at our opponents' pleasure, and that we are somehow on the defensive. In the second case we say to those opponents, as Burke would not have hesitated to say to the French revolutionaries, Sirs, you have lost your sense of the fitness of things; it is you who are burning to persuade us, not we who have a society to run who are burning to persuade you; you must, therefore, let us choose the terrain on which we are to be persuaded, and let us determine the point at which the discussion ceases to be profitable. In the first case, we agree to act as if we did not know that discussion can go forward only in the context of shared premises, and, as I have already suggested, end up will-we nill-we accepting those of our opponents. In the second we say flatly to those opponents, again echoing Burke, We must insist that you refer your proposal to the premises on which we understand our society, and along with our society our civilization, to rest; that you either prove that your proposal is consistent with those premises, or, having failed to prove that, agree with us that we have no alternative but to reject it. In the first case, we permit the energumen to call into question even those premises on which, as I have just put it, we understand our civilization to rest, and adopt for the sake of argument the fiction that the discussion in which we are about to engage might result—as the energumen wishes it to—in our setting those premises aside and adopting new ones. In the second case, still paraphrasing Burke, we lay it on the line: We look upon the frame of our civilization, such as it stands, to be of inestimable value; and we shall not lightly alter the frame, or risk the civilization.

The following "Conservative statement" on Christian pacifism is, as the reader will have guessed, intended as a venture in the second not the first of these two types of argument. The general reader will find in it no attempt to "meet" the "case" for pacifism, no attempt to show the pacifist, or even those who are attracted by his arguments, where and how he is wrong. The Conservative reader will carry away from it no thunderbolts that he can use in his next dinner-table set-to with the man who favors unilateral disarmament because it says in the Bible "Thou shalt not kill" and because Jesus taught that we should love our neighbor as ourselves. The assumption throughout is that we do not have any "decision" to make over against the pacifist proposal, that because of "our" commitments the decision is already made, and that as far as "debate" with the pacifist is concerned, there is, quite simply, nothing to debate about.

Nor do I make any apology for having dwelt so long over the distinction between the two types of argument. Conservatives in America must learn to eschew the first and to cultivate the second, and must, now that pacifism has impudently reared its head within the Conservative movement itself, do so especially when the topic before the house is the "use of force." Indeed, one way to put it is to say, I humbly offer the following statement as a "model" that Conservatives should imitate in day-to-day political discussion. My purpose in the present chapter, then, is to set forth—not for the pacifist, but for those of us who already believe in them—the reasons that have led Western civilization in the past, that will lead Western civilization for so long as it exists, to reject the basic proposal of the pacifist. Now: in order to go at the matter in that way we must make certain assumptions, which we may profitably pause to get down in black and white: We must assume (and I do assume it unabashedly) that when we speak of Western Civilization, the "West" as many call it today, we mean something that *exists* and has existed through a past reaching back at least to Moses and to Homer; something that is, in the last analysis, definable; something that, though it changes, as civilizations must change, remains recognizably itself through its changes. We must assume (again I do assume it unabashedly) that we may properly speak of a tradition of Western Civilization, or an *orthodoxy* of Western Civilization—that is, of a complex of beliefs, of commitments, of notions of good and evil, of truth and untruth, of beauty and ugliness, all subject, like the Civilization itself, to change. This changing, to be sure, is by no means necessarily always for the better, but again is of such character that the complex endures through the changes, has at least up to now remained recognizably itself. We must assume (and once more I assume it unabashedly) that we most accurately identify the tradition or orthodoxy by seeking out those beliefs, those commitments, those notions of good and evil that survive through all the changes. And that we are nearest to the core of the tradition when we touch upon those beliefs and commitments and notions of good and evil that (a) have perdured in recognizable form over the longest period of time, and (b) have proved themselves genuine by being consistently acted upon and, at the margin, *fought* for. And fought for, both against enemies from beyond the gates of our Civilization, whom by a long tradition and with strict accuracy we call *barbarians,* and now against enemies within the gates, whom by a long tradition we call *heretics.* We assume, finally, that it is part of our business as carriers of Western Civilization to call a spade a spade—

even if there are persons around or within earshot whose experience of Civilization is so limited that they do not know what a spade is, have never had any occasion to call a spade anything, and therefore dislike hearing the word used (as many today dislike such words as "tradition" and "orthodoxy" and "barbarian" and "heretic"—all of which, however, are indispensable for any discussion of the topics we have in hand). Even, I say, if there are such persons within earshot, and even if, regretfully, we must injure their sensibilities a little. We must assume these things because they are themselves part of the tradition that they help to define—or, if you like, because they have been taught to us by our experience of Western Civilization, and because Western Civilization is our most sacred and most cherished inheritance. And, having assumed them, we shall have brought out into the open the vocabulary we need—tradition, orthodoxy, barbarian, heretic—in order for me to formulate my major theses in this chapter. These are twofold:

A. That while there are many variants of pacifism, many forms its proposals may take, many rationales its proponents may put forward, they all have at least this major emphasis in common, namely, that they demand the principled rejection of force, of the recourse to arms—even by legally constituted states attempting to defend their just interests, including survival itself. We find differences, from pacifist to pacifist, as to how far to go in pressing this or that kind of demand, as to the situations, if any, in which to permit the use of force, and as to the new twists or nuances to be injected into the age-old arguments for the pacifist position with a view to getting around the objections that have always led Western Civilization to reject it. These differences, however, are unimportant as far as the central issue is concerned. The essence of pacifism, that which all pacifists have in common, is the principled rejection of force—not merely by legally-constituted states, but by Western Civilization itself in its current struggle with Communist barbarism.

B. That pacifism is alien to the tradition of Western Civilization because that tradition is primarily though not exclusively a Christian tradition and because pacifism is alien to the Christian tradition. (More concretely, pacifism—though it appeals to the Christian doctrine of love—is the very negation of that love, that is, a manifestation of a kind of self-love that is hostile to the very meaning and heart of Christianity.)

Although it insinuates itself into the body politic as a higher expression of Christian selflessness, it is marked throughout by irresponsibility and callous indifference towards the wants and needs and rights of the pacifists' fellow-men. And finally, so-called *Christian* pacifism, though often no doubt motivated by a good-will whose roots are indeed to be found in the Christian tradition, is in fact a Christian heresy and by that very token a sign of barbarism in our midst.

We shall not understand each other about these theses, about why Christian pacifism must be judged a heresy, until we have said something more about the meaning of orthodoxy. At least this much must be said: The mark of a mind civilized by our primarily Christian inheritance, and therefore pervaded through and through by *civility*—a term I take from Dr. Johnson—is its ability to entertain intellectually and experience emotionally a complex of propositions whose unity consists, difficult as the idea may be for some persons to grasp, in the very *tension* among them. We confront here the paradox of intellectual opposites caught up together in a unity that gives vision and therefore peace to the man who possesses it. Precisely what makes a man an orthodox Christian is his *will's* assent, under the impetus of the Grace of God, to a vision of reality based upon a fusing of opposites. The man who fails to be moved to that assent by the Grace of God, the man who fails there but is still able to entertain the vision intellectually, is what we may call a civilized unbeliever and not, in our terms, a heretic at all. The heretic is a different kind of man altogether, and his delineation is of central importance for our topic. The heretic is the man insufficiently civilized to understand—to get through his head—the complex of propositions that make up orthodox Christianity, and are thus a major part of the intellectual inheritance of Western Civilization. He is not, let us note carefully, an unbeliever. The heretic believes, but believes only a portion of the deposit of faith;

and he believes *this* portion to the exclusion of *that* because (I repeat) he is temperamentally or intellectually incapable of getting hold of that fusion of opposites that is the fullness of the Christian faith.

For example, orthodox Christianity maintained from the beginning that Christ was not a being apart from God and man (as an elf is), nor yet a being half-human and half not (like a centaur), but both at once and both through and through—*very* man and *very* God. The inability to believe this is not heresy, but rather incredulousness. Total rejection of the Incarnation, of the doctrine we have just stated, is easy to imagine in a mind and will annealed in the Judaic experience of civilized order, and is not, therefore, an evidence—if I may invert Dr. Johnson's word —of uncivility. It is easy to imagine also in a mind and will annealed in the classical experience of civilized order, where again it would not be an indication of uncivility. But it is quite otherwise with the mind and will that partially accepts the doctrine and at the same time partially rejects it. For here we have a mind and will both inside and outside the Christian experience of the order of being, both inside and outside our primarily Christian civilization and, insofar as he is outside, by definition a barbarian. The stigmata by which he is to be recognized are the various forms of the wish to live *off* our Civilization and benefit from the commitments it imposes upon others, but not live within them. And since that wish derives from his failure to grasp that complex of propositions, to entertain that paradox and to assent to the mystery inherent in it, he is a double threat to Civilization. He consumes the produce of fields that he does not help to till—that are, indeed, tilled by his enemies; he draws his strength from that which he rejects; and society is the weaker both because of that which he consumes and because of that which he should have nurtured but did not nurture. The heretic is a parasite.

Heretic, barbarian, parasite. That is the profane trinity that sums up the pacifist. Christianity—so Chesterton puts it—taught the lion to lie down with the lamb; but the lion did not thereby cease to be leonine, or become lamblike. The paradox of orthodoxy is this joining together of lion and lamb that remain lion and lamb, of war and peace that are truly war and peace, of force that is force and resignation to evil that is resigned. The Christian pacifist, by contrast with the orthodox Christian, seizes upon Christ's injunction to bear evil for His sake, and forgets or ignores or cannot comprehend the massive truth that Christ himself used force when he scourged the money-changers out of the temple. And that He was fond of the company of Roman soldiers. And that He paid one of His highest compliments to a centurion.

We learn from Augustine that the first serious manifestation of the heresy known as pacifism is to be found in the Manicheans. They insisted that there are two principles in reality, the Good and the Evil; that the material universe is the work of Evil and therefore itself evil warp-and-woof; that whatsoever the body does and suffers has no essential bearing upon what the soul thinks and knows and loves—all of this issuing logically in an indifference towards civil society that in due course hardened into opposition, obstruction and, eventually, into hatred. They were, in any case, pacifists, and punctuated their lives of lethargic indifference to the world with periodic orgies and excesses and then, pure spirits that they were, denied all responsibility for the consequences of their debauchery. We have it from Waldensis that the Manicheans' pacifism was in due course handed down (which brings it a deal closer home) to Wycliffe, who probably received it from the Catharists, a sect whose doctrine on the evil of marriage struck at the very roots of civilized order and the decency of human love. Also in the fourteenth century, pacifism reared its head in the Rhine Valley, where it signalized the internal breakdown of medieval Christendom and the spread of that religious individualism, the negation of Christian charity, which I believe to be the root—both philosophical and theological—of the pacifist malady.[1] (A great deal of foolishness has been talked, and by persons who ought to know better, about the alleged pacifism

[1] See *The Decline of the Intellectual*, by Thomas Molnar (Cleveland: Meridian, 1961), for an analysis of what has happened to the "Christian synthesis" since the Middle Ages.

of the early Christians. They did indeed refuse to serve in the Roman armies, but not because they regarded the recourse to arms as evil; rather because as Roman soldiers they would have had to burn incense to the gods. As for the martyrs, they did not, to be sure, resist; but the martyrs were precisely not pacifists but saints, and did not pick and choose among the Beatitudes.)

Let us speak now of traditional Christian doctrine concerning the just war, which we may safely cite as one of Western Civilization's major defenses against the heretical preachments of the pacifists. In brief summary, it runs as follows: The state is a natural society; being that, it possesses under natural law the right to use the means necessary for its preservation and proper functioning. In certain conditions, moreover, the only means by which it can preserve itself, or perfect or recover its lawful rights, is the recourse to arms. And, given those conditions, it possesses under the natural law the right and the duty to wage war.

The traditional reasoning here has as its underpinning, let us notice at once, a profound metaphysics of Being itself, and one that has nowhere been better articulated than in Abraham Lincoln's blunt assertion that "No state voluntarily wills its own dissolution." The state—so runs the reasoning—has as its end the common good of its citizenry; it therefore is an order of Being, and of the Being appropriate to a complex relationship. To say that it must not have recourse to armed might even when its existence is threatened by aggressors from without or within is, in other words, to demand that an order of Being voluntarily will its own nothingness; and such a demand is contrary to the structure of reality itself. Or, as Thomas Aquinas puts it: every order of Being, and every being as well, *by its very nature* strives to keep itself in being. As Paul Tillich puts it, Being is identical with its own power to be, is its own affirmation against its own non-being. In a word, when we say that the lawfully-constituted state must bare its neck to the executioner, must do so though it exists to promote the common good of its citizenry, we as good as say that reality must have a tendency towards non-reality, that existence is one with nothingness. The pacifist in his heresy approaches the heresy of the suicide, and both are powerful artillery pieces trained upon the structure of existence itself. The Jewish tradition of Spinoza, the Catholic tradition of Aquinas, and the Protestant tradition of Tillich are all at one in this conception of the fundamental metaphysics. And the fact that they are at one bespeaks an orthodoxy common to the *entire* West, wholly incompatible with pacifism—a doctrine so irresponsible that it refuses to salute even the Flag of Being, and so represents a sharp break with that orthodoxy. It is the Jehovah's Witness *par excellence.*

Let us put the point a little differently: A state which will not wage war in any circumstances, however serious, would condemn itself to extinction. Now, if the natural law demanded that, then God, who is the Author of the natural law, would both will and not will political society. He would will its purpose, its *end,* and at the same time forbid it the means necessary for attaining that end—and I say "necessary" because the state that cannot protect the life, liberty, and property of its citizens fails in its appointed function. If, therefore, the state can sometimes perform its function only through the use of force, it must have the right to use force. And, naturally enough, the common orthodoxy of the West has always maintained that among the most precious rights of man is the right to go to war.

In this context, we readily see what is wrong with pacifism as a doctrine. If the pacifist were merely an opponent of militarism, of the use of aggressive war as an instrument of imperialistic expansion, the West would not always have turned a deaf ear to him. But the pacifist contents himself with nothing so modest or sensible. He condemns *all* war, even defensive war, and in doing so logically plunges himself into anarchism—an anarchism which, implicitly and often explicitly, wills the nothingness of civil society. This is a nihilism as dangerous as that of *Zarathustra*—nay, more dangerous, because it masks itself under the cloak of the very Christian responsibility that it denies.

Let us, however, pass on to another chapter of our topic. War, says the common tradition of Western Civilization, is not only not intrinsically wrong; it is very often intrinsically right, intrinsically moral. This also emerges from the doctrine of the just war—the conditions for which, under natural law, are as follows: (1) The just or legitimate war must be declared by a lawful authority. (Killing, the doctrine teaches, is clearly wrong when the killer is an individual acting in a private capacity, though no longer wrong when the killer kills in self-defense against private aggression. As for the soldier, he has a clear right to kill when he acts as the legal and publicly-designated agent of his country in the prosecution of a just war; and even public designation is not necessary if the war is a purely defensive one.) (2) Resort to force is permitted only on behalf of a just cause, where we must confess at once that the definition of just cause has given rise to very considerable differences of opinion, though not so many as to prevent our pointing to certain just causes about which there has been general agreement—namely that of the state that is fighting for its very existence; that of the state which moves to recover that which is rightfully its own; and that of the state whose honor has been wounded so grievously that inaction would plead it guilty of cowardice in the eyes of the world. (3) The use of force is permitted only as a last resort. That is to say, before a nation launches its just war, it must have exhausted every peaceful means consistent with its dignity: negotiation; mediation; arbitration; diplomacy; economic sanctions; ultimatums—in a word, every means short of war known to enlightened statesmanship. Otherwise, the doctrine holds, there exists no clear proof that the war is unavoidable, and that there is a proper relation between the good hoped for from the war and the means of achieving that good. (4) The state resorting to war must have a fair hope of success. Here again, however, the doctrine is not entirely clear, since it recognizes that there are times when men are so pressed—or oppressed—that resistance, even hopeless resistance, is the only means by which men can preserve their common dignity. By signing history with their heroism, as the Hungarians did yesterday and the Tibetans are doing today, noble men not only go to God but remind other men everywhere of what it means to be a man. To die on the streets of Budapest, a machine-gun in hand, is not only to save one's dignity and therefore one's soul; it is to offer an example to a timid and even cowardly world. And such a death, our tradition recognizes, may express a love that passes all understanding: "Greater love hath no man," it says, than "that he lay down his life for his friend." The Hungarian freedom fighters, I like to think, died not only to save themselves, but to save us; their names should pass into the speech of all whose tongues still utter decency in a disintegrating world. The doctrine teaches, finally, that (5) even a punitive war, a war undertaken to punish a guilty nation, may be a just war. Right order and the future peace of the world may well demand, for example, that gangster nations not be permitted to commit mass-murder with impunity—that, rather they be taught a lesson in morals here and now. (There is, however, no blanket authorization in this regard; the right to wage a punitive war may well be counterbalanced by other considerations. The remitting of punishment, for instance, which is an act of mercy, might in certain circumstances be the higher duty.)

This traditional Christian doctrine, which, I repeat, is also that of the whole Western heritage, has both restrained the arrogant and given spirit to the timid. It has been articulated step by step, within the Christian West and *nowhere else*—which suggests, if it does not prove, that its roots are in the Christian experience itself. It owes as much to philosophic reason as to Revelation, and thus illustrates the Christian baptism of the Greek philosophical experience. It is of crucial importance for the preservation of Western Civilization, and only a man weary of both the burdens and the glory of the heritage of that Civilization would seek to undermine it or call it into question. And that is the point about the pacifist; he is weary, and weary of both the burdens and the glory; and the consequences of his abdication of responsibility are visited not so much on him as on his society or civilization.

Let me make that clear. If the Christian pacifist were an isolated Ebenezer in a frontier society, we could let Bill take care of him—as Bill does in Hilaire Belloc's delightful refrain:

> Pale Ebenezer thought it wrong to fight;
> But roaring Bill who killed him
> Thought it right.

But the Christian pacifist is not a pale Ebenezer, who seraphically turns his face towards a lonely aggressor. He is a heretic within a society that his actions weaken and, were they to be multiplied, would destroy. The only thing to do with him is to unmask his pretensions, if only to be done with his constant moralizing. Unmask them how? One possibility would be for us to imitate Hilaire Belloc's delightful Bishop of old Auxerre, who:

> . . . With his stout Episcopal staff
> So thoroughly thwacked and banged
> The heretics all, both short and tall,
> They rather had been hanged.
>
> Oh, he thwacked them hard, and he
>   banged them long,
> Upon each and all occasions,
> Till they bellowed in chorus,
>   long and strong,
> Their orthodox persuasions!

But however we unmask him, unmask him we must, and soon. Appealing as he does from the doctrine of brotherly love and Christ's injunction to "turn the other cheek," he has confused them both and confused them badly.

Let me pause a moment over that injunction to "turn the other cheek," and let me go for assistance once again to Thomas Aquinas—not of course because of his supposed authority, but because his teaching on the matter appears to have imbedded itself deep in the conscience of Western Civilization, to have entered into and become part of the Western way of life, and to have guided the actions of countless millions of Westerners—countless millions who certainly could not have put the teaching into words, but have not, for that reason, acted upon it any the less surely or any the less confidently. Who, asks Thomas Aquinas, has the *right* to turn the other cheek?—not, mind you, the duty, but the right, since unless we have the right we clearly cannot have the duty. Who has the *right* to submit to unjust aggression? And Aquinas answers, Only the man upon whom no higher responsibility falls; only the man who owes no other duty, in justice or in charity, to a friend or a wife or a child or a society that would be adversely affected by the aggression. Now, for the sake of argument let us grant that such an isolated man, a man liberated from the responsibilities that normally attach to the Christian way of life in society, might exist. Thomas wishes us to ask farther, Does even he have the right to turn the other cheek? And we get not a "Yes" answer but the answer "Yes, but." Yes, but not always, not in all circumstances. Such a man has the right to turn the other cheek *only if his act of submitting to the aggressor will, or possibly could, deter the aggressor from his evil act;* only if his act of bearing injustice for the sake of Christ may become a symbol of righteousness that might sign itself within the conscience of the aggressor. Then, and then only, says Aquinas, ought the Christian to refrain from resistance. If non-resistance clearly cannot effect this end—as who but the pacifist supposes it could against a Hitler, or against the disciplined hordes of World Communism?—then resistance becomes a duty. And this duty is not primarily a means by which the man unjustly attacked may save himself, but a means of preventing the aggressor from carrying out his act and, by striking back, teach the bully a lesson. Given the circumstances, resistance would be demanded by the *law of Christian love itself.* In a word, I ought to be concerned enough about the moral and spiritual health of my enemy *to fight him for his own good!* And the principle is, I repeat, important not because it is Aquinas', but because it is and will continue to be the rule of action of Western Civilization. It is the rule of action that sent us out to destroy the abomination known as Nazism; and it has much further work to do.

A Conservative Statement on Christian Pacifism

The issue of pacifism, let me repeat, is less important for us than the locus in which it is argued. And the point to grasp becomes this: the reasoning, on which the doctrine just summarized rests, moves from a spiritual emphasis that is unknown to and unknowable by the pacifist. It originates in what Sombart and Weber and Dawson call the "ec-static" structure of Christian Love, which is a love that seeks not the self but the perfection of the other; a love so strong that, as we have just seen, it will strike a man down in order that he may rise up the better for the blow! And we cannot, I think, overemphasize the fact that modern Christian pacifism grew up within the climate of that Christian individualism which is an utter distortion of the meaning of Christian love. Should we seek its origins, or at least its earliest full expression, we might well look to that same Rhine Valley gnosticism that produced both Mennonite pacifism and Thomas à Kempis, whose *Imitation of Christ* preaches a strange new doctrine of Christian perfection. It holds that I am called to love my neighbor because God has thrown him my way as an occasion, as an instrument, for *my own perfection*. Its emphasis is, clearly, upon the self. It teaches a self-centered Christianity, the essence of which is that it would sacrifice society, even the life of one's own sons and daughters, on the altar of personal perfection—and this for the sake of personal identification with a misunderstood ideal of the Christian life. Such a Christianity inverts not only the psychological and theological but also the ethical dimension of the human spirit. And the ideal that it distorts, the true ideal of Christian love and thus of Christianity itself, is that caught up in St. John's magnificent injunction, "As the Father so loved you that He gave you His only Begotten Son, so do you love the world." The orthodox Christian loves the other —including his enemy—not because *he* will thereby be perfected, but because the other so needs his love; and in the background of this ec-static doctrine of love, Christ's injunctions to bear suffering and to turn the other cheek take on a transcendent meaning that is one with the sacrifice, even unto death, demanded by the Christian life. When resistance to aggression is the only means whereby I can cure a man of evil, then the love I owe him demands that I resist him. The sword ought to be taken up in love; and Chesterton is there to remind us that the cross and the sword are, paradoxically, the same symbol, pointing to the same Reality.

Another point or two, and I shall have done. The pacifist insists that Christian history fails to reveal any instance of a war's having achieved the ends for which it was waged. The assertion is altogether false, of course, in its understanding of the history of the West. To take the simplest and most obvious cases: Had Charles Martel not taken up the sword against the Mohammedan barbarians, the crescent and not the cross would surely be planted where today there stands Notre Dame de Paris. Had Charlemagne not hurled back the Germanic pagans to the East, we might well be worshipping Odin and Thor and living in a forest of barbarism and blood. Had Don Juan of Austria not turned back the Turks at Lepanto, and had not John Sobieski halted the Turks at Vienna, our civilization would have gone down in a twilight of the gods that would have left the world empty of decency and bereft of law. These men are the heroes of our cradles; tales of their valour have always been the substance of the childhood dreams of Christian men everywhere. And "we" of the West value our Marlboroughs and George Washingtons—value them and revere their memories, as we value and revere the memories of our Beethovens and our Shakespeares. Each has contributed a kind of knowledge and a kind of devotion without which the West could not have become the West as we know it.

It is objected that the medieval Church forbade the taking up of arms by clerks regular and secular, and on the ground that hands that consecrate at the altar ought not to be stained by blood. Indeed it did; but let no one try to transform this into a leg for pacifism to stand on. The leading theologians of the period are at one in justifying and praising those religious orders whose mission was the defence of the Holy Places against the barbarians. The position is crystal-clear: for the "defence of religion and public safety" and out of love for "the poor and the oppressed," men of God were raised up who carried shields and lances. And the tradition approved—as approve it must in view of the teaching of Ambrose, who praised those who would defend the fatherland against barbarians; those who would shield the hearth against thieves; those who would stand as living swords between murderers and persons who are sick and infirm. And Ambrose praised them precisely because of their love of *justice*.

Christian love—it is this which is the pretended strength of pacifism, and it is this which makes of pacifism a peculiarly hideous heresy. For its love is a pale and fraudulent imitation of the real thing. It loves neither its enemy nor its friend, neither society nor home. To its claim that peace is its end, we have the answer of Christ Himself that "I bring you not peace, but a sword." Peace is something waged for, fought for; and the reason our world today may well find itself forced to wage war again is not that it cannot rise to the pacifist love of peace, but that it loves peace really, and knows it to be inseparable from the obligation to maintain order. God has made it our business to protect justice and law and liberty, and this out of love for our neighbor. Another teaching of Aquinas that has entered into the conscience of the West drives the point home: Even if I knew infallibly, Aquinas argues, even if I knew by a Revelation of God that my efforts to save my dying father were doomed to failure, that God Himself had willed my father's death, it would not affect my obligation to try to keep him alive. In a word, God's will for me would remain what it was before the Revelation, namely, that I live up to my obligations. God may have willed the destruction of the planet in an atomic *Gotterdämmerung* (I do not know, of course, and can never know); but *we* are still obligated to use the means at our disposal in order to preserve justice in the situations in which we are involved, to fulfill our duties in all their concreteness and detail. That preserving, that fulfilling, is God's will for us, and whatever else He may have willed as a consequence of what we do is, I repeat, God's business and not ours. In acting accordingly we would have behind us the full weight of the only tradition—the Christian tradition—that has made life bearable for man within time.

The temptation to give way to the pacifists—who have now added to their other skills a mastery of what let's call the art of nuclear-weapons blackmail—is very great, and great especially in those quarters where the Scripture the pacifist diabolically cites is held in contempt (except, of course, as a stick with which to beat non-pacifist Christians over the head). The temptation, I say, is very great; it will become greater as time passes; it will be at its greatest on that future day when the Soviet Union delivers to us the ultimatum that, back in 1946, we should have delivered to it. The thought of surrender on that day—not, I repeat, on Christian pacifist grounds, but out of sheer funk—is indeed present in the atmosphere, is already sapping our national will to resist the Communist enemy, is already pushing further and further into the future the moment when we shall discover, not too late I hope, that our duty to strike down the Soviet aggressor, our duty to prevent him from doing the wrong he is doing, is not different from but identical to the duty we shouldered a few years ago with respect to the Nazis. And not less urgent, but much more urgent.

Christians themselves may come to feel the temptation—not, as today, in small numbers, but in the large numbers that are the stuff of the so-called Christian pacifist's dreams. And we must say to them, You must resist the temptation. Let me, this once more, fall back on Chesterton:

> "It is easy to be a madman; it is easy to be a heretic. It is always easy to let the age have its head; the difficult thing is to keep one's own . . . To have fallen into any of those open traps of error and exaggeration which fashion after fashion set along the historic path of Christendom—that would indeed have been simple. It is always simple to fall; there are an infinity of angles at which one falls, only one at which one stands. To have fallen into any one of the fads . . . would have been obvious and tame. But to have avoided them all has been one whirling adventure; and in my vision the heavenly chariot flies thundering through the ages, the dull heresies sprawling and prostrate, the wild truth reeling but erect."

Chapter 8

Conservative Appraisals of
Recent Works on Politics

THE CONSERVATIVE ILLUSION. By M. MORTON AUERBACH

(New York: Columbia University Press, 1959.)

Like Seurat, Professor Auerbach likes a big canvas (Plato to the present day). Like Van Gogh, he prefers bright colors, especially purple. Like Gauguin, he has a sharp eye (no "contradiction" escapes it), and concerns himself little about the sensibilities of his less-emancipated fellows. Like Toulouse-Lautrec, he seems to mix a little venom with his oils—to correct against any possible "slip" in the direction of kindliness or understanding. *"Patience, mon coeur; doucement, doucement,"* the critical reader must keep saying to himself as he watches the argument unfold; and if he thinks of himself as a Conservative, he must do more than that, namely: see to it that Auerbach doesn't get his goat—the more urgently because, if he is a Conservative in any intelligible sense, Auerbach not only has no right to get his goat, but rather deserves his thanks. The Almighty tempers the wind to the shorn lamb—which, according to Auerbach, is what the Conservative always is; and in this case He has done so by sending the perpetual sufferer an avowedly anti-Conservative book which can only redound to the benefit of Conservatism. First, by helping it dissociate itself from the Clinton Rossiters, the Peter Vierecks and Peter Druckers, the Herbert Agars (Auerbach calls them the "adjusted" Conservatives), who write books showing how you can be a Conservative and yet agree with the Liberals about everything not demonstrably unimportant. Second, by saying what needs to be said, from the Conservative point of view as well as from Auerbach's own, about what let's call the rhetorical Conservatives (who in practice tend a little to be "adjusted," or at least a "little-adjusted"). Instead of going on and on about "unbought grace," and so on (however much meaning such expressions may have back and forth among hearts that beat as one), let them come out and say what they mean, so we can all decide whose side they are on. Third, by reminding Conservatives of what goes on in the heads and hearts of their opponents, including the adjusted Conservatives, thus confirming them in their determination to keep on being Conservatives. And fourth, by forcing on them the distinction between political debate and political philosophy, thus sending them back to the latter—which is where they belong.

In political debate we seek to discomfit, to refute, with an eye to the presumed audience; in political philosophy we seek to understand, to arrive at truth, to teach and at the same time learn. In political debate, we seize upon the weaknesses of the positions of those with whom we disagree, thus *need* a sharp eye for "contradictions," for "dilemmas" that they can be forced into; in political philosophy we are concerned primarily with the strength of those positions, because our hope is to clarify the problems and drive them to ever-deeper levels. Now on such a showing, any similarity between Professor Auerbach's book and political philosophy, for all that the names of Plato, Aristotle, Cicero, etc., do turn up in it, is merely coincidental. Auerbach's procedure (I do *not* say his intention) is to set up a definition of Conservatism (it places a supreme value on "harmony" as opposed to "freedom," it asserts that the central fact of history is that of moral degeneration, it seeks to "minimize" human desires, when all else fails it is prepared to hand "the problem" over to God) which makes it sound silly to begin with. He takes up one by one political writers whom he regards, now with reason now without it, as having asserted such nonsense, and crucifies them—with nails fashioned out of contradictions—on an old rugged cross made up of the two questions, "What's your program for achieving the harmony you desiderate?" and, "What, really now, are your chances of bringing your program off?" This, of course, is mere political debate, in which the question "What succeeds?" replaces the question "What is true?", and the more regrettably because of the truly vast literature Auerbach has put himself through in order to write the book (some writers have done better home-work about, e.g., the so-called "New Conservatives," but none has done more home-work), and because there are seven whole pages (238-245) that suggest that the fates intended the author for better things. It is also the easiest kind of political debate, which accordingly Auerbach always wins hands down (and winning, as he is at great pains to point out, is what counts in this business, besides which nothing wins like winning). As for political philosophy, I think it not unfair to say that the author, burdened as he is with the "findings" and ideology of contemporary social science, knows the answers to too many questions that political philosophy continues to treat as problems (because they are problems), and thus too little about the few things that are obvious in political philosophy (e.g., the difference in "rank," as Strauss puts it, between Plato and, say, Auerbach, or Plato and, say, Drucker—whose names Auerbach joins with an "and" without batting an eyelash), to give political philosophy the time of day.

The Conservative Illusion is not, however, an unscrupulous book. For one thing (dead Conservatives apart, since anything goes there), the author holds himself rigorously to the maxim of justice that forbids us to pick on people that aren't our size. Only the small-fry among contemporary exponents of views differing from his own turn up in his pages; one seeks in vain names like Jaspers, Löwith, Strauss, Voegelin, Guardini, as also any recognition of the major issues—positivism, historicism, the authority of the Bible and of classical political philosophy—that they have drawn with the age they live in. For another thing, one sees by the end of the book that Auerbach's attributing to the Conservatives a patently absurd position is a matter of honest if not very workmanlike intellectual error. Although on the main point—whether the Conservative seeks harmony *tout court* or harmony on certain terms (Yes, his), which terms, whether religious or philosophical, become the essence of the Conservative position—the truth finally flies up and hits him in the face: he does see, though too late to do anything about it, that Burke, while he might go along a while with the forces Auerbach glorifies, would at some point have had to draw the line (i.e., quit being "adjusted"). Not, I hasten to add, that I regard the *term* "conservative" as worth fighting over. Auerbach can have it, to apply to anything he likes. What he and this reviewer can agree on whole-heartedly, and what is more important by far than the meaning we assign to "conservative," is: who are the anti-Conservatives, and what are *their* supreme values? Had he but cottoned onto the fact that the Conservatives in the modern period are simply those who resist the revolutionary program Burke identified and opposed in the *Reflections,* that the question is not whether they have a program and can carry it out but whether they can continue to frustrate the Machiavellians (the program Burke identified hasn't been carried out anywhere yet), he would have written a very different book, one that might even have done hurt, as surely he wished to do, to the Conservative cause. As for Auerbach's confidence that he and his *copains* are riding the crest of the wave of History, and that the Conservatives always represent History's "tail-end" (can't, as we used to say in poker games, win for losing), this reviewer contents himself with four observations.

Nobody knows how the story is going to end. Pride goeth before a fall. The fortunes of Liberalism may begin to worsen even in the short term if many of its spokesmen throw its mind and heart open to inspection as Auerbach does. And I can cite authority *he* likes to the effect that the goddess he has handed the problem over to is a Bitch.

DEMOCRACY AND THE CHALLENGE TO POWER.
By DAVID SPITZ
(*New York: Columbia University Press, 1958.*)

If there be such a thing as a good Liberal (other than a dead one), then in this reviewer's book, political theorist David Spitz is—and has been for a long time—it. He writes out of a vast first-hand knowledge of the literature of politics; he is clear-headed, unsentimental, *sérieux*. He would not, one gets to feel, try to have it both ways on an intellectual issue, even if nobody were looking and he could easily get by with it. He is aware that there are points of view different from his own that might be worth listening to, and makes a patently honest effort to understand them and come to grips with them. Best of all, he writes with respect, warmth and affection of those who disagree with him: he really means it about freedom of thought and speech—to the extent, for example, that one senses in him a man who on his campus would insist that academic freedom extends even to Conservatives. He would, I think, even leave out the "even."

Spitz' preoccupation in this book is twofold. First, our alleged failure, here in the United States, to discover and maintain a "mode of government that respects the principle of consent as *the* legitimate source of power" (the italics are mine, but should be his). And, second, the continued denial, within our political system, of "certain [inviolable] rights which are indispensable to the very principle of democracy—namely, such freedoms as the freedoms of speech and political association, and such equalities as equality of citizenship and equality of opportunity, . . . [which are] minimum rights without which no state can be termed democratic."

With respect to the first of these propositions, his logic appears to run as follows: the principle of consent is *the* valid principle of authority; that principle calls as a matter of course for democracy; democracy calls for majority rule; and majority rule calls for the elimination of the non-majoritarian features of our political system (separation of powers, staggered elections, over-representation of particular constituencies in our bicameral legislatures). Spitz recognizes, in a word, that democracy is *stuck* with majority rule (a thesis upon which this writer has been hammering for many years), and that, therefore, those who defend democracy as something other than a *pis aller* (i.e., as valid in and of itself), must also defend majority rule and its foreseeable consequences as something other than a *pis aller* (that is, as something it is possible to make out a case for). Whence—and Spitz travels the whole road—the "barriers" to majority rule have, in principle, to go.

Unlike most writers who take this position, however, Spitz does not demand that we rush out and do something about it. He sees that the majority of the American people simply do not want majority rule (as the majoritarians define it), and that for a minority to impose majority rule upon the majority would be "undemocratic." So for him to demand that we rush out and do something about it would run him afoul of what, officially anyhow, is the only ethic he has: namely, the notion that right is whatever the majority in a democratic society decrees. He is, in short, prepared to bide his time about the barriers—so long, of course, as everybody is perfectly clear that they are unjustifiable; which, however, has the effect of leaving his argument just a little up in the air.

There is a better way out for him, incidentally, which he can learn about from Bertrand de Jouvenel's *Sovereignty,* wherein it is argued that the "sovereign" can set up procedures for the exercise of his sovereignty which from one point of view may seem to limit his authority but from another are seen to increase it; that at the height of the French monarchy such procedural limitations abounded; and that they were not, and rightly were not, regarded as inconsistent with the monarch's complete supremacy. That is how this reviewer thinks of the barriers to popular rule in our constitutional system.

What lies heaviest on Spitz' heart is Phase Two of his pre-occupation—that is, the continued denial of rights, the continued "abuses of power," the continued "oppression," that he sees as he examines our politics and our society. He regards democracy as demanding a way of life in which there is *no* discrimination, *no* favored position for any creed or idea; and he will not, one gathers, be satisfied until we have all learned to live that way of life. Here also, however, he places himself a cut or two above other Liberal political theorists by recognizing that "oppression" pretty certainly can't be eliminated (it is always a matter of more or less, of lessening this abuse of power or that one); and that one abuse of power is sometimes eliminated at the cost of increasing other abuses of power. He therefore shies off the socialism to which his logic might easily have led him, and concedes that (even where the enforcement of "civil rights" is concerned) giving the government full enforcement powers might expose us to grave dangers.

"Oppression," let us be clear, is for Spitz what stands in the way of the "open society," made up of individuals who are politically equal. And we must have such a society, he never wearies of saying, because "democracy" requires it—there being no criterion external to democracy by which to decide what behavior, whether individual or institutional, is oppressive. Spitz' democracy, in a word, is democracy pure and simple; it generates its ethical principles as it goes along, and denies that there is any other source from which ethical principles might derive. "Suppose," he writes, ". . . we grant the right principles are those revealed by God. The obvious question is, which god?"

Well, let us answer him: The God of the "In God We Trust" on the nation's coinage. The God of the chaplains in the nation's armed forces. The God Whose name is Yahweh, and around Whose revelation, united in St. Paul with Greek philosophy, has grown up that which we know as Western Civilization—which, accordingly, does not need to ask the question, "which god?" And it is that civilization that has created and preserved the intellectual virtues which David Spitz exemplifies. Despite himself he keeps appealing, quite inconsistently, to notions of justice

145

and decency that do lie outside, far outside, his miserable little game of majority rule. It would be nice if he would come aboard, where he's needed.

LIBERALISM: ITS THEORY AND PRACTICE.
By Theodore M. Greene
(Austin: University of Texas, 1957.)

We have been needing a book that tries to talk sense on the question, Can a man be a Christian and a Liberal at the same time? Been needing it, but not likely to get it, because the Christian Liberals tend to deny that the problem exists, and because non-Christian Liberals are not yet ready to drive the Christians out of the Liberal camp with an honest No. (Because one good way for the Christians who deem Liberalism incompatible with true religion to keep out of trouble is not to write books saying so.) We may, therefore, count ourselves fortunate that a professional philosopher like Theodore M. Greene should have come forward at this moment with a book that does try to make sense of the problem from one side, and that no future writer who addresses himself to the problem from the other side will dare ignore.

Professor Greene does not, to be sure, pose the problem in the terms I have just used. He writes as a Christian Liberal who is quite certain that the good Christian must be a Liberal, that the good Liberal ought to be a Christian and in due course probably will be, and that any apparent incompatibilities between Christianity and Liberalism are due, quite simply, to troublemakers who misrepresent the one or the other or both. His purpose is to state a Christian Liberal position, to explain how he can hold it without betraying either his Christianity or his Liberalism, and to urge others to help him discover any possible weaknesses

146

in it and correct them. So, even without posing my question, he gives an affirmative answer to it that at least takes into account some of the major issues involved.

These are, make no mistake about it, genuine issues—not the less sharp because they are so rarely talked about. The essence of Liberalism (as Professor Greene recognizes) is commitment to free thought and speech, to toleration of all points of view that are not themselves intolerant, and to the idea that each of us is finite and fallible, possessing therefore at most a modicum of the truth, and so having no business attempting to substitute his freely-arrived-at judgment for somebody else's. Liberalism demands, moreover, that society be ordered conformably to freedom and toleration thus conceived—ordered in such fashion as to leave no room for the man who is so certain of his modicum of truth as to insist that it is true for others as well as himself.

But how—and this brings me to at least one of the issues—if I believe that *my* modicum of truth is not the expression of my finiteness but of the infinity and omniscience of God, so that in insisting upon its truthfulness for you I insist not upon my own infallibility but upon His? How if I believe that the institutions and public policy of my society should reflect the truths of my revealed religion, which, if not the whole of the truth (a kind of point Professor Greene makes much of), I believe to be true as far as they go? How if, as a consequence of freedom and toleration thus conceived, I find that my society is rapidly transforming itself into a secular society, whose institutions and public policy will predictably *not* reflect the truths of my revealed religion? How if, again as a consequence of the Liberals' kind of freedom and toleration, I find my society descending into a diversity of basic belief that I see to be incompatible with the very existence of society, and so fatal to the protection I expect society to offer to truth? (Professor Greene appears to concede the premise here: "Any society seems to tend . . . toward creedal diversity when real freedom of speech and worship prevail.") How, in a word, if freedom and toleration produce results that are outrageous to my Christian conscience? Do I, because Liberalism bids me to, cling still to freedom and toleration? And if so, do I nevertheless tell myself that I am *not* preferring my Liberalism to my Christianity?

Professor Greene, I repeat, sees some of the issues. He sees, for instance, that the United States, in changing from a predominantly Christian to a "half-Christian, half-secular" society, has developed some minorities with beliefs that any Christian must find disturbing. He deplores those who entertain relativist views about "values," and assures us that values do possess objective reality. And he seems about to say, But no, over there are those who entertain absolutist views about values and think that some of those values that do possess objective reality are actually *known*, so that further discussion of them is beside the point. And the absolutists are at least as wrong as the relativists.

He has at the determinists with all the eloquence possible to a man who writes such graceless prose, and possesses so little talent for making a platitude sound other than platitudinous. There is, he insists, such a thing as moral freedom, and seems about to say, But no, over there are those libertarians, who believe that "the soul . . . which constitutes man's true essence . . . is free and responsible, and . . . is destined for immortality"; and the libertarians have no better case than the determinists.

He speaks with profound respect of "what can only be called man's religious experiences," of "rich and disciplined encounter with a God of righteousness and love." One expects him, in a moment, to be speaking of revelation, and to be saying why those who believe in it must, at some point, draw the line about freedom and toleration, But no, over here are the "honest" religious skeptics who believe that life has no ultimate meaning ("Our society would be infinitely impoverished without [their] gallantry, . . . enthusiasm, . . . creativity, and . . . **devotion**"). Over there are the "men of trust[!]," who "distrust[!] equally all 'proofs' and 'disproofs' of God's existence," and "with stature and humility pay homage to the faith they cannot share"; and it seems a fair guess that Professor Greene thinks society the richer because of both. (That, indeed, he regards both as capable of making a needed contribution to the final synthesis to which "we," along the paths of freedom and toleration and to the

148

cadence of a drum beat—one suspects—by Professor Toynbee, are moving.)

To say that Professor Greene solves all his problems by identifying the extremes and taking the middle course between them would be an over-simplification. His is the middle course between the middle course and the extreme Right: objective values, about which some may speak with greater assurance than others, Yes; but no nonsense about absolute values, or any "authority" capable of deciding disputes about them. God, a God of righteousness and love, and the moral law, perhaps even salvation, Yes; but no extremist talk about revelation that might render further discussion with those skeptics and men of trust impossible. The Right-most course always, except where it leads (as it almost always does) to positions that are uncompromisable, at which time he veers to the Left—and as far toward the Left as he can go without reaching a position over *there* that is uncompromisable, and so forces him to veer again to the Right.

This traveler, who likes the course at the extreme Right and thinks zig-zag drivers to be menaces, wishes Professor Greene would get 'way over in the middle—and stay there.

DEMOCRACY AND CATHOLICISM IN AMERICA.
By Currin Shields
(New York: McGraw-Hill, 1958.)

One of the many virtues of American politics is that we in this country believe in both majority-rule and minority-right.

We are, to be sure, constantly being told that we must choose between the two, and remake our institutions accordingly. We must, for instance, get rid of the filibuster: it frustrates the will of the majority. We must abolish the electoral college: it gives us Presidents who cannot point to a majority mandate for their policies. We must bid farewell to our traditional political parties: they fail to draw sharp issues at election time, and thus make it impossible for the majority will to express itself. Or, conversely, we are told that we must cling to and re-enforce these things: they are bulwarks against "majority tyranny," the indispensable guarantees of our "rights" as American citizens. But we turn a deaf ear to the "majoritarians" and the anti-majoritarians, and for good reason. We want to be majoritarians, on and on through an indefinite future, when we think the majority is, or is about to be, right; and anti-majoritarians when we find ourselves in, or with, the minority. That is the game of American politics as we have always played it, and intend—or so this writer likes to believe—to keep on playing it.

That is why the Liberals, increasingly committed as they are to all-out majority-rule, to the idea that the rights of the minority are merely the rights the majority chooses to concede to them, *and that that is just as it should be,* are something new under the sun of American politics. And it is why such a book as Currin Shields' *Democracy and Catholicism in America,* the first full-dress attempt by an American to state a "case" for majority-rule, is long overdue. It deserves, bad political theory though it is, the most serious possible attention as a portent of things to come. The Liberal propaganda machine has been needing a Shields—that is, a political theorist foolish enough to take on the task, impossible on the face of it, of proving that majority-rule is a good thing *as such.* The machine now has one; and we may safely predict that it will, by adopting his argument over the years, make the most of him. Let us, then, listen to what he has to say.

Decisions about the exercise of a "community's authority," states Mr. Shields flatly, "should be determined by a vote of a majority of [its] members." The members—all of them presumably—should regard such a decision as the "decision of the entire community." Because the majority has a "right" to rule? Well, no. To put it that way would be to withdraw our attention from the interesting and important question, namely, "What form of decision-making is likely to lead to the most desirable 'effects'?"

We must not let ourselves fall for the "trick" played upon the American people by the Framers of their Constitution.

What trick? Well, first the Framers equated "legitimate authority" with "constitutionality," and then they "substituted the principle of constitutionality for the principle of majority rule," with the result that officials in the United States are "bound by the higher law of the Constitution rather than by a mandate from the majority of the people." What is wrong with our Constitution, in other words, is that it forbids the majority to "exercise authority contrary to constitutional provision," and, on top of that, "discourages" the majority from pressing any wish on its part to change the Constitution. The Constitution, in a word, "restrains" majority-rule; and that, in practice, has always meant restraint of the majority either by a mere minority, a violation of the "principle of political equality," or by some authority "outside and independent of the community," a violation of the "principle of popular sovereignty."

The restraints, then, have to go. And along with them all attempts by present majorities to bind the hands of future majorities, since—insists Mr. Shields—"if it is legitimate to adopt restraints by majority vote, it is legitimate to abolish them in the same way." And since, again, restraints imply that "the authority to make a decision affecting the community is not located in [its] membership." Judicial review, for example, must go; and the whole "principle of constitutionality" must go, too. A constitution is not, properly, "a legalistic device for muffling the expression of popular desires"; a constitution is nothing more nor less than a "convenient evidence of agreements shared by the members of a constituted political community."

We must, then, declares Shields, get away from the whole "source of authority" approach, and face *ab initio* the key question, "Why should a minority consent to a majority's decision?" And the answer to that question is, quite simply, this: "no member of a community knows with certainty what is right"; that being the case, "two heads are better than one, and many better than a few"; and the majority is, *a fortiori*, "more likely than a minority to make the right decision."

What if the majority uses its power merely to impose its private desires? Shields has, it soon appears, no answer, but also no intention to lose any sleep over the problem. "A decision about exercising authority determined by a majority vote is more likely to advance the general welfare of a community than a decision made according to any alternative principle." Two heads are better than one, remember?

Well, there you have it—all naked, be it noted, in its reliance upon dogmatic relativism. But the Liberal propaganda machine couldn't use it if it relied on anything else.

FREEDOM IN CONTEMPORARY SOCIETY.
By Samuel Eliot Morison

(*Boston: Atlantic Monthly Press, 1956.*)

This reviewer thought he knew what this book was going to say before he read a word of it. The author is Professor Emeritus of American History at Harvard, the former collaborator of Henry Steele Commager, and the World War Two historian of the stuffiest and most respectable branch of our armed services. He is, in a word, a man not renowned for the fusses he has kicked up with the Establishment, and not likely, therefore, in writing on political, economic, and academic freedom, to rise above what might be called the Zechariah Chafee level of penetration and originality.

And sure enough, Admiral Morison talks of our "great peril," of our liberties that are about to be subverted "at the hands of foolish and wicked Americans—by whom I do not mean those commonly called 'fellow travelers.' " He refers to that "obscene" phenomenon known as McCarthyism. The TVA, we learn under the topic of "Economic Freedom," is the "greatest constructive and permanent achievement of the New Deal," and the latter, let there be no question about it, "saved the capitalist system . . . and democratic government as well." The Great Depression "discredited *laissez faire,* a resort to which, now, is even less likely than a return to neolithic civilization following an atomic war"—which seems to put the familiar relax-and-enjoy-statism theme as forcefully as the Establishment could wish. And on "academic freedom" we hear, as we expected to, about those "frightened conservatives" who are attacking our colleges as centers of Communism.

I could, I suppose, cite some further examples of the kind of thing I expected to find in *Freedom in Contemporary Society;* but I am not going to because it has been mighty hard work turning up the ones I've just given you, and because the time has come to confess: I couldn't have been more wrong about Professor Morison's book. Though no great shakes as political theory, it has more good sense in it about freedom, especially academic freedom, than anything I've read—from within the Establishment or from outside it—in recent years. It is, because of the esteem in which its author is held, a major windfall for those of us who have been trying to raise a little hell with the civil libertarians, the academic freedomites, the all-questions-are-open-questions characters, and, above all, those who suppose that American society can cut itself off from its religious basis and yet remain decent and viable. For it is a book by a man of courage and conviction, Conservative conviction furthermore, who sees political and social life with the innocent and accurate eye of a child. But that, as Gerhart Niemeyer has reminded us, is Conservative too.

For one thing, when he writes "economic freedom" Professor Morison means not "security" or "equality" or "industrial democracy" but, simply, *freedom:* "freedom to choose your profession or occupation, free competition at all levels, freedom to grow rich, or go broke, freedom to make all the profit you can, acquire a fortune, and to bequeath or inherit said fortune." Moreover, he's *for* that kind of economic freedom, thinks it will survive just about to the extent that we as a nation retain "character and wisdom," and—a note that this reviewer has been waiting for someone to strike for a long time—believes we have lost a lot less of it than our pundits would like us to think. He estimates the proportion we've kept at 79 per cent, and concludes: "Free enterprise, like Mark Twain, may remark that the rumor of its death is exaggerated." And he knows who in American society are the true enemies of free enterprise: "The unions have battled their way so successfully that their members have become the privileged class . . . comparable to the *rentier* of the nineteenth century." And, back to that point about "character and wisdom," he lays it on the line about the relation between religion and liberty: "Only a Christian commonwealth is capable of preserving freedom; and without freedom nothing in what we call civilization is worth preserving."

Secondly, Professor Morison believes in natural law and believes that natural law is divine law, and remembers (and reminds us at every turn) that our natural rights derive from our natural duties, rather than the other way round. For no emphasis, in the political theory we normally get these days from the Liberals, is so confusing as its failure to recognize that the man who does not perform his duties thereby divests himself of his rights.

Thirdly, his views on academic freedom and Communism reflect throughout that profound conception of rights and duties —with the result that he says all the things that, in those areas, need saying in a book on liberty. Academic freedom, he writes, "is but one of the many freedoms that come from God, who gave us our minds that we might rise a little nearer the angels; and without whose grace we are powerless for good." It is, however, a freedom that "must be exercised in a framework of academic discipline, which includes good manners, good taste and a decent respect for the opinions of the non-academic world." Those who are concerned about the future of academic freedom, he insists further, should fear neither the Reds nor the Red-baiters, but *"the attempts of professional 'educators' to control higher education,"* and *"the general mediocrity of the teaching profession"* (italics added). As for the Communists, they "are not entitled to civil rights, so long as they deny them to others," and that, he adds in effect, goes for "Communists on college faculties" and for Communists in organized research. "The scientific community has too much taken for granted that a scientist's political and social beliefs are irrelevant to his professional competence. [They are] . . . under the impression that these matters of belief were nobody's business. They had better make it their business. . . ."

Our big problem, in short, is the *trahison des clercs,* and the relevant question, Professor Morison is saying, is not how much academic freedom ought people as a matter of course to have, but how much have they deserved? The answer, he makes clear, might be "None at all."

This is one I'd say to go read for yourself. It's that exciting.

WHO GOVERNS? By ROBERT A. DAHL
(New Haven: Yale University Press, 1961.)

The branch of political science called "comparative government," whose lineage reaches back through De Tocqueville, Montesquieu, Machiavelli, and Polybius to Aristotle himself, always knew this: before *generalizing* about government we must make ourselves familiar with *particular* governments. That branch has at present fallen on evil days; we have no contemporary Bryce, and the monographic literature about particular governments that a contemporary Bryce would use as his raw materials is in a sickly state. But the books it produced remain; and they are, apart from the literature of political philosophy itself, the nearest thing we have to a "science of politics" that students can be required to master without, for the most part, wasting their time.

Now in the United States, political scientists have poured considerable energies, over the past fifty years, into a branch called, because it deals with the governments of counties and munici-palities, "local government." We ought, therefore, to "know" as much about "local government" as about "comparative govern-ment." But in point of fact we know little or nothing about it, in large part because the study of local government has not taken comparative government as its model. Rather it has sought to "compare," and to generalize, without first knowing thoroughly the things being compared—that is, without exhaustive prelimi-nary inquiries into particular local governments, despite the fact that the investigators had them to hand by the thousand, and for all that it was only a matter of applying to them the techniques that Bryce had used in *The American Commonwealth.* To put the point otherwise: nobody ever got around to "doing a Bryce" on an American city or town, and "local government" (for a num-ber of reasons that want discussing in their proper place) re-mained a "science" of generalizations based on uninvestigated particulars.

Robert A. Dahl's *Who Governs?* is, for these reasons and any way you look at it, a major breakthrough in American political science, and a work destined, deservedly, to influence profoundly all future investigation of our politics. Casting aside the inhibi-tions that have made political scientists postpone such a study fifty years beyond the date at which it should have been attempted for the first time, Dahl *does* a Bryce on an American city (New Haven, Connecticut), treating its history, its problems, its poli-tics just as seriously, just as attentively, just as thoroughly, as we are accustomed to see those of the Nation-State treated. That is, he proceeds without apologies for the narrowness of the investi-gation, without haste to pass along to some broader inquiry capable of yielding broader generalizations, without doubts as to the relevance of the findings to our knowledge of how politics work. Within its limitations moreover, of which more later, the book is masterful, imaginative, and courageous. I recommend it unreservedly to the attention of all students of American politics, alike for what they will learn from it and for the further think-ing it may cause, and even help, them to do.

Who, according to the author of *Who Governs?*, does govern?

One summary answer (which perhaps does not do too much in-justice to Dahl's rich and complex solution of the problem he sets himself) is, "Nobody in particular; New Haven is governed 'pluralistically.' " Another is, "Certainly not the 'boss' to whom the findings of earlier investigators of local governments seemed to point; certainly not the covert 'oligarchy' that figures so promi-nently in what we may call the mythology of American local government; and certainly not the greedy and implacable 'mass,' demanding pork chops and ever more pork chops, which we learn about from contemporary anti-democratic political theorists; the evidence, once you have it before you, bears out none of these hypotheses." Another is, "Different people for different purposes —one set of leaders, assisted by sub-leaders and standing in a com-plex but comprehensible relation to such and such a constituency among the led, one for one purpose, another for another." But these answers, if they do not do excessive injustice to Dahl's full answer, also do not do it adequate justice, because no statement in a brief review possibly can. (Indeed one of the reasons I should like to see the book widely read is that it may discourage know-it-all pronouncements, as to who governs, by persons who do not know what they are talking about.)

Where does whoever governs govern? Dahl's most circumspect answer here is, "In New Haven, Connecticut, which is where I got my evidence." But he clearly believes (and leaves me con-vinced—as, however, I was before I read him) that the correct answer to the question "Who governs in New Haven?" is, with descending degrees of probability, applicable, as far as it goes, also to (a) the politics of any American city, (b) the politics of the United States in general, and (c) democratic situations, that is, democracies in general (though he would be the first—and I the second—to enjoin great caution here, and to say that before attempting any sweeping answer we need many, many more studies comparable to his about New Haven).

A word now about the "limitations" within which Dahl can be said to have "done a Bryce" on an American city. The major limitation is, if I may put it so, moral. Having cut himself off from Aristotle in favor of the nice "objectivity" of contemporary "social science" (never mind that the sharp reader can see soon enough whose side, in contemporary political struggles, he's objective on), Dahl can go on and on forever about a local community without ever reminding himself that its function (for the local community, not the Nation-State, *is* the modern equivalent of the *polis*) is to provide for the good life. He can go on and on, that is, without any standard by which to judge its performance as a political system; and also (for such *is* the connection between morals and political science) without a point of view from which even to cognize its performance. Another, almost equally great limitation (no matter that in the end, though too late, he transcends it) is methodological. Officially, he can use only evidence that is "observable," "confirmable," and, potentially at least, "quantifiable," and this ends him up equating *politics* and the *political process* with *elections* and the *electoral process,* that is, treating as relevant only those matters that relate in some sense to the contesting of elections. And one consequence of the latter is, he never touches the question that has dominated much of our best local government literature in the past; the question whether the American local community is so completely in thrall to the state legislature that (a) it *cannot* provide for the good life, and (b) its politics, concerned as they necessarily are with merely the police department, the fire department and a school system so devised as to have no relation to the good life except that of undermining it, *must* deal exclusively with trivia—*must* fail to capture the sustained interest of the citizens. Such limitations, sure as they are to be perpetuated and made increasingly restrictive by the very influence of Dahl's book, are a grave matter, and should be kept in mind by all who read the book.

One further point: Dahl is, off at the end, unable to explain the politics of New Haven without appealing to an entity, the "political stratum" of the community he calls it, so using a theoretical construct in the purest sense of the term—and attributing to that stratum what I at least should call the crucial political functions of the community. (That is what I mean when I speak of his finally "transcending" his methodological limitation.) That is well. *Because* he is willing to appeal to it (i.e., to be uncircumspect methodologically), his picture of New Haven politics ends up making far more sense than it otherwise would.

It enables an answer to the question, "Who (all that being the case as to 'who governs?') *rules?*". Or, that being the case about "decisions" concerning the police department, "To whom do we look for community 'decisions' about the things that matter?" Let us, then, not twit him for it, unless by asking a question that, on Dahl's method, does not arise: namely, "Doesn't the system work—as regards giving the 'people' the *power* to rule without letting ourselves in for the horrors to which popular rule would actually lead—pretty much as the Framers intended it to?" Yet Dahl, whose previous book, *Preface to Democratic Theory,* showed that the political thought of the Framers is incomprehensible to him, never mentions them in connection with the New Haven system.

THE AMERICAN PRESIDENCY. By CLINTON ROSSITER

(*New York: Harcourt Brace & Company, 1960.*)

Clinton Rossiter sings in this book, like Virgil, of arms and the man—of the instruments of power concentrated in the White House, and of each President, from Washington to Eisenhower, who has wielded those powers. His mood is one part ecstasy, evoked by the sheer beauty and efficaciousness of those instruments, and one part adulation, which with even-handed justice he confers upon those Presidents who have enriched the White House armory and smitten the enemy hip and thigh. And his song (which here as in his last book, *Conservatism in America,* frequently echoes the rhetoric and rhythms of the late Harold Laski) is rich in metaphor and gypsy phrase.

Rossiter's avowed purpose is to examine "coolly at a hot time the powers and limits, the strengths and weaknesses, the past and present and future of the American Presidency." "Ecstasy" is, nevertheless, the *mot juste:* the Presidency "unites power, drama, and prestige as does no other office in the world. Its incumbent sits, wherever he sits, at the head of the table." The power of the Presidency "moves as a mighty host . . ."; that power "has not been 'poison,' as Henry Adams wrote in scorn; rather, it has elevated often and corrupted never, chiefly because those who held it recognized the true source of the power and were ennobled by the knowledge." The President enjoys an "aggregate of power that would have made Caesar or Genghis Khan or Napoleon bite his nails with envy."

And "adulation" is the *mot juste* too: "If [the President] is not widely and predictably[?] accused in his own time of subverting the Constitution, he may as well forget about being judged a truly eminent man by future generations." "Franklin Roosevelt . . . must . . . enjoy a long head start toward the eminence he surely wished for in his heart . . . Like [Jackson] he considered the independence of the office to be its most precious asset, like [Theodore Roosevelt] he thought of himself as a steward of the people, like [Lincoln] he made himself a 'constitutional dictator' in time of severe national emergency." Not one—not one, mind you—of Truman's "grave steps in foreign and military affairs . . . has yet been proved wrong, stupid, or contrary to the best judgment and interests of the American people." Truman "defended the integrity of the Presidency against the grand challenge of MacArthur and the sabotage[!] of McCarthy." And as for Eisenhower, he will no doubt learn with relief from Mr. Rossiter that "his times are less exacting than Roosevelt's or Truman's . . . , the kind in which a President may win fame and gratitude but no immortality." "He has very little sense of history to begin with, and even if he had it to the full measure of Harry S. Truman, he is too modest to do an imitation of one of the earthshakers."

In speaking of "smiting the enemy," I use the word "enemy" advisedly. Mr. Rossiter's "great" Presidents are precisely those who have put Congress in its place. His "modern" Presidency is preeminently a Presidency that, because it is "resilient" and "resolute," has "outstripped" Congress (and the Supreme Court as well) in the "long race for power and prestige." The counterpart of his adulation of Presidential power, and of Presidents who edge it along toward omnipotence, is, as we should expect, contempt for Congress. That contempt he loses no opportunity to inculcate upon his readers (who, particularly in our colleges, will be as the sands of the sea).

Congress, he asserts, is a "cumbersome, overstaffed pair of assemblies that speak in a confusion of tongues." The next President to be impeached, Mr. Rossiter predicts "confidently," will have "asked for the extreme medicine by committing a low personal rather than a high political crime—by shooting a Senator, for example." "The imagination goes limp," he cries, "before the thought of what the Presidency would be today"—if the Framers had really succeeded in subordinating the President to the Legislature. And the notion that the President's task is to carry out the policies determined by Congress (or rather, as he characteristically puts it, an "all-wise Congress"), he dismisses as a piece of nineteenth-century Whiggery—than which, one gathers, there could be nothing worse or more ignorant.

Rossiter's major theses are more or less as follows:

1. The modern President has tasks and powers immeasurably greater than those granted him by the Constitution. He is Chief of Party ("the Party that makes him," however, "also brakes him"). He is the Voice of the People ("the leading formulator and expounder of public opinion"). He is Protector of the Peace (he takes "forceful steps" in behalf of any "section or city or group or enterprise that has been hit hard and suddenly by disaster"). He is Manager of Prosperity (he is called upon to prevent "runaway booms and plunging busts"). He is Leader of a Coalition of Free Nations (with a constituency "much larger . . . than the American electorate"). And he is Commander in the "ongoing struggle for civil liberties and civil rights" (his task is to "inspire those who are working for a more democratic America and to rebuff those who would drag us backward into the swamps of primitivism and oppression").

2. The Presidency is going to grow more and more powerful.

161

"In the face of history, it seems hard to deny the inevitability of the upward course of the Presidency. . . ." To oppose the growth of Presidential power is to take on some of the "major forces in our history"; the growth of the "positive" state, our involvement in world affairs, and the unavoidable incidence of crises in our destiny. All of these, we are assured, require a stronger and stronger Executive.

3. Despite all the loose talk about power corrupting, and despite the "loud dissenters" in "deep right field," there is nothing in this increase in executive power to worry about. The President is checked to some extent by Congress and the Courts; a "more reliable" restraint is the "natural obstinacy," the "politics and prejudices of, let us say, the top twenty thousand civil and military officials." Another check is the opposition party; still another is the "opinion of the people of the United States, which pressure groups express with zeal" (the President, says Mr. Rossiter, cannot make headway against the grain of our "private liberty and public morality"). Most important of all, the President is checked by his conscience and training. "He, like the rest of us, has been raised in the American tradition" (as, one supposes, Lenin was raised in the Russian tradition and Batista in the Cuban). He therefore subordinates himself to "the accepted dictates of constitutionalism, democracy, personal liberty, and Christian morality."

I have quoted Rossiter at such length in order to let him make for himself what would otherwise have been the point I should myself have endeavored to make: namely, that *The American Presidency* is a venture in myth-making, not analysis; in polemics, not political science; and above all in eristical not dialectical discourse. And all that the less pardonably, for my money, because the first seven pages of Mr. Rossiter's chapter on "The Presidency in History" will bear comparison with the best writing we have on this topic, and because of the following remarkably keen sentences toward the end of the book:

In point of fact, the struggle over the power of the Presidency, fierce though it may seem, is only a secondary campaign in a

political war over the future of America . . . Arguments over
its powers are really arguments over the American way of life,
and the direction in which it is moving.

Exactly! Mr. Rossiter puts his finger on *a basic weakness of current political discussion.* But he writes on the powers of the President as a professional scholar, and we may fairly expect him to
set others an example—by *not* confusing categories, by *not* palm-
ing off policies on immediate issues as usages of the Constitution,
and by *not* proceeding as though no reasonable man could possibly disagree with his position—or, if he did, be worth listening to.

Mr. Rossiter shows no understanding whatever (and here his
claims to scholarship are certainly at stake) of what goes on in
the minds of advocates of congressional supremacy. Hence his
facile dismissal of the Bricker Amendment as an expression of
old-fashioned isolationism, of the wish to prevent the United
States from playing a vigorous role in world affairs. Hence, too,
his failure to take cognizance of the fact that some people have
sober reasons for opposing the amendment of the Constitution
by executive fiat, and the further fact that some people who support the Bricker Amendment would have the United States play
a more vigorous role in world affairs than ever Mr. Rossiter
would.

Thus, again, his evasive failure to anticipate the obvious reaction to his remark about the twenty thousand top bureaucrats
who exercise a restraining influence. Mr. Rossiter evidently does
not know that critics of executive omnipotence are worried
somewhat less about a future President's making like a Batista
and getting away with it, our tradition of private liberty and
public morality notwithstanding, than about a President's being
captured and used against both his will and knowledge by a
bureaucracy that has (as some of us increasingly suspect ours has)
no respect for either. Mr. Rossiter can, therefore, concede the
President's inability to control the bureaucracy, which he as good
as does, and satisfy himself that he thereby *eases* our minds concerning the dangers of Presidential power.

Recommended for Clinton Rossiter: a month's good hard reading in the literature of legislative supremacy. And a lifetime of redoubled effort over the grammar of freedom.

PARTIES AND POLITICS IN AMERICA.
By CLINTON ROSSITER
(Ithaca: Cornell University Press, 1960.)

Clinton Rossiter's *Parties and Politics in America* is (1) a witty, skillful, "up-to-now" summarization of the burgeoning literature on American political parties; (2) a shrewd attempt to influence the political opinions of the thousands of college students and paper-back-book-store customers who will be reading it this year; and (3) an attempt, indispensable to (2), to adjudicate some of the continuing "issues" about political parties that have arisen over the decades in American political theory.

As the first of these, the book is a remarkable accomplishment. It compresses into less than two hundred pages of lucid, fast-moving prose all that the general reader and the beginning college student need to know about what the political scientists have written on American political parties. Had the author let it go at that, the book might have performed a much-needed educational function. Book-reading Americans, who certainly need to know more about their political parties, are estopped from learning about them by the dullest and most illiterate shelf of books that American political scientists, with their unlimited capacity for dullness and illiteracy, have yet created. Rossiter brings the findings of that literature to life, makes them intelligible, drives them home. *Parties and Politics in America* makes a couple of evenings of indispensable reading for anyone sufficiently sophisticated about politics to realize, before reaching the grape-arbor, that he or she is being led down the garden-path.

That brings us to (2), Rossiter's assault on the political chastity of his readers, the lust and relevant skills for which seem now to grow within him from book to book. He uses as his seductive lure what I like to call the planted axiom: the proposition of dubious validity put forward in the context of an impressive array of footnotes as just plain fact, in the presence of which the learned author stands helpless, resigned, and with nothing left to do except pass it on to the reader (who, he manages to suggest, must, being an intelligent man, already know it). All Liberals of course use the planted axiom; but Rossiter, unlike the others, knows better than to do it, and once upon a time was too good to do it. As he himself would put it, he once scraped the stars and at least approached glory, in a book called *Seedtime of the Republic*—the most loving, objective, scholarly account we have of the roots of the American political tradition.

Rossiter will not believe me—not at first, anyhow—when I say that what is at issue here is *not* the fact that I dislike his particular planted axioms and their political tendency. I do happen to dislike them, and do very much hope, in opposition to Rossiter, that America will not move in the direction in which it would move if everybody accepted them. But that is not the point, which is, rather: by pretending, under the mantle of scholarship, to know all the answers both about what America *ought* to do and what it is *going* to do, Rossiter stacks the cards, and goes to a lot of trouble to deal them to people who have no way of guessing when they are being cold-decked.

As for (3), Rossiter's adjudication of certain issues that American political theorists like to debate about, his procedure is remarkably similar to that of the men who write the platforms of our political parties—namely, the accommodation of *all* points of view. Each of the many authors he cites will, in consequence, if he but looks at the right page (as, proceeding from the index, he is very likely to do), go away feeling that Rossiter has mercifully confirmed his own most deeply-meditated conclusions.

At the beginning of the book Rossiter wrings his hands over the terrifying numbers of our voters who stay away from the polls. At the end of the book he is quite sophisticated about "non-voting," recognizing that it is *not* an index of the health of a democracy (though not so sophisticated as to concede that which is obvious to this reviewer: namely, that given what we know about the kind of people who do not vote, we owe the health of our democracy in large part to their abstention). On one hand, we get the straightest of straight bread-and-butter-and-pork-chops explanations of American politics; on the other hand, he speaks as if it involved the highest moral and spiritual aspirations of the soul of man.

In one section the Democratic and Republican parties really are "different," so that it really does matter (independently of the personalities "up" in a given election) which of them you vote for; in another section he gives us a "prescription" for making them still more different. Look elsewhere and you will find the confession that in "important respects" (*the* important ones for Rossiter, incidentally, and for me) they are as much alike as two textbooks on American government . . . plus the concession that that is how it has got to be . . . plus the concession that it'll be a bad day for our democracy when it has ceased to be.

Here we learn that we Americans are deeply united ideologically, so deeply that really major issues cannot become issues between our parties; there we find refreshingly frank recognition of the ideological chasm that divides our Goldwaters and Hruskas and Byrds and Russells from our Douglases, Humphreys and Mansfields. Here we seem about to face up to *the* big fact of American politics—the continuing clash over the deepest issues between the Executive, which tries to bring about a revolution, and the Congress, which tries to prevent one—and to the relation of that clash to the way in which the two are elected. We seem about to probe into the reasons, about which we all know so little, why the same electorate chooses *that* kind of President and *that* kind of Congress (that is, we seem about to get somewhere). There we learn that it is all quite simple, the result of the "gerrymander" (as Rossiter says, one good gerrymander deserves another), which in our presidential elections gives the green light to one part of the electorate, and in our congressional elections to another (which is to miss the problem altogether).

My point is not that Rossiter contradicts himself in a way possible only to the man unspoiled by theory—this being merely the vice of his age and of his calling. Nor is it my point that the contradictions are inexcusable; most of the dilemmas in question are real dilemmas. My concern is his refusal to let the dilemmas drive him to those deeper levels of discourse on which contradictions are translated, as in the American political system so many contradictions are, into the tensions of meaningful paradox. The effect of that refusal, here as in so much Liberal writing, is simply to forswear discussion—in favor, of course, of planted axioms: the future is the welfare state; the future is internationalism; everything's decided, except the moment at which the decision is to be promulgated.

CONSERVATISM IN AMERICA:
THE THANKLESS PERSUASION.
By CLINTON ROSSITER
(New York: Alfred Knopf, 1962.)

Professor Clinton Rossiter's *Conservatism in America,* published between hard covers in 1955, will henceforth be available in a revised paperback edition that, professedly, takes cognizance of the "comings and goings on the stage of American conservatism" in the intervening seven years. The new volume, in view of the current popular interest in Conservatism and Conservative ideas, will predictably have a large sale, especially on college and university campuses—where one can even imagine its being used on occasion as a secondary textbook. The question whether Rossiter's enterprise is valid has, therefore, a kind of urgency that it did not have back in 1955, when the book was too expensive to get into many people's hands and when, because there was a great deal less at stake politically, the harm it was capable of doing was very considerably smaller.

Well, let us be clear at the outset that the enterprise is invalid: (a) because the 1955 version, whose major vices are preserved in the paperback, was invalid already; and (b) because Rossiter's handling of those *recent* "comings and goings on the stage of American conservatism" is, apart from his excellent bibliography, even more ignorant or perverse (let us not try to say which) than his handling of the pre-1955 data. His book is, in either version, one that can only mislead most persons who read it, on most of the questions with which it deals.

Rossiter's strategy, in both versions, boils down to this: Set up a definition of "conservatism" (he distinguishes always between "conservatism," an American phenomenon, he says, and "Conservatism"—that is, Burkean Conservatism, of which he finds at most a smidgin in our politics) that reduces the differences between "conservatives" and "liberals" to mere differences in emphasis and mood. Conservatives and Liberals (so he at least professes to believe) substantially agree on what we in America are trying to accomplish—which we may identify, for most Conservative readers at least, as what the Liberals are trying to accomplish or, simply, what Rossiter himself is trying to accomplish. Treat any "conservative" idea or position that involves meaningful opposition to Liberal goals as, therefore, not properly "conservative" at all, that is, as "ultra-conservative" or "reactionary" or "standpattist" and, in consequence, wide of the real business of American politics, unrealistic, quixotic. Insist that the real question for Americans, the only question, is always, How soon, and by what means, do we carry out the Liberal program? Ignore any facts indicating that principled opposition to the Liberal program is a universally observable phenomenon of American life (let Rossiter have a sober look one day at the House of Representatives, or at most of our state legislatures)—and that what is really wide of American politics is the idea or position openly predicated on Liberal premises.

Go on and on, therefore, as if the "important issues" have already been politically decided for America; for instance: the issue of the open society versus the consensus society that comes down hard on opinions contrary to the consensus; the issue as to the future of the American Presidency, of which Rossiter is a shamefully slavish cultist; the issue as to whether the American university is to remain the property of its present positivist-relativist captors; the issue as to whether the United States is to contain or "compete with" Communism on the one hand, or set out to remove it on the other; the issue as to the role of popular "will," as opposed to natural law, in determining the shape and tendency of American policy and legislation; the issue as to legally enforced desegregation of the Southern schools and, indeed, as to the future of the white Southerners in our national life; the issue as to "reapportionment" based on French-style political "equality"; the issue as to whether we are going to continue to enact "social reform" legislation in an age when the affluent society has rendered it unnecessary on the face of it; and, as a final example, the issue as to the future of the Supreme Court.

Rossiter's basic contentions about the "comings and goings on the stage of conservatism" during the past seven years, dictated as they are by the strategy just outlined, we may put briefly as follows: The major developments have been, so to speak, "literary"—that is, in the realm of "ideas." The big one is a burgeoning literature (much of it, he thinks, of high quality) which has called into question, and subjected to relentless criticism, the soft-headed Liberalism of a dozen years ago and, at the same time, deepened and freshened our knowledge of the principles upon which the American Republic was founded. That literature, whose authors occupy a spectrum reaching all the way from, say, Chodorov and Chamberlain to (if you please!) Adlai Stevenson and George F. Kennan, is a great "conservative" achievement, alike because (a) it has already made, and will continue to make, American intellectual "history," and (b) its effect has been, and will continue to be, that of "toughening" the Liberalism against which it is aimed. He welcomes and even applauds this literature, even the part of it that is "ultra-conservative"; one gathers that he would not even be sorry if it kept on burgeoning.

A lesser development is the "conservative revival" in American politics itself, but that, as we should expect, he sees as a matter of the rise to power of Dwight Eisenhower (whose name Rossiter links, impudently, to the names of Robert Taft and Herbert Hoover). Rossiter is, he confesses with disarming candor, disappointed in it, so that a tidy part of the new material in the new edition is given over to an exposition of what the "conservatism" that informs the "revival" must do in order to disappoint him less in the future.

Both developments, in Rossiter's treatment, are merely squid-ink with which to obscure the really major developments of the last years, which are of course the rise of *National Review* and its readership to, almost overnight, the status of a national movement; the resurgence of the Right—but what Rossiter would have to call "ultra-conservatism"—among American youth; the continuous stiffening of the anti-Liberal coalition in Congress; and— most important of all, perhaps, because a development in the realm of actual events—Liberalism's own entry into a phase where the bankruptcy of its basic public policies has become simply too obvious to escape notice. Of none of these developments does Rossiter have a word to say—nor, I might add, *could* he have without blowing his whole enterprise high as a kite. He writes about a political world that exists only in his own head.

Since Rossiter must know more about what is going on around him than he lets on, one is tempted to attribute his major misrepresentations to the twofold political purpose of discrediting the genuine American Right in the eyes of the uncommitted, and of helping feed that Right's own perpetual mood of defeatism. One is tempted, that is, to explain the book in terms of perversity, *not* ignorance. But that might be ungenerous, since the book is shot through and through with methodological confusions: as to the relation in politics between thought and verbiage; as to what *a* conservatism (any conservatism, in any country) *is,* to begin with; as to what a tradition is and how you find out in any given time and place what the tradition "holds" and does not "hold." Political purposes entirely apart, this must lead to comparable misrepresentations; so the suspicion that Rossiter's trouble is, after all, ignorance, will not down.

"CONSERVATISM AND PERSONALITY."
By HERBERT MCCLOSKY
(*American Political Science Review*, March, 1957.)

McClosky's procedure, as I understand it, comprises the following steps: (1) Compile, by reference to that on which there is "astonishing agreement among the disciples, and among disinterested scholars as well," a list of the "characteristic . . . if not quintessential elements of the conservative outlook." (2) Take note of, and deplore (via the adverb "unfortunately") the fact that "some of the points . . . are . . . distinguished more for their rhetoric than for the clarity and crispness of their content." (3) Break down the "creed" so arrived at into 43 items, most of them "fairly [!] straightforward statements of the conservative beliefs just discussed." (4) Submit the 43 items to a "large general sample of persons in the vicinity of the Twin Cities," asking them to agree or disagree with the items. (5) Analyze the responses, with a view to identifying the items that "[cluster] sufficiently to convince us that they [belong] to the same universe," and so derive "scales" made up of items that in fact measure "some degree of the same attitude dimension." (This, it appears, took two years of what at least sounds like very hard work.) (6) Satisfy yourself that the twelve-item scale you end up with is a "tighter," more "refined," scale, with "greater internal consistency," than that "found in the original 43-item pool." (7) Submit the new scale to an "advanced senior-graduate class in political theory" and accept the fact that 44 of 48 members in the class describe the "sentiments expressed" as "conservative" or "traditionalist" as significant "validation" of the items (that is, as evidence that it is really "conservatism" you are soon going to be measuring). As further validation, appeal *en passant* to the scale's "face validity" (note, that is to say, that the "items it includes express on their face the values that *most knowledgeable people would designate as conservative* [italics added]"). (8) Submit the items at different times to two "entirely different samples of the population." (9) Divide the respondents into four categories, "Extreme Conservatives," "Moderate Conservatives," "Moderate Liberals," "Liberals" (not, let us notice, Extreme Liberals, as we would expect for purposes of symmetry), according to the quartile in which their scores (on the items) fall. (10) Take note of differences among the respondents in Education, Awareness, Intellectuality, and recognize (as, these being the findings, you are clearly called upon to do) that "conservative beliefs are found most frequently among the uninformed, the poorly educated, and, so far as we can determine, the less intelligent." (Explain, however, that you don't mean for a moment that "all conservatives are uninformed, [or] . . . all liberals knowledgeable, [or that] . . . all the unlearned are conservative," but merely that "the most articulate and informed classes in our society are preponderantly liberal in their outlook.") (11) Break the respondents down again, according to their scores on "social personality traits" such as submissiveness, excessive feelings of guilt, etc., noting incidentally that one end of each of your trait scales is "desirable" (no need to say to whom), the other "undesirable." Again accept that which the data fairly force upon you: "conservatism, in our society at least, appears to be far more characteristic of social isolates, of people who think poorly of themselves, who suffer personal disgruntlement and frustration, who are submissive, timid, and wanting in confidence, etc." (12) Break down the respondents once more, this time according to their "clinical" personality traits, and again yield to the unavoidable conclusion: "the extreme conservatives are easily the most hostile and suspicious, the most rigid and compulsive, the quickest to condemn others for their imperfections and weaknesses, the most intolerant, . . . the most inflexible and unyielding in their perceptions and judgments

. . . [They] apparently set far less store upon rigor or precision of thought. . . ."

I propose here to challenge neither the "objectivity" of all this (that is, the researchers' indifference, in "setting up" the project, to the conclusions they might arrive at), nor the statistical methods employed, nor—tempting though it be—the confidence they have in existing techniques for measuring personality traits. Rather, I wish to fix attention upon a single point, namely, the grounds on which McClosky, *on his own showing as to what Conservatism is,* assumes that he is measuring his respondents' "degree of conservatism." For the crucial step in the procedure summarized above, if his conclusions are to have any relevance to the "conservative-liberal distinction," is surely the one which gets him over from (1) to (3), i.e., from the "characteristic . . . if not quintessential elements of the conservative outlook" to the "items" he is going to submit to his respondents. Either there is some reason to expect that agreement with the items will be predictive of agreement with the creed, or there is not. I submit that (a) no such reason exists, and (b) the researchers' "validation" of the items, as McClosky describes it, is—particularly given the size of the bet they are about to place on them—casual beyond belief. If, for example, we are going to take the judgment of a political theory class as to what beliefs are Conservative, why introduce the creed (the class was not asked about the possible correspondence between the items and the creed) at all? And if we can establish "face validity" for the items by merely appealing to the "values which most people would designate as conservative," again the creed is superfluous; or else it embodies those same values and the question must still be faced: Do the items in fact reproduce the emphases of the creed? For, if we are obliged to answer that question No, McClosky must go back to step (3) and start all over again.

Here, as it seems to me, is how the items emerge from confrontation, in accordance with traditional procedures of textual analysis, with the creed:

The first of the items (that is, of the items McClosky sees fit to divulge) states that there must be "much wisdom" in "something" (which if it means anything must mean *anything*, that is, *everything*) that has grown up "over a long time." The creed, as the most cursory glance will convince the hastiest of readers, says nothing of the kind. It says that "society" (not everything in society, not even everything old in society, but society) embodies the "accumulated wisdom of the past" (which, be it noted, does not exclude its embodying also the accumulated folly of the past; let us remember, moreover, that Liberalism itself, to which Conservatives attribute no wisdom at all, is one of those "some-things" that have grown up "over a long time"), and that there is a *presumption*, but only a presumption, in favor of that which has "survived," and so of institutions "that have been tried and *found to work* [italics added]." (That is, there is more accumulated wisdom than accumulated folly in society, and the way you tell the difference between that which is wise and that which is foolish, where institutions are concerned anyhow, is to ask: do they work?) In the creed, in a word, there is not a whisper of the suggestion that there is "bound" to be "much wisdom," or even any wisdom, in that which "grows up over a long time."

Take the second: "If you start [why, incidentally, "start"?] trying to change things very much, you usually make them worse." The relevant passage in the creed speaks not of "things" but, as we have noted, of "institutions that have been tried and found to work," and of "innovation" as being "more often"— not "usually," but "more often"—a "devouring conflagration" than a "torch of progress." Clearly this is consistent, as McClosky's item is not, with, e.g., the proposition that change is in nearly half of all instances a "torch of progress," that is, a means of making things better. McClosky's item is a straight-out caricature of the point in his creed.

Or the third: to "recognize that the world is divided into superior and inferior people" is "not really undemocratic." While the creed certainly warrants the proposition, "Some people are superior to other people," it is silent as the tomb on the question, What is democratic and what undemocratic? It asserts the proposition, "Men are naturally unequal," but makes no predication about it.

For the fourth item ("All groups can live in harmony . . . without changing the system in any way"), I find *no conceivable textual basis* in McClosky's creed. In the fifth we leap from the creed's assertion that "private property" is a "stabilizing institution of society" to an item which asserts that men who own property can be "depended . . . on" more than men who don't. In the sixth we must get over somehow from "Society is . . . inordinately complex" *and* "There is a presumption in favor of whatever has survived" *and* that "innovation" is "more often a devouring conflagration, etc.," to the item—a very different matter, surely—"if you try to reform parts of [society] . . . you are likely to upset the whole system" (which is taking liberty enough in all conscience) and then to the assertion that the reason why that is true is that society is "so complicated." No such connection—complicatedness: unwisdom of reforming parts of society —is present in the creed.

Not all the items, to be sure, are so remote from the creed. "It's better to stick with what you have than to be trying things you don't really know about" is a not inaccurate restatement, perhaps, of "There is a presumption, etc." "Political authority comes not from us but from some higher power," bears no doubt a cousinly resemblance to "Society is ruled by 'divine intent' and made legitimate by Providence" and to "Religion is the foundation of civil society" (only cousinly, however, because of the injection of "not from us" in the item, which many might interpret as presupposing, as the creed certainly does not presuppose, a necessary choice between authority deriving from divine intent and authority deriving from the people—that is, from us). "It is never wise to introduce changes rapidly, in government or the economic system," is possibly a fair enough rendering of "Man's traditional inheritance is . . . not to be cast away lightly."

But all the other items in the first of McClosky's two lists are, in one way or another, cruel distortions of the relevant propositions in the creed. "I prefer the practical man anytime to the man of ideas" will pass muster only for those who equate "ideas" and "reason." "I'd want to know something will really work before I'd be willing to take a chance on it" is acceptable only if "There is a presumption, etc." be taken to mean, as evidently it does not, that nothing should ever be tried until it has been "found to work" (cf.: "There must always be three taxis on this three-taxi taxistand"). "A man doesn't really get to have much wisdom until he's along in years" can, so far as I can see, be tied back to no proposition in the creed. Nor can "Private ownership of property is necessary if we are to have a strong nation," since the creed does not address itself at any point to the question of national strength. McClosky's score for the first of his two lists: three hits out of thirteen trips to the plate, that is, a batting average of a little less than .250, which simply won't do for a lead-off man in the majors.

Nor do we get a different result from McClosky's second list:

Does "Duties are more important than rights" restate the idea, indeed present in the creed, that duties are "superior" to rights? Only if "superiority" and "importance" are interchangeable concepts. Does "You can't change human nature" catch up the meaning of "Man is . . . doomed to imperfection" and "All efforts at levelling are futile . . ."? Only, it would seem, if to change and to perfect and to level are (things equal to the same thing being equal to each other), all three of them, synonyms. Can "The world is too complicated to be understood by anyone but experts" be expected to tap the beliefs expressed in "Society is . . . inordinately complex" and "The superior classes must be allowed to differentiate themselves and to have a hand in the direction of the state"? Not unless the words "superiority" and "expertise" say the same thing. Besides, is it not notorious that the cult of expertise is a characteristic of Liberal, not Conservative, political theory?

And to what paragraph in the creed can McClosky point as justification for "We have to teach children that all men are created equal, but almost everyone knows that some are better than others"? The idea that some are better than others is indeed there (as also in the heads of most grown-ups), but McClosky's item does not say that. It says "almost everyone" knows that some are better than others, a notion that is not present in the creed, and says on top of that that we must teach our children that "all men are created equal." The creed does not address itself to what we must teach our children. McClosky then connects the two propositions with a "but" in such a fashion as to leave the affirmative respondent asserting neither of them, but rather the very different proposition, "We must teach our children that which is false" (wherefore what the item tests is not Conservatism as McClosky defines it, but parental cynicism). Where in the creed can McClosky find "The heart is as good a guide as the head"? Only, it would appear, by latching onto "Theory is to be distrusted" and "reason . . . is a deceptive, shallow, and limited instrument." Both of these, however, in the context in which McClosky himself presents them, point the way to reliance not on the "heart" but upon tradition, and in any case assert that something *x* is better than, not as good as, something *y*. Even, then, if we concede McClosky the remaining two items ("No matter what the people think, a few people will always run things anyway," and "People are getting soft and weak from so much coddling and babying")—concede them, that is, as recognizable baby-talk for "All efforts at levelling are futile, etc."— he still gets only two for eight, or the slightly-improved batting average of .250 exactly.

We conclude: McClosky—on, we repeat, his own showing as to what Conservatives believe—has no warrant for speaking of "conservatives" and "conservatism" in his conclusions.

OUR PUBLIC LIFE. By Paul Weiss

(Bloomington: Indiana University Press, 1959.)

"The assumptions that made the idea of natural rights intellectually defensible have tended to dissolve in recent times." So reads the most widely-discussed sentence in the most widely-praised of recent American political science treatises. "The logic of natural rights," the passage goes on to say, "seems to require a transcendental view in which the right is 'natural' because God directly or indirectly wills it. God wills it as a right men ought to be (but not necessarily are) permitted by their fellows to exercise in society." And the author concludes (he is Robert A. Dahl, Chairman of the Political Science Department at Yale University, and the book is *A Preface to Democratic Theory*): "Such an argument inevitably involves assumptions that at best are difficult and at worst impossible to prove to the satisfaction of anyone of positivist or skeptical pre-dispositions."

The tacit premise, you will notice, is that what is "intellectually defensible" in "recent times" is what can be proved to the satisfaction of positivists and skeptics. Or, conversely, that one is entitled simply to read out of the recent world of the intellect those who countenance the idea of natural right, and of a God who (directly or indirectly, whatever that may mean) wills it.

The question of how many such men are left in the world of the intellect is one about which I think the positivists and skeptics are much too optimistic, and their opponents are far too pessimistic.

I think this especially when I hold in my hand such a book as *Our Public Life*, by Paul Weiss, which is the handiwork of a teacher of philosophy at Professor Dahl's own university; one who notoriously packs 'em in and gets himself listened to and who has given a lifetime of loving study and meditation to the problems that the positivists and skeptics think to brush aside (as they are brushed aside in the passage I have quoted). He has won his spurs in the scholarly literature relating to those problems and is there to prove that there's a dance or two yet in the old gal the positivists and skeptics wish to see laid out in the parlor. So long as Paul Weiss is about—and he looks young and spry in the photograph on the dust-wrapper—there's hope.

No, I am not about to do Professor Weiss and his book the disservice of extending to him an unsolicited welcome into the ranks of academic Conservatives, much less into the ranks of political Conservatives, though the overlap between the academic and the political here is more common than not.

For one thing, *Our Public Life* has, like most—but not all—books that attempt to deal soberly and systematically with the important problems of politics, a programmatic aspect. It advocates more equality; more do-gooding; more desegregation of the Southern schools (though I must say Professor Weiss is more generous to the Southerners than anyone else I know of who likes to agitate this issue); more United Nations with more power to coerce more recalcitrants (it "represents the greatest advance ever made in history toward the achievement of a world state," so that we are today closer than ever before to the time when Civilization will be a reality); more Red China therefore in the United Nations; more acting and talking on as if there were no such thing as World Communism (I believe it is not so much as mentioned in the book).

All of this Conservatives must deplore, and all of this, other things being equal, might have caused great joy in whatever place it is the positivists and skeptics celebrate in the room of Heaven. But other things are not equal; and I predict, with a chuckle I wish I knew how to set down on paper, that *Our Public Life* will get far deeper under the skins of the positivists and skeptics (make them more hopping-mad) than ever it will under those of Conservatives. And for several reasons:

1. Its sweetly reasonable but nevertheless confident insistence that we cannot talk meaningfully about politics in the absence of the idea of Natural Law—that is, in the absence of a standard of justice to which questions of right and wrong may ultimately be appealed; which is to say that positivists and skeptics cannot talk meaningfully about politics.

2. Its air of circumspect piety about the Framers of the Constitution of the United States and, in general, the roots of the American political tradition—a piety that may one day lead Professor Weiss to keep better company politically.

3. It is true that Professor Weiss is very difficult to pin down about God (he can write "whatever God there be"), and Christians will seek in vain for any recognition that the central problem of politics arises in that nexus between the transcendent and the immanent that is the soul of man (or that the central task

of politics is being accomplished only when men with well-ordered souls seek to bring law into attunement with the will of God). Indeed, Christians will want to remind Professor Weiss, when he speaks of the new religion just over the horizon in language that suggests he is thinking of founding it, that first you have got to get yourself crucified and rise from the dead. Nevertheless, his Christian readers will be far less offended by what he says than the positivists and skeptics. The latter insist on hearing what they cannot hear from Professor Weiss: not only that God is dead but that God never existed. They will never forgive him for his in many respects admirable and brilliant discussion of the Jewish and Christian conceptions of God, a discussion which commits the outrage of taking them both seriously—that is, not assimilating them to superstitions.

4. The Christians and Conservatives will, as I have said, find much to disagree with. What they will not find is any position so defended, any form of words so chosen, that it might operate to close the door to further friendly discussion between them and Professor Weiss (who accordingly stands forth as that Liberal we've all been looking for who truly values the discussion process, with whom therefore discussion is possible and could not fail to be rewarding). That, neither the positivists and skeptics nor his fellow Liberals will ever forgive him for.

And shouldn't. Lest they fail to be true to themselves at their best.

CITADEL. By WILLIAM S. WHITE
(New York: Harper and Brothers, 1957.)

This exasperating and pretentious book puts itself forward as the "Story of the U. S. Senate," told out of a deep conviction that the "kind of society we are to maintain" depends upon the

"vitality and honor" of the upper chamber of our federal legislature. But in point of fact it redeems neither of the commitments implicit in these claims. Save on the level of anecdote, it
adds little or nothing to our knowledge of Senate history, and
rehashes in only the sketchiest and most casual manner the findings
of earlier Senate historians. Its thesis as to the relation between the vitality of the Senate and the character of our society
—surely the former depends on the latter, rather than the other
way 'round?—is merely asserted, not demonstrated. Nor are we
ever told what kind of society the author thinks we *ought* to
maintain. He would like it, clearly, to be equipped with a Senate
much like the one we have, but he seems to have given not
one moment's thought to those current trends in public policy,
strongly entrenched moreover in the Senate he so much admires,
that by undermining the power and significance of our several
states may, before long, deprive the Senate of its traditional—
and only possible—meaning. His book should have been called:
*Random Notes on the Senate: The Story of a Times-Man's In-
fatuation with an Institution.*

Institution, mind you, with a great big capital I—which of
course is how it should be written, and how Mr. White always
writes it. Which brings me to the book's one considerable
strength, namely its clarity and vigor. First, in setting forth what
I have just called the traditional and only possible meaning of
the Senate. Second, in defending those characteristics of the
Senate that are inseparable from that meaning.

"The Senate," Mr. White writes, "though the Senate of the
United States, is in fact [*in fact,* not also] the Senate of the
States, so that never will the cloud of uniformism roll over the
sun of the individual and the minority. . . . For the Institution
protects and expresses that last, true heart of the democratic
thesis: the triumphant distinction and oneness of the individual
and of the little State, the infinite variety in each which is the
juice of national life."

He recognizes—no, proclaims—that those who would like representation in the Senate to reflect differences in population have
as little right on their side as, say, the man who seeks to nullify

his marriage contract on the grounds that his wife has got fat less rapidly than he: "Deliberately [the Institution] puts Rhode Island, in terms of power, on equal footing with Illinois."

And he asserts unabashedly what political theorist you have to go to for a vindication of such arrangements. Calhoun of South Carolina, he writes, laid down "the most classical, and still the most irreplaceable dictum of our practical politics. This was the Doctrine of the Concurrent Majority . . . [which] postulated that this was a country of so many harsh and fundamental divisions that the central demand of the art of politics was to accommodate and merge and thus ameliorate the divergences lest they become inflamed beyond cure."

And again, "We must not press upon any minority, sectional or otherwise, policies or laws that are quite literally intolerable, though of course care must be taken not to equate the truly intolerable with the merely repugnant [e.g., one suspects, desegregation of the public schools]."

Moreover, he regards the filibuster as an indispensable corollary of the Concurrent Majority, approves of the seniority principle, and has no quarrel with the kind of power the two together confer upon Senators from the South: ". . . the Senate might be described as the South's revenge upon the North for Gettysburg." And he takes delight in the Senate hierarchy: "The inner life of the Senate is controlled by the Inner Club [which] . . . makes the decisions as to what *in general* is proper in the Institution and what *in general* its conclusions should be on high issues." Nor will he have any truck with the notion that the Senate's majority- and minority-leaders should be "responsible" to the political parties whose labels they bear: ". . . such an arrangement . . . is . . . demonstrably heretical unless one wishes to overturn the triune system of government that is fundamental to all."

These unfashionable sentiments will predictably earn Mr. White a quick reputation for being a "Conservative"—justified in the sense that he states with genuine conviction many of the tenets of a true Conservative's credo about the Senate, unjustified in the sense that they seem to be the only matters on which he fails to go all the way with the Liberals. Thus:

He hero-worships Hubert Humphrey and, out of the past, George Norris. He heaps scorn on those—those Senators even—who have questioned the "wisdom and *honor* of the action of the Executive in the China crisis that . . . left the mainland in Communist hands."

He deems the censure of Senator McCarthy and the defeat of the Bricker Amendment as two of the Senate's great historic achievements. And he seriously believes that General MacArthur precipitated a constitutional crisis when he sought to create popular sentiment in favor of more vigorous prosecution of the Korean War. So that the Senate Committee that did MacArthur in saved the principle of civilian supremacy over the military, and thus the Constitution itself!

He thinks it ill behooves even Senators to dream dreams of investigating the Central Intelligence Agency—on the grounds, if you please, that "the work of the . . . country's lawful intelligence agencies" would be "complicated" by such an investigation. Indeed, he deplores the very idea of "punitive" Senate investigations, conducted in a "spirit of prosecution"—no matter who is being investigated, and no matter what he is suspected of being up to.

Finally, White believes that some Senate inquiries have performed a useful educational function, but, astonishingly, would not include in their number the McCarran Committee. And he can write, with both McCarthy and McCarran in mind, "the Senate Office Building . . . stank with the odor of fear, and the odor of monstrous silliness. The presumed and alleged objective was to seek out and destroy what was supposed to be [but was not, of course] a vast Communist 'apparatus' that was gnawing at the Republic's vitals."

Mr. White's "Conservatism," his apparent devotion to tradition, his seeming reverence for the intent of the Framers, are all as spurious as store teeth. On the great issues of the age—e.g., the growth of Executive power and centralization—he aligns himself consistently with forces—and Senators—that are bent on so transforming our society as to make nonsense of the Concurrent Majority.

Mr. White leaves no room for doubt as to how much he loves the Senate. What he fails to do is explain why he loves it.

IDEAS HAVE CONSEQUENCES. By RICHARD WEAVER
(Chicago: University of Chicago Press, 1948.)

Ideas Have Consequences is an indictment of something called "modern man" and, at the same time, a statement of the beliefs and preferences and hopes and fears upon which that indictment is predicated. Its author, a University of Chicago humanities teacher, feels as little at home in the society in which he is living as Rousseau felt in that of the eighteenth century Europe. Like Rousseau, he is deeply convinced that his society is sick to the death, and that he knows the secret etiology of its disease; like Rousseau again, he conceives his own diagnostician-therapist's role as that of leaving the patient with no scrap of an illusion as to the gravity of his condition or the severity of the regimen he must adopt if he is to get well.

Mr. Weaver's argument covers a wide range of problems, most of which we cannot possibly bring up for discussion here; at most we can record the main points in what we have called his indictment. He sees "modern man" as a "moral idiot," incapable of distinguishing good and evil or of grasping the meaning of the word "duty"; as a "spoiled child," blind to the relation between effort and reward; as an "egotist," unwilling to concede to anything he has not himself contrived even the right to exist. This ill-tempered name-calling emphasis is, however, only a single phase of Mr. Weaver's bill of particulars, into which, in a more thoughtful mood, he writes such items as these: Modern man is committed to the view that it does not matter what a man believes. He has put aside the idea of mission, and therefore has no recognizable goals towards which to strive. He is no longer able to assign any intelligible meaning to such words as "justice" and "truth." He is the prisoner of the "endless induction of empiricism." He is obsessed with the isolated parts of his now wholly fragmented world, and fondly supposes that factual accuracy concerning small matters adds up in the long run to valid judgments concerning large ones. He takes his separate self as the measure of value, and his neighbors (who are doing this also) have no principle upon which to rebuke him for this effective withdrawal from the (or any) community—from which, in this sense, they also have withdrawn. And so on.

The indictment has many other particulars, but the reader now has before him enough of them to let him do a certain amount of justice to the present reviewer's primarily marginal quarrel with it. What Weaver has done here is to subsume under a single concept (as Ortega y Gasset, a few years ago, did with his concept "mass-man") a number of convictions and attitudes that he thoroughly dislikes, and (like Ortega, with whom, on a number of counts, he invites comparison) attribute the relevant state of mind to a much broader group than the intellectual map of his world warrants. For one thing, his illustrations are mostly American, i.e., non-European, and one does not get the impression that he knows other modern societies than our own (e.g., England or Scandinavia) well enough to justify his having included them in the indictment. And, for another thing, the state of mind of which he is speaking is demonstrably less general (though in all conscience general enough to lose lots of sleep over, even in American society which he appears to know extremely well) than he is inclined to suppose. One result of this incaution is that Mr. Weaver rarely calls his real enemy, the more or less typical American Liberal, by name. Another is that he has no opportunity, as he proceeds, to identify those who are more or less his friends. Indeed one suspects, sometimes, that he would prefer to think he has no friends.

Ideas Have Consequences, in short, includes the principal elements of (but is itself far from being) the book Mr. Weaver should write next. In it he would call the American Liberals by their name on every page. In it he would be careful to emphasize that no-one, not even a *New Republic* editor, believes all the propositions that must be included in an account of the Liberal's state of mind. In it he would report (but would not exaggerate) the extent to which the strategic positions in American society —the positions from which the effective decisions regarding our politics and our culture and our mores are most deeply influenced —have been infiltrated by persons who must enter a demurrer to most of Weaver's indictment. In it he would distinguish between the Liberal and the democrat. And in it, finally, he would insist rather less upon certain incidental emphases of his *Weltanschauung,* and confine the discussion to the major issues—not because the major ones can really be separated, in the long run, from the minor ones, but because if we can win the major engagements we can send out some of our less talented combatants to mop up. Meantime, however, with respect to two of the major issues, *Ideas Have Consequences* can do useful service as an *esquisse,* however ill-organized and badly executed, of that future book—about which the resistance movement that must one day be directed against the Liberal occupation might well be built.

What are these two issues? One of them is the issue between those of us who believe and those of us who deny that all questions are open questions (Mr. Weaver says the Liberals doubt their premises even when they are acting on them, and clearly thinks that this does not make sense). The other is that between those of us who believe and those of us who deny that a society must, in order to be a society at all, possess a minimum consensus of "value" about which it means business. The second of these issues (as Weaver shows himself to understand in his discussion of Communism) is the Achilles' heel of the Liberals (it is, incidentally, the theme of Mr. Faulkner's new novel, which is a convincing artistic expression of a state of mind and heart much like Mr. Weaver's); and Weaver has, further than any other American writer this reviewer knows, developed at least a vocabulary in which it can be discussed. Wherever the debate turns on either of these issues, Mr. Weaver has one vote for the captaincy of the anti-Liberal team.

PUBLIC SCHOOLS AND MORAL EDUCATION.
By Neil Gerard McCluskey, S.J.
(*New York: Columbia University Press, 1958.*)

In the year 1639 the town of Dorchester (in Massachusetts) levied a land tax for the support of a "free school." Two years later the Massachusetts General Court decreed that all "masters of families" should "once a week (at the least) catechise their children and servants in the grounds and principles of religion." And six years after that the General Court provided that every township must, "after the Lord hath increased them to the number of fifty householders," name a teacher and furnish a school for him to teach in, enabling the act on the following grounds: "It being one chief object of that old deluder, Satan, to keep men from the knowledge of the Scriptures," etc.

In 1789, and again in 1827—when it re-enacted the 1789 statute —the Court charged the "President, Professors, and Tutors, of the University at Cambridge, and of the several Colleges of this Commonwealth, Preceptors and Teachers of Academies," with responsibility

> to take diligent care . . . to impress upon the minds of children, and youth . . . the principles of piety, justice, and sacred regard to truth, love to their country, humanity, and universal benevolence, sobriety, industry, and frugality, chastity, moderation, and temperance, and those other virtues, which are the ornament of human society, and the bases upon which the Republican Constitution is founded.

Even as late as 1837, when Horace Mann became secretary of the Massachusetts Board of Education, everybody understood the Court's mandate to mean, quite simply, that the public schools were to instruct their charges in the Christian religion. As Mann himself put it, twelve years after he became secretary:

I could not avoid regarding the man, who should oppose the religious education of the young in the public schools, as an insane man: and were it proposed to debate the question between us, I should desire to restore him to his reason, before entering upon the discussion.

The record, in a word, is clear. Through the first two centuries of our history Americans thought of themselves as building, and handing down to their descendants, a *Christian* society. They intended their public schools to provide the religious and moral training appropriate to such a society. Nor do any of them seem to have seen where the grand project of public education had to lead—namely, to a moment when those public schools (having got around to virtually monopolizing the childhood and adolescence of well-nigh the entire population) would have become the major instrumentality of that same "old deluder" against whom they were directed: for keeping man from the "knowledge of the Scriptures" and, we might add, from knowledge of anything else worth knowing over and beyond the capacity to tease meaning out of road-signs (in order, of course, the better to disobey them).

Or did they see, without of course admitting it to themselves, and actually will the triumph of the democratic dogma (which I suppose is what gets you into the idea of public schools in the first place) over the Christian religion? How, to put the point a little differently, will you have those ancestors of ours—merely stupid, or perverse? Unable to see the dilemma, or wicked enough to choose the wrong horn of it? Me, I prefer them stupid—doubly stupid because one suspects that their (and their descendants') attachment to the idea of public schools was based in large part on bad economics. They must have believed—as most of those good folk in Atlanta must believe who ride about now with windshield stickers reading "We *Want* Public Schools"—that by not going down in their pockets for money with which to pay for private education for their youngsters they somehow saved money, beat the game, got something for nothing.

In any case, the dilemma was there, and it emerges most clearly when we ask ourselves whether anything could have been done to forestall it. Actually, something could have: The people of Massachusetts could have had it both ways about public schools and Christian education had they been willing to divide up into religiously homogeneous communities, ghettos if you like, in which little or no disagreement over the proper content of religious education would have occurred. That, however, they not only didn't do, but apparently did not even think of doing; so that the "sectarian problem" (the schools proliferated during just the period when the established Congregational Church was splitting every which way over differences about dogma) produced, from an early date, controversy over what the schools were to teach (though not, curiously, about the principle that ought to govern the matter—namely, that the schools should teach the Christian religion, but in such fashion as not to "favor any particular religious sect or tenet"). And I say "curiously" because what that prescription called for, even at the first stage, was the reduction of Christianity to the lowest common denominator of *all* the sects, i.e., the exclusion from the schools of precisely the doctrines that, over in the religious sphere of their lives, men regarded as worth fighting about; and with the predictable result that, as the sects multiplied and got further and further apart, the common denominator must sink to an ever lower level.

Public Schools and Moral Education is a thoughtful, balanced history and analysis of this working out of the problem to its present-day "solution." The latter, of course, has been dictated by the fact that in due course the sectarian problem ceased to be the sectarian problem and became what Rousseau calls the problem of "dispersion of belief" about fundamentals. In terms of the scheme of Father McCluskey's book, Horace Mann, who strove bravely to have his schools teach a Christianity short of everything that any sect might object to, gave way as *the* philosopher of the public school system to William Torrey Harris, who sought a solution in terms of a rigorous separation between religion and morality. And Harris gave way to John Dewey, who solved the problem (once and for all?) by divorcing morality from principle, and desiring the schools merely to inculcate "behavior patterns" appropriate to a democracy.

Always, the lowest common denominator—off at the end, that common to Christians, Jews, atheists, agnostics, and Jehovah's Witnesses—was what got handed along to future generations. Always, instead of doing the obviously sensible thing—which was to abolish the public schools and have people send (or not send) their children to private schools, free to impart such religious education as their patrons might wish—men chose to abstract from their most jealously-guarded beliefs and settle for an artificial uniformity. Always, therefore, there was a nearer and nearer approach to a public school system which, unless just ineffective, produces atheists and agnostics; and always the system produced the Harris or Dewey it needed in order to ease it into the next stage of degradation.

Is the Dewey solution indeed once and for all? Of course not; truth can be divorced from true religion no more than morality can. Or, to put it a little differently, there is a lowest common denominator for non-religious truth as there is for religious truth; and the genius of democracy as we practice it can be counted on to produce and then minister to the demand that that common denominator be taught in its public schools—and to frown even on the thought of the schools' little prisoners being given a moment of "released time," now and then, to learn something above the common denominator.

Father McCluskey is too unangry a man to write the book that should have been written on this topic. But he has provided a treasure-house of information and implicit guidance for the angry man who will one day write it.

NEA: THE BUILDING OF THE
TEACHING PROFESSION.
By EDGAR B. WESLEY
(*New York: Harper and Brothers, 1957.*)

The National Education Association was founded in 1857. It has now celebrated its one-hundredth birthday. What more natural, what more clearly inevitable, than that it should have improved that occasion with a book about itself? Well, here it is, under the sprightly title *NEA: The Building of the Teaching Profession*—the record of NEA's growth and "achievements," executed with an inexhaustible wealth of dreary detail in prose that will make every half-educated schoolmarm and high-school principal in the land feel *comme chez soi,* and (the ultimate testimonial to NEA's power) with the footnotes printed not in a publisher's graveyard over at the end but smack in the body of the book! It should have been called, like Dreiser's novel, *An American Tragedy;* and it belongs on your bookshelf beside that other book in which stupid crimes and criminal stupidities are related as deeds to be proud of—namely, Rousseau's *Confessions.*

Make no mistake about the growth. NEA has today "nearly 700,000 members," who "function" through 66 state organizations and 6,000 local associations, elect 4,000 to 5,000 delegates to a Representative Assembly (a little vague that, but who cares about a thousand delegates more or less?), and act through an executive secretary with a 440-man staff. Time was (1870) when NEA had only four departments through which to accomplish its two-fold purpose ("elevate the character and advance the interests of the profession of teaching, and . . . promote the cause of popular education in the United States"); today it has thirty. It is, in a word, a whopping big pressure group (though Mr.

Wesley never gets around to noticing this), which knows what it is after, and has quite a history of getting what it is after. The gates of Hell may one day prevail against it; but Mortimer Smith and Arthur Bestor pretty certainly won't. For NEA has what it takes—that is, numbers, and a full-time bureaucracy to jump those numbers through the hoop.

Make no mistake, either, about the character of those achievements, which Mr. Wesley chronicles under the general heading "Development of American Education." A notable series of NEA "actions," he says, brought the American people to accept the "ideal of secondary education for *all* youth," and so made way for the "rise" of our present kind of high school. "The public high schools," stated an NEA resolution of 1908,

> should not be chiefly fitting schools for higher institutions, but should be adapted to the general needs, both intellectual and industrial, of their students and communities, and we suggest the higher institutions may wisely adapt their courses to this condition. The high schools must become the "poor man's colleges," because the amount of latent and dormant power; of wealth-discovering and wealth-producing energy; of beauty-loving and beauty-inspiring taste and skill, that lie concealed and slumbering in the brains and hearts of the keen, shrewd, capable, but untutored millions of our youth, is beyond computation.

Victory, to be sure, did not come easily; as recently as 1900 Latin was "exceeded in popularity as a high school study only by algebra"—a state of affairs that "reflected the persistence of the classical illusion and the power of . . . the 'dead hand from the tombs of culture.' " For a while, indeed, it seemed possible that the country might "indulge the anti-republican idea" of "two systems of education, one for the ordinary citizen, . . . the other for the 'highly cultured few.' " But, happily, the American people, freed from the domination of the academies, from the narrow theological dogmas that had pervaded the schools, and from the superstitious awe of the classics,

worked out "their own educational salvation." And the high schools were accordingly rescued from the absurd notion that "whatever a pupil studied he should study thoroughly."

Similar NEA actions fostered the normal schools and teachers' colleges, and made of them "an integral part of the American pattern of public education." Yet others, a little later, contributed to the establishment of departments of education in the nation's universities, stimulated the rapid multiplication of higher educational "facilities" in general, and influenced the higher educational curriculum in the direction clearly indicated by the needs of American society. For the latter, Mr. Wesley tells us, has been

too *democratic* to accept an aristocratic tradition, too *competitive* to tolerate one program however efficacious, too *practical* to be content with theoretical values, too *intense* to endure the arid drill of formal grammar, too *impatient* to wait for deferred values, too *progressive* to study outmoded languages, too *nationalistic* to acknowledge dependence upon foreign studies, too *modern* to be awed by ancient lore, too *cosmopolitan* to depend upon . . . small segments of its heritage . . .

The NEA, in short, has spared no effort, neglected no project, that might hasten the transformation of our public school education into (what it is today) a continuous assault on the intellectual skills of the population.

The "seven subjects of the elementary program," according to an NEA president speaking back in 1882, "spelling, reading, writing, arithmetic, geography, grammar, and American history, [have] won their place by chance. . . . Neither arithmetic nor geography [throws] light upon the great moral, social, and political issues of the day." But, exults Mr. Wesley, "through the years both the curriculum and the process of making it changed fundamentally. The guidance of tradition, the influence of abstract principles, the weight of authority . . . gradually lost favor and were replaced by studies of the social setting, the principles of learning, and student capacities."

But let us not be unfair to Mr. Wesley. His Chapter 5 is a brilliant demonstration of the contribution statistic-frequency studies can make to our understanding of the past. The NEA, he assures us, held 94 conventions in the years 1857-1956. At the typical convention, he further states, 200 speeches were delivered, making a total for the 94 of about 19,000 speeches. Now, asks Mr. Wesley, "who delivered those 19,000 speeches [and] what were the speakers talking about . . . ?"

As for the first half of the question, Mr. Wesley concludes that some of the speakers were from inside the teaching profession and some from outside; that some of the speakers from outside provided "both entertainment and information"; and that "frequency of speaking" (the highest score of any speaker was 145 appearances) is "not necessarily an index of ability and effectiveness," but is "an indication of prominence and status."

As for the second half of the question, "some topics (1) waned in frequency, (2) some increased in frequency, and (3) some remained fairly constant." The group of topics that waned most in frequency were the "school subjects of Latin, Greek, grammar, algebra, history, and physics." "Education as a profession" also waned, as did the "fervent and vehement speeches on the use of the Bible in schools." Typical of the topics that "rose markedly in frequency of discussion" were business education, physical education, democracy and citizenship, and administration and supervision; and of those that "remained constant," the "nature of public education and its relation to government, democracy, and civilization in general."

But at this point this reviewer's interest, far from rising markedly or remaining constant, waned.

PROTESTANT AND CATHOLIC.
By KENNETH WILSON UNDERWOOD
(*New York: The Beacon Press, 1956.*)

Like the Lynd's famous *Middletown*, Kenneth Wilson Underwood's *Protestant and Catholic* is a book about an American city.
Like *Middletown* again, the book summarizes findings arrived at
in the course of an intensive "sociological" survey of the city in
question—or, as the author would prefer to put it, a "study in
depth" of that city, involving "more than a thousand interviews,"
analysis of everything available in the way of documentation,
and a vast and heroic effort on the investigator's part to live himself into, and understand, the problems of the people he brings
under his microscope.

The Lynds studied Muncie, Indiana, because they regarded it
as somehow average and typical. Dr. Underwood studies Holyoke, Massachusetts, because he deems it exceptional and not typical—because, concretely, it is a city in which "Roman Catholicism . . . [is] the dominant religious force in the culture" (some
Roman Catholic leaders, he tells us, have called it "the most
Catholic city in America"), and seems, therefore, an excellent
laboratory in which to investigate the "over-all social and religious impact" of the Catholic Church, and so throw light on the
"basic issues of freedom and order which people [face] in all of
Western society."

The Lynds were interested, so to speak, in everybody in Muncie
or, if you like, in everybody's "relations" (economic, social, cultural, political, etc.) with everybody else; their avowed purpose
was to show how Muncie as a going community "works"—and,
if their Left-wing bias, subsequently notorious, showed sometimes under the skirt of their "impartiality," their study did not

in general reflect preconceived notions as to how the good folk of Muncie ought to behave.

Dr. Underwood, by contrast, though he leaves this reviewer convinced of his detailed knowledge of Holyoke in general, is for purposes of his book directly concerned with only one aspect of its life ("the *relations* of Roman Catholic and Protestant churches and peoples"); he approaches his interviewees, therefore, in their capacity as Catholics or Protestants. Yet for all his sociologist's apparatus of impartiality, for all his determination (he is a Protestant minister) to be scrupulously fair and accurate about his guinea-pigs, his study suffers at every point from the difficulty that he does have preconceived notions as to how they, and people all over the world, ought to behave. Not (or at least not avowedly) Protestant preconceived notions, but rather preconceived notions drawn from his conception (erroneous in my opinion) of democracy and the democratic process, and of "freedom."

Unlike the Lynds with their Muncie, he has something he can't keep from wishing to do to his Holyoke—and he studies Holyoke (called "Paper City" in the book) because that which he wishes to do to cities everywhere clearly needs doing in Holyoke more urgently than in any other city within his reach.

The story of how the book came to be written goes back, it seems, to a "brief period in the fall of 1940," when this "industrial city of some 54,000 people held the rapt attention of many religious leaders in the United States." "The members of the Roman Catholic and Protestant faiths," our author continues, "were set in conflict by the attempt of Roman Catholic clergy to keep Margaret Sanger, America's foremost birth-control advocate, from speaking in the First Congregational Church. . . . The local Protestant clergy [pled] for . . . investigation of the forces set in operation by the effort of a Protestant church to permit a public dissent to the dominant ethos of the community."

That is why I say that Dr. Underwood's bias is not a Protestant or even a religious bias, but rather a *political* bias—a bias, quite simply, in favor of unlimited freedom of thought and speech. So far as one can tell from his book, he is willing for debate in Holyoke—on birth-control, on religious authority, on whether Communism is really so wicked and dangerous, on any question whatever—to produce whatever results it may happen to produce.

What matters to him, and matters supremely, is that the debate should occur; that everybody should participate in it; that no one should try to hold back, as not subject for discussion, any doctrine or problem or issue; that everyone should recognize that the debate, based on unrestricted liberty of "public dissent to the dominant ethos of the community," is *the* thing.

Dr. Underwood is, first and foremost, not a Protestant but a Liberal, committed to the view that all beliefs and ideas must start out equal in a competitive struggle for public approval, and that no belief or idea should be given a head start or an inside run in any area of a community's life.

Indeed, his outlook on specifically religious questions seems to this reviewer to derive from his politics, rather than the latter from the former, so that to call his bias "Protestant" would be to beg all the interesting questions about the "relations" between the beliefs and behavior of Catholics and those of Protestants. For there is, I believe, no conclusion we should be more hesitant to draw about Protestantism than that it regards coexistence with Catholicism as out of the question; or that in the impending struggle over the secularization of American life it will take its stand with the Liberals. If our author's position were indeed the Protestant position, we should have no alternative but to draw that conclusion, and to rethink our views as to the probable immediate outcome of that struggle.

This brings me to the two major comments I wish to make about this book.

Dr. Underwood, as we have seen, writes about Holyoke because it is a predominantly Catholic city, and his major point appears to be that the Catholics in Holyoke use the power that accrues to them in virtue of their numbers to inhibit the discussion process, to influence public policy in a sense favorable to the point of view of the Catholic Church, and to force the Protestant members of the community to adopt (out of fear concerning the consequences of refusal) certain patterns of behavior that are themselves uncongenial to the development, particularly the religious development, of free society. And even he, I think, would concede that his book moves from the premise that Holyoke would be a better place to live in if the Catholics did not use their power in these ways, if they would act in Holyoke as they do in an American community in which they are the minority —or, as I am tempted to put it, if they would only be a little less Catholic. In *that* sense, the book can be said to embody an anti-Catholic bias.

Beyond that—the author being only human—one might have thought to catch him, now and then, stacking the cards a little and making Catholics look less capable of participating in his kind of public discussion than they in fact are. I give it as my opinion, however, that no such charge can be leveled against the book. Some Catholic beliefs, to be sure, are difficult to translate into Dr. Underwood's sociology-of-religion jargon—which tends to avoid, for example, the word "Revelation." Other Catholic beliefs clearly set Dr. Underwood to wondering how any grown-up man or woman could possibly accept them, so that he writes of them with overtones of enforced objectivity reminiscent of the anthropologists' accounts of superstitions in, say, the South Sea islands. Yet others seem to have been explained to him by persons either too hurried or too inarticulate to explain them fully (he always speaks of absolution, for instance, as if a priest could forgive sins quite independently of the attitude of the sinner).

But, in general, no Catholic should fail to recognize himself and his fellow Catholics in Dr. Underwood's account of Catholic beliefs and practices. And none needs feel other than pride and satisfaction at its publication over the signature of a Protestant minister not open to the accusation of trying to make Catholics appear more serious, more loyal to the Church and its clergy, more ready to bear witness and to stand up for what they believe, than they in fact are.

By the same token, Protestant readers, aware both of Dr. Underwood's calling *and* his prepossessions about the discussion process, might wish to keep an eye on him lest, being only human, he seek to have it *two* ways about Protestantism. That is, they might want to satisfy themselves whether he recognizes the extent to which Protestants *also* possess an identifiable and firm position about the purport of Christian teaching, and thus the extent to which Protestants, were they to participate in the kind of debate he regards as characteristic of the healthy community, would have to give up something *they* value in order to improve substantially on the behavior of their Catholic neighbors. On Dr. Underwood's showing, I submit, no such dilemma exists. He might have been tempted to make Protestants sound as serious and committed as Catholics, but to a different set of beliefs and doctrines, so as to lead up, and lend the color of plausibility, to the question, "Why cannot the Catholics, who have no more at stake, act as the Protestants do about full ventilation of all issues?" But if any such temptation was ever present to Dr. Underwood's mind, he clearly resisted it with the fortitude of a saint, for his account of Protestant belief and practice is one that no opponent or critic of Protestantism could have published without raising the suspicion that he had falsified his data—and the further suspicion of having done so with the self-evident purpose of discrediting Protestant beliefs in the eyes of all persons who deem religion something other than an arena for indefinite personal improvisation.

Dr. Underwood's Protestants "assert that God cannot be identified with any act or object of worship." They "localize the manifestations of the holy in the individual, in his act of personal decision." They believe that "the more complex the development of doctrines, worship, and organization, the greater is the compromise and corruption of the gospel, and the less vital the Protestant protest against Catholicism." They meet "occasionally for social fellowship, and for participation in a service of worship or cultus[!] which has as its major act the expression by a professional leader of his personal convictions."

Their own leaders recognize that they "live in a society in which men are increasingly confused as to what they believe about God and about their responsibilities in the world." They declare that there is "nothing binding on man except what he receives in his own study of the Scriptures and meditation upon the insights and experiences of fellow-believers." They conceive the proper role of the minister as "that of clarifying the general moral and religious goals for men, and leaving to each individual the working out of the specific relation of the goals to his life . . ." They affirm, clergy and laymen alike, that "their most pressing doctrinal problem is to develop a Protestant concept of the nature and role of the church in man's salvation."

In their typical church "it is difficult for the pastor to find a consensus of belief that is the product of a religious community; there does not seem to be any priesthood of believers, . . . the main categories of analysis and occasions of disciplined study [having] been supplied by the special political and economic associations of the city." Their polity is "represented by individual subjectivism, an unrecognized institutionalization of personal charismatic leadership among the clergy, inability to achieve expression of religious conviction disciplined enough to influence effectively a highly organized society." They believe that a "community and a nation with diverse religious structure are essential for the discovery of truth, maintenance of freedom, and development of strong religious commitment."

In a word, they believe not in any particular religious truth or truths, but in a proposition about the relation between individuals-in-general and religious truth-in-general—namely, that if any of the former ever achieves any of the latter, they will do so unaided by authority, doctrine, or institutional commitment. The one rule in religion is to play by ear; the one forbidden act, to look at the composer's score.

One cannot but shudder, I repeat, at the thought that this is what American Protestantism has come to; and we shall surely want better evidence than Dr. Underwood's "thousand and more interviews" before we accept so insulting a picture of one of the major components of Christian civilization. (The Lutheran and Episcopal Churches, we may note in passing, disappear again and again from Dr. Underwood's purview; and it is never clear to what extent his statements about Protestants are intended to apply to their members.)

Back, however, to 1940, and Margaret Sanger, and the question whether Dr. Underwood's is a Liberal bias or a Protestant bias. Mrs. Sanger did make her speech in Holyoke, but to a mere handful of people, and in a small trade union meeting-place, not in a Protestant church.

When the Catholics—I follow Dr. Underwood's own account —first took exception to her delivering her lecture in the First Congregational Church, some Protestants, including the minister of the church in question, made remarks very much in line with Dr. Underwood's views concerning the discussion process in free society: Truth, they alleged, is arrived at through free and open discussion, with no topics barred and all participating; the man or organization seeking to prevent discussion of some topic is claiming for him or itself a monopoly of the truth, which by hypothesis no man or organization can possibly possess; Mrs. Sanger *must* be permitted to speak, to be heard, else we must ask, "What becomes of freedom, of the capacity for public dissent to the dominant ethos of the community?"

An innocent bystander might even—to judge from Dr. Underwood's citation—have got the impression that the Protestants really meant business, really did value "freedom of discussion" in the way he would wish them to. But all it took to get First Congregational's invitation to Mrs. Sanger withdrawn was a hint or two—for I do not understand Dr. Underwood to be saying there was more than that—of an economic boycott by Catholics of certain Congregationalist businessmen who were in position to exert pressure on the minister; and in the end no other Protestant church was prepared to offer Mrs. Sanger its hospitality.

So the question arises, What—on Dr. Underwood's own showing—are we to make of this incident in Holyoke's history? What Dr. Underwood would like us to make of it, of course, is that the Protestants, confronted as they were by Catholic power, had no alternative but to back down—that, therefore, we can make no inference from their behavior as regards their attitude toward unlimited discussion. But the more indicated conclusion would seem to be that the Protestants discovered in the pinch (men living in communities often discover surprising things about themselves in the pinch) that there were some things—whether the peace of the community or profits or Christian teaching we need not ask—that they valued more highly than unrestricted free debate.

In short, the question that Dr. Underwood is tacitly asking about Holyoke's Catholics (whether the "rigidity" and "absolutism" of their beliefs render impossible for them a proper "democratic" attitude concerning the demands of his discussion process?) needs to be asked about Holyoke's Protestants as well, as also about anyone in Holyoke who believes, in George Bernard Shaw's phrase, that some things are worth more than others. No community whose members value it enough to wish to perpetuate it will submit the basic tenets of its "dominant ethos" to untrammeled discussion by persons avowedly hostile to it; and no dominant majority aware of the responsibilities that accompany its power will, or should, hesitate to place barriers in the way of those who seek to undermine the community's basic beliefs.

Let Dr. Underwood, if he doubts that, examine the statistics in another recent sociological study, Stouffer's *Communism, Conformity, and Civil Liberties,* where an overwhelming majority of the respondents, a "representative sample" of our population, gave one and the same answer to the question, "Would you permit an atheist to speak in your town?" Namely, No.

FREEDOM, VIRTUE AND THE FIRST AMENDMENT.
By WALTER BERNS
(Baton Rouge: Louisiana State University Press, 1957.)

There is a new breed of political scientists abroad in the land, as different from the old breed as chalk from cheese. The old breed has its roots, at best, in Madison and Hamilton and Jefferson and Wilson and the late great Charles A. Beard, and at worst in Harold Lasswell and those of his adepts who have encouraged the idea that we improve our understanding of politics through statistical analysis of the phenomena of political "behavior." The new breed has its roots, by sharp contrast, in Plato and Aristotle and Thomas Aquinas. The old breed, officially at least, are cultists of "scientific" "impartiality"; the new make no secret of the fact that they take sides. The old breed never touch the English language except to slaughter it; the new tend to a high degree of literacy: they can write, and their products show that they can read, and even like to read. The old breed has given us a professional political science literature projected on a level of intellectual difficulty more appropriate to a Chinese laundry than to a scholarly discipline, and dull beyond belief; the new think both before and while they are writing, work their readers hard, and even tickle their fancy now and then with a chuckle or a witticism.

The old breed are obtainable in quantity, any June, at any of the nation's Ph.D. factories; the new breed are still *rara avis,* and come, for the most part, from a single institution, namely the University of Chicago, and for a good reason. Most of them are pupils of one of the two or three great teachers of politics of our day, Professor Leo Strauss, who communicates to them, as if by magic, his own love of learning, his own sense of the gravity of the great problems of politics, and his own habit of thinking deeply about a problem before rushing into print. The old breed are riding high, and make and unmake reputations for professional achievements; the new breed are unlikely, for a good long while anyhow, to cut much ice in the political science profession's most exalted counsels. But they may well do something far more important—namely, to revive the habit of political thought in the United States, to set standards for it that the old breed (because of the patent inadequacy of their training) cannot live up to, *and* bring under challenge the Liberal orthodoxy that is the main burden of the bulk of our current political science literature.

Freedom, Virtue [virtue, mark you] *and the First Amendment* is the first full-dress book we have from the new breed in which the author addresses himself to a traditional problem of American politics (as contrasted with a problem in "pure" political theory). Its thesis is fourfold:

1. That the constitutional law of the First Amendment—that one of the amendments that forbids Congress and (as interpreted) the states to make any law "abridging the freedom of speech, or of the press" is today a "shambles," in "hopeless confusion."

2. That the confusion is due to the fact that the relevant Supreme Court decisions, over the past decades but particularly of late, have been dictated by the Liberal (Berns writes "liberal") "notion of law."

3. That the Liberal notion of law reduces itself, on one side anyhow, to the idea that "freedom is not a problem"—that men are born free in the sense that they have inalienable rights derived from a nongovernmental source, that the protection of these rights against interference by the government is the supreme political good, and that (this being why freedom is not a problem) it is all very simple: when a claim to freedom clashes with a claim on behalf of any competing good *except* national security, you resolve the clash in favor of freedom.

4. That a constitutional system can assign to freedom that kind of priority only by sacrificing justice and certain other goods that are indispensable to a decent society. That, most particularly, a decent society does not hesitate, when occasion arises, to deny to its citizens the freedom to utter that which is evil and must, to that end, know and be prepared to act on the distinction between good and evil (which our Liberal-dominated Supreme Court persistently refuses to do). And that the only reason the Liberals think otherwise is that they possess neither the wisdom nor the knowledge nor the skills imparted by political philosophy.

In a word, freedom, Berns insists, *is* a problem; and if we ever solve the problem that is freedom we shall do so not with catch-phrases out of a constitution, but by hard thinking that must begin by recognizing the complexities the problem involves— and, ultimately, by hard thinking about "what men of another era called virtue." The Supreme Court, that is to say, must mend its ways. This calls, first of all, for abandonment of the Liberal idea that "the word virtue carries overtones of authoritarianism [and] bigotry," and that the "one unexpiable sin is for government to get into the business of distinguishing good and evil." Berns continues: That sort of thing leads, so it is claimed, "to the imposing of orthodoxies, and an orthodoxy imposed by government is the dirty work of totalitarianism. Strict adherence to the Constitution will prevent this. Government will never have the opportunity to impose a definition of good and evil . . . [because] the [clear and present] danger test is available to solve all problems. And the danger test does not recognize virtue."

But, says Berns, it is precisely the danger test that has led to the confusion that this book proceeds to document:

The test originated as an attempt to get around a difficulty that is inherent in our Constitution in its original form, and has become more formidable by far since the adoption of the Fourteenth Amendment—namely this:

The First Amendment *seems* to forbid any and every abridgment by Congress of certain "rights": freedom of speech, press, religion, assembly and petition. But the First Amendment is part of the *Constitution,* the purpose of which is to vouchsafe to the American people certain goods—justice, for example—that are set forth in its Preamble. Now, unless freedom and justice are one and the same thing (which pretty clearly they are not) the "absolute prohibition" of the First Amendment must, on occasion, be set aside—so as to "free" Congress and the Executive to take action on behalf of those other goods. Freedom may be—probably should be—the rule; but there must be exceptions—and clear and present danger was intended as a rule to cover the exceptions. There are, the doctrine runs, certain evils that Congress has a right to prevent; when freedom of speech is so used as to pose a "clear and present danger" of one of those evils, the government's—that is the federal government's—hands are no longer tied by the First Amendment. Whatever it *appears* to say, the First Amendment permits certain speech and prohibits certain speech. The dividing line between the permitted and the prohibited is clear and present danger; and the effect of the dividing line—as we have long been assured by our constitutional lawyers—is to place a certain area of discourse well within the absolute prohibitions of the First Amendment, and so beyond the government's reach. And, ever since the Fourteenth Amendment, which seems to have extended the First Amendment prohibitions to the states, beyond the reach of the state governments as well. The clear and present danger test becomes, therefore, a bulwark of our freedom—a guarantee of our rights "against" the federal government and the state governments.

Berns thinks that the test, in its original form and used for the purpose for which it was originally conceived, has much to be said for it—but precisely *not* what previous scholars have said for it. For in its original form it was a means of letting the federal government, despite the First Amendment, send people to jail for abusing the right to free speech—which Berns, unlike most of his predecessors, thinks it a good thing to let the federal government be in position to do. In a word, the Supreme Court does not, in practice, enforce the First Amendment prohibitions in any case to which the federal government is one party and someone accused of abusing free speech is the other party. And the proof is that the accused always goes to jail. Berns finds *not a single case* in which the "test" has saved somebody from being imprisoned by the U. S. government.

Berns, I repeat, thinks that is all to the good, so when he speaks of the "shambles" of the law of the First Amendment he does not include the fact that everyone always goes to jail in his indictment (as one wishes he would). But his main points—that the federal government's hands must not be wholly tied by the First Amendment, that the danger test untied them at a moment when the free-speechites might well have tied them completely, and that the *test* was, therefore, a healthy development—are brilliantly argued and, in my view, unassailably sound. So also are his parallel points concerning the First Amendment and the states: just as the test rescues nobody when the federal government is the plaintiff, so it rescues everybody when a state or municipality is the plaintiff. And the states and municipalities of course have far more impact upon the quality of our freedom than the federal government.

Let us be quite clear what Berns means by this. During a long period of recent Supreme Court history, as he shows by patient and skilful analysis of the cases, the free-speechites used the danger test to enforce the First Amendment as an absolute prohibition against state or municipal interference of *any* kind with freedom of speech or religion. They used it, as this writer would prefer to put it, as a means of declaring the United States, as far as local authority is concerned, an "open society"—in which no kind of speech, no sort of so-called religious practice, could be prohibited or punished save on the grounds that it was a clear and present danger. Worse still, the free-speechites always refused to be convinced that any kind of speech or religious practice was a clear and present danger. On the state-municipal level, that is to say, they made the test one that nobody ever fails— that is, no test at all. And even if sometimes they were outvoted, they caused the Supreme Court to fail in its central function in this area, which was to maintain a situation in which state and municipal officials can with fair certainty know beforehand what, under the First Amendment, they are and are not empowered to do. Yet, insists Berns, they are the custodians of community interests that, if less urgent, may well be more important than national security—interests that, in any case, must be protected against abuses of freedom of speech and freedom of religion if we are to have a decent society.

And Berns will leave few readers unconvinced—whether he intends this or not—that these interests can be protected only if we take the Supreme Court away from the Liberals.

Berns' book would be a "must" for Conservatives even had he contented himself with doing that which we have already noticed —namely, making clear the incompatibility between the Liberal cult of freedom as the highest good, and the requirements of good government as defined in the Preamble of our Constitution. Actually, however, he does much more than that: he pursues Liberal constitutional thought and practice to their very bases in Liberal political theory, and reads the Liberals the sternest lectures they have ever heard from an American political scientist. And the sternest of these lectures is in connection with the problem of loyalty.

Berns holds that the Smith Act, under which Eugene Dennis went to jail, adds a "new dimension" to our constitutional law. Congress, with the blessing of the Supreme Court in the Dennis case, has now given us a statute that makes it a crime to hold certain ideas. The "evil that Congress sought to prevent" in passing it was not the overthrow of the government by force and violence, but "advocacy of this idea." The Act "does not say that such advocacy is bad only when there is a danger that it will lead to the overthrow, but . . . that such advocacy, like heresy of old, is always bad." The question in the Dennis case, therefore, was whether, in passing such a law, Congress had exceeded its constitutional powers. "The case represents the end of a one-way street for our Liberal justices who have regarded free speech as a right of American citizenship . . . [and it] might possibly contain a lesson worth our while to find and reflect upon."

As we would expect, Berns—unlike most persons who have spoken of the Dennis decision in such terms—thinks Congress did *not* exceed its constitutional powers; his target is not the Supreme Court majority that upheld the Smith Act, but Justice Douglas' dissenting opinion, which held that "Full and free discussion has indeed been the first article of our faith."

Berns' major point is that like "all faiths unsupported by reason . . . [faith] in full and free discussion is . . . contradicted . . . by reflection upon its unwarranted presuppositions . . ."

Berns forces the issue with all his might. The Smith Act, he argues, defines loyalty "negatively"—as the "absence of disloyalty"; Douglas would add to this a "positive element," namely, the "belief in full and free discussion." So, he notes, would Sidney Hook, who writes: "The liberal stands ready to defend the honest heretic no matter what his views against any attempt to curb him"—a "heresy" being, on Hook's showing, a "set of unpopular ideas or opinions on any matter of grave concern to the community." Berns summarizes the position as follows: "In America, despite the fact that Communism, cannibalism, and head-hunting are unpopular, honest Communists, cannibals and head-hunters must be given a fair shake and the liberal will help them get it . . . Except that they are denied to conspirators, civil liberties are indivisible. Having turned from judicial opinions in order to find a more philosophical . . . discussion . . . we achieve a conclusion . . . in no way superior to that culled from judicial opinions."

But, Berns proceeds to show, the Douglas-Hook position will not do. If *"the* cause to which the liberal is loyal is the cause of full and free discussion," then it should be "a matter of indifference to him which of the competing doctrines or ideas emerges triumphant." But it isn't a matter of indifference. Hook, for example, does not conceal his fear of "the systematic corruption of the free market by activities which make intelligent choice impossible." And, Berns reasons, once that word "intelligent" gets into the discussion, the position becomes repugnant to reason: ". . . if it is intelligent choice the liberal wants, would it not be reasonable and feasible for him to exclude the unintelligent proposals . . . ? . . . If Professor Hook is prepared to define 'intelligent' (his word), he can also define 'unintelligent,' and why anyone should permit the community to choose an unintelligent doctrine like Marxism or Fascism, if there is a chance he can prevent it, is one of those liberal mysteries comprehensible only to the initiated."

And then the lecture: "The purpose to which liberals ask us to be loyal is not really a purpose but an empty process. . . . Before any reasonable man can give his loyalty to such a purpose he will want some assurance that the doctrine that will achieve popularity is one with which he is sympathetic . . . [The Liberal] cannot say that Communism is evil because it commits terrible deeds . . . He cannot say that anything is unjust, because he refuses to concede that one definition of justice is more reasonable than another . . . So it is we are told that the good American is loyal to a process . . . But . . . a process . . . is not a cause unless one has no concern with the results, and it is not a reasonable cause in any case. Freedom cannot be that cause to which we can be loyal; there must be another cause to which the good American is loyal."

What cause? Berns takes his answer from Aristotle. "The good man," as Berns puts it, "is a good citizen in a good regime. . . . [And we] must ever be alert to maintain the identity of a good man and a good American." If we do that, he continues, what we end up with is both the idea that the good American is loyal not to a process, not a freedom, but to moral principle, and with the answer we need for Justice Douglas: ". . . [A] good regime cannot trust bad men . . . The United States cannot trust Eugene Dennis. [And] this means that it is legitimate and on occasion necessary to deny [bad] men the freedom to perform bad acts, such as teaching and advocating an immoral political doctrine."

COMMON SENSE AND THE FIFTH AMENDMENT.
By SIDNEY HOOK

(New York: Criterion Books, 1957; republished, Chicago: Henry Regnery, 1963.)

"God, James," Wilde once said in response to a Whistler epigram, "I wish I'd said that." "Don't worry, Oscar," Whistler replied, "you will." This reviewer, similarly, wishes that the political scientists of America, himself included, had not left to someone outside their profession the writing of this book. And he confidently predicts that they, himself included, will be plagiarizing its contents for many a long day. Or, failing that, will go on talking the kind of nonsense about self-incrimination that all of us were brought up on, and that has enabled the Communists to transform the privilege against self-incrimination into one of their most potent weapons.

"No person . . . shall be compelled in any criminal case to be a witness against himself." So reads the non-self-incrimination clause of the U. S. Constitution. But nothing could matter less:

our present law of self-incrimination, as laid down by the courts, is related to it only as a broad overhang is related to its foundation. The "privilege," today, is by no means confined to criminal cases—or even (since it applies in congressional hearings) to cases in the courts of law. It applies now not merely to defendants, but to *all* witnesses. It excuses witnesses from answering not merely questions the replies to which would be directly self-incriminating, but also any question a truthful answer to which might provide a "link in the chain of evidence" that might result in prosecution, *and* any question about the witness' grounds for thinking that truthful answers might incriminate him. It extends to many "questions in which by common agreement his answer could not possibly incriminate him." And it has been held to include not merely the privilege of refusing to answer, but the privilege of doing so *without giving rise to any inference about one's guilt,* no matter how inescapable, in pure logic, that inference may be.

Professor Hook's main contention in this book is that the time has come when we must rethink this whole matter, and (since we are always free to raze that which we have built on a foundation) perhaps undo some of what the courts have done, or even (since we can also root up foundations) ask ourselves whether the Constitution should contain a non-self-incrimination clause at all.

Certainly, he believes, we must rethink the part about no inference of guilt.

Few Conservatives, anyway, will need much of Professor Hook's persuading on that last. But let all of them remember that this book is the place to go for a corpus of argument in support of a position they have long defended—and, in any case, let all of them who have mourned the simultaneous passing of the stiletto and the 16-inch cannon take care not to miss the show. The regnant anti-interference-of-guilt doctrine, Hook insists, rests either:

First, on question-begging hypothetical examples: an innocent man takes the privilege, an inference of guilt is drawn; is not the inference wrong? Indeed it is, Hook replies in effect, but not necessarily unwarranted.

Or, second, on arguments that prove merely that taking the privilege is "not necessarily *sufficient* or *conclusive* evidence of guilt or involvement with respect to the issue under inquiry."

Or, third, on an indefensible extension of the maxim that a man is innocent until proved guilty. (Hook's answer: The real issue is whether the fact of taking the privilege can properly be regarded as part of the proof of his guilt.)

Or, fourth, on the false contention that we shift the burden of proof onto the defendant when we permit the inference of guilt. (Hook's answer: The burden must indeed remain with the accusers; but in making out their case the accusers can, "in the interest of truth and justice, question him . . . , ask for a truthful answer, and draw an adverse inference, prejudicial to him, if he refuses to reply on grounds that a truthful answer would tend to be self-incriminating.")

The refutations are, in each case, devastating and, as nearly as can be in such matters, definitive—thus reminiscent (though Professor Hook may not thank me for the comparison) of the late F. H. Bradley at his best. "Common sense," Hook concludes, "recognizes that evidence against a man acquires a greater force when it is not denied, particularly when a man is in a position to deny or refute the evidence. *Whose* common sense? the reader may inquire. Literally, the common sense of the moral tradition of at least the Western world. . . ."

Should the privilege itself be withdrawn? Here Professor Hook shows himself at *his* best—that is, as a legal and political theorist forcing the discussion of a difficult and involved problem over into hitherto unbroken ground, and delicately weighing, *against one another*, principles and interests for each of which there is something to be said. He is always aware of his indebtedness to earlier writers (Bentham, J. S. Mill, Wigmore, and *National Review's* Dickerman Williams), but deeply troubled by the present condition of the relevant literature, and profoundly convinced that the issues *can* be resolved by right reason illuminated by political knowledge and understanding.

Hook concludes (here we cannot possibly follow out the details of the argument):

That the stock justifications for retention of the privilege (forcing a man to testify against himself is cruel, abolition of the privilege would encourage third-degree methods at the police station and the court house, protection of the innocent should take precedence over the apprehension and punishment of the guilty) simply will not hold water.

That we had better retain the privilege, though subject to the limitation that *illegitimate* use of it (to protect persons other than the user, to prevent damage to the user's reputation, to extricate the user from difficult situations in which "there is not the remotest danger of self-incrimination") is "as much a form of perjury as lying under oath."

That current objections to immunity statutes rest for the most part on "a politically confused sentimentalism."

That the best contemporary justification for the privilege runs in terms of the nature of the contemporary state, namely: "The state has become so powerful *today,* so many techniques are at its command in proving its case, that it is wise to lean over backward and permit individuals the benefit of withholding pertinent evidence if it tends to implicate them."

That *my* privilege against self-incrimination may conflict with *your* right to compel the testimony you need in order to protect yourself against injustice.

That the objective of our judicial system is—or should be—to see justice done after the fullest possible canvass of the available evidence.

And by justice Professor Hook seems to mean, for all the Deweyite trappings of his argument, that same good that preoccupied those old absolutists Plato and Aristotle and Thomas Aquinas.

THE NEGRO IN AMERICAN CIVILIZATION.
By NATHANIEL WEYL
(*Washington: Public Affairs Press, 1960.*)

No one can read *The Negro in American Civilization* by Nathaniel Weyl without realizing: (a) that we have long needed a compendious and objective survey of the *facts* about the American Negro (not least of all because many of those facts have been systematically suppressed and misrepresented); (b) that we—not merely "we" in America but "we" in the West—do have a "Negro problem," the mishandling of which may be the instrument we shall use to destroy ourselves; and (c) that the author, clearly a man of intellectual honesty, is attempting to perform a signal service for us all, and especially (though he will surely be accused of the contrary) for the American Negroes themselves.

Let us speak first of the author's intellectual honesty. Just as Columbus did not set out to discover America, so Nathaniel Weyl did not set out to write this book. What he intended, he tells us, was a modest little study of the "changing status" of the Negro under the American Constitution. Moreover, it was to be predicated upon and to document the prevailing mythology as to what constitutes "justice" for the Negro—and hence to justify the Supreme Court's *Brown* decision. His subject-matter, however, grew and broadened under his hand, carrying him into areas that he had "intended to ignore." He discovered that "material which passed for the objective findings of social scientists could more accurately be characterized as rationalizations and propaganda wearing academic cap and gown."

Above all, he found that the evidence accumulating in his hands warranted his changing his mind on some of the major

214

issues involved—*not,* I hasten to add, on one: *the imperative need for "policies . . . designed to achieve harmony between the two races on a foundation of justice and freedom"* (italics added). Rather, he found the need to reshape his ideas on the *form* those policies are going to have to take and the political theory that is going to have to guide them. A less honest man would have found a means of papering over the cracks in the wall he had selected to work on; a man less bold would have chosen—as, if he had his wits about him, Weyl must have felt tempted to do—not to write and publish the book he found germinating within him. (This reviewer's *a priori* guess, for what it is worth, is that he will pay dearly for it.)

I shall not attempt to summarize the evidence to which the questions burgeoning in Weyl's mind led him, if for no other reason than that my readers owe it to themselves to go to the book itself and examine it in detail. Suffice it to say that in "area" after "area" the evidence Weyl has assembled is vastly more discouraging, with respect both to the Negro's own future and to his future impact upon American society, than most of us have permitted ourselves to fear in our most pessimistic moments. And suffice it to add that the cumulative effect of the evidence in the several areas is appalling—doubly so because the author is apparently himself appalled.

On Weyl's showing, the Negroes, on the average (happily, the propositions can be stated, and should be for Weyl's kind of purpose, without using any such judgmental terms as "inferior"), just plain do chalk up lesser scores on intelligence tests than whites. They just plain do learn less than whites, and with greater difficulty than whites, at school. They just plain do commit fantastically more crimes proportionally, and more violent crimes, than whites. And Weyl believes that these statistical tendencies have—at least at our present stage of knowledge and understanding—to be explained in large part (never mind how often you have been told this can't be) in terms of specifically biological inheritance. In which case, not only do these statistical tendencies apply to the present generation of Negroes, they will be found applying to the next and the next generation (which, incidentally, will be much larger proportionately than the present one).

All this, or at least all except the "biological" part, most of us knew in a sense already—even those of us who rely for our information upon sources that supply information of *this* kind most grudgingly. So the value of Weyl's book lies elsewhere. Namely: (a) in his handling of the ten thousand Liberal expedients for explaining all of it away on so-called "environmental" grounds, that is, as the wages of our sin in not having done more *for* the Negroes, and (b) in his treatment of what, ultimately, is the only interesting question, Where, for the sake of all of us, white and Negro alike, do we go from here?

As for (a), Weyl's general answer is along the following lines: From the standpoint of income, comfort, the means to health, access to the goods of civilization, the present generation of American Negroes is a *privileged* class—by comparison either with most of the population of the world, or, more importantly, an entire series of "underprivileged" groups in the United States which have responded successfully and fruitfully to the challenge of American life: the Russian Jews, the Chinese and the Japanese, to take only a few of the examples that come most readily to mind.

Here again Weyl's statistics are breathtaking and, in the opinion of this writer, formidable. Could it be we shall never do justice to the Negroes in our midst, nor the Negroes to themselves, save as we all recognize that as a group they may have a lesser capacity than the rest of us for civilizational achievement? When we impose upon them equal responsibility for civilizational achievement we may be doing them not justice but injustice.

As for (b), Weyl's major thesis would seem to be this: American civilization cannot survive without, first, an educational system that offers maximum opportunity for students of extraordinary ability to grow and learn in an academic environment that is both congenial and so structured as to bring out of them (*e ducere*) the best they have in them; and, second, cities capable of performing the indispensable urban function of providing facilities for intellectual and aesthetic communication. We are sacrificing both these goods to our ignorance and sentimentality and vicarious guilt (guilt, let me add to Weyl, that is always greatest in those quarters of American life that have *no* ethic over against which to feel guilty) about the Negroes. Or, to return to the point about political theory, we are sacrificing them to our determination to subordinate the American dream of liberty to new-fangled notions of equality.

The American educational system must be rescued from those who would treat it as an adjunct of the Negro problem (on this point Weyl tellingly cites Mrs. Agnes Meyer, and so enables me to say: this even Mrs. Meyer can see). We must reverse the trend that is making the American city an all-Negro city, in which the rule of life is, quite simply, have more children because more children mean bigger relief checks. The alternative may be no less than the self-destruction of America—with the Negroes themselves as the chief sufferers. And these possibilities call, in Weyl's view, for simultaneously learning to think of the Negroes as a group that pose very special problems, and, paradoxical though it seem, ceasing to treat the Negroes as a group.

"Southern racism believes," Weyl writes, "or pretends to believe, that *all* Negroes are mentally [and morally?] inferior to *all* whites. . . . In the North, [the] fundamental creed is that all races are equal in innate intelligence [and moral capacity?] . . . Negro shortcomings are therefore . . . due to an unfavorable environment. . . . [Now:] . . . Being equal, the Negro should produce his share of Einsteins, Freuds and Picassos. . . . Yet the really outstanding Negro intellectuals can be counted on one's fingers. . . ."

And then: "Today, the intelligent and capable Negro finds that he is carrying the stupid and delinquent one on his back. . . . He is not permitted to . . . demand that he be treated solely on the basis of . . . individual merit. . . . The American system . . . does not [properly understood?] offer equality of reward where inequality exists in ability or effort. The capable

Negro . . . demands merely the full privileges of citizenship without regard to race. He is not entitled to more, nor are any of us."

CONSTITUTIONAL REASON OF STATE.
By C. J. FRIEDRICH
(Providence: Brown University Press, 1957.)

Suppose you are convinced (a) that there can be no Christianity without the Christian Church, and (b) that the Church's survival is threatened by rising heretical movements. You may, says C. J. Friedrich in this book, react as he says the Jesuits do, and think yourself entitled to violate the Church's own moral law in order to put down the heresies; that is, you may adopt a "reason of Church" policy.

Or suppose you are convinced (a) that your State is necessary to the survival of morality itself, and (b) that it faces enemies, within or without, that threaten its very existence. You may, thinks our author, react like those in America today who are "excited about the Communist danger" (as he clearly is not), and think yourself entitled to "go to any length to defend the United States"—that is, adopt a "reason of State" policy. So the political theory of the modern constitutional State has got to pose for itself the problem, "Can you justify the violation of the law, when the survival of the legal order is at stake?"

Professor Friedrich, upon whose heart the problems of the modern constitutional State lie heavy, steps forward to straighten out our thinking about this—partly by conducting a scholarly song-and-dance through the work of the political theorists who have addressed themselves to the issue, partly by giving deep thought to it himself. One sort of knows, however, from the middle of page one or thereabouts, where he is going to end up—

that is, striking a blow for the curious kind of "freedom" that our contemporary Liberals have settled for.

Not, to be sure, much of a blow, because the enemies at whom the blow is directed do not exist. It simply is not true—the nearest parish priest could have told Professor Friedrich so—that the Catholic Church "has been prepared, since the days of St. Augustine, to take that horn of the dilemma which says that in fighting the enemy all bars are down, that while at war the laws are silent." Nor is it true that our Republic is today "rocked to its foundations" by a controversy along the lines that Professor Friedrich alleges. The question actually at issue between "civil libertarians" and their opponents is not whether the rights guaranteed by the Constitution are to be maintained, but the very different question, "What are those rights, and what does the Constitution authorize us to do in order to maintain them?" And this being, in all conscience, a difficult enough question already, anyone who complicates it by falsifying the issues is doing the nation a signal disservice. Especially since the persons on the American horizon who believe that "the State is the highest value" have, in your reviewer's experience, consistently ranged themselves on Professor Friedrich's side of this, the real controversy. And precisely because they recognize no competing high value (unless the UN or coexistence with the USSR) to which they could possibly subordinate themselves.

Professor Friedrich's major target, of course, is the internal security program, and the length to which he is prepared to go in fighting it may be gathered from his contention that the "objections recently raised against the Fifth Amendment in the United States are very subversive, and should be stopped." As, I might add, the length to which he is prepared to go in doing his homework about such matters may be gathered from the fact that he misspells the name of the author of the Internal Security Act, both in his text and his index.

The question Professor Friedrich—like other civil libertarians —refuses to face is, "Can we keep house with an open and avowed Communist minority?" Some of us, in answer to this question, say "No; we must create a constitutional order that will somehow exclude the Communists." They—and this reviewer is one of them—flatly deny that the United States is committed to the "capacity of human beings to work together effectively by granting to each member of the Community a substantial amount of freedom . . . to search out the truth for himself. . . ." They —including this reviewer—deny that the United States is committed, through its Constitution, to the proposition that we "do not know the truth, except in comparative terms." They, and this reviewer, refuse to agree that while we "know that one proposition may contain more truth than another . . . we do not know that this proposition is final, and the presumption is that it is not."

We believe that the proposition "Communism is evil, and must be prevented" is final, and final precisely because of a "value" infinitely higher than that of "the State"—this State, or any State. And any time the "constitutional order" gets in our way, as regards combating the evil of Communism, we shall seek a change in the constitutional order—not for "reason of Church," or "reason of State" or "constitutional reason of State," but for reason of God.

THE NEW DIMENSIONS OF PEACE. By CHESTER BOWLES

(New York: Harper & Brothers, 1955.)

The Liberals *are* anti-Communist. Nowadays they come right out and say that Communist intentions are wicked, that Communist dreams of world empire are a threat to the long-term security of Americans (anti-Liberals and Liberals alike), even that something has to be done to prevent those dreams being realized. They are, therefore, not merely anti-Communist: they are even pro-United States.

Chester Bowles' *The New Dimensions of Peace* we may fairly

call the current authoritative, full-dress exposition of the Liberal line on anti-Communism. *New Dimensions* is at one and the same time (a) a summons to all of us to take cognizance of the "real" world and how it ticks (as contrasted with the world as seen by, for example, military men), (b) a carefully elaborated program for defeating the world Communist movement without firing a shot or mussing a shirt-cuff, and (c) an eloquent demonstration of the happy coincidence between what Americans must do in order to defeat world Communism and what the American political tradition commits us to do as a matter of course.

Mr. Bowles' world is above all a world in which history is made by the masses of the people. Lenin won in Russia because he enunciated ideas (Land, Bread and Peace) that "moved" the masses and therefore "proved to be the decisive factor." Mao won in China because he saw that "the broad base of revolutionary power in China lay among the peasants." (Similarly, Chiang lost because he too often neglected "the importance of ideas and the stubborn power of people caught up by their influence.") The ideas that move men are, moreover, everywhere the same, though they get stated differently from place to place (Mr. Bowles himself is at pains to state them in terms likely to conceal their central tendency, so that it takes a bit of swinging from limb to limb in the tree of his argument to feel it all out). One formulation, that of the mid-nineteenth-century Chinese revolutionary leader Hung Hsiu Ch'uan, runs thus: "All shall eat food, all shall have clothes, money shall be shared, and in all things there shall be equality." Another comes from the pen of Gandhi, to whom Mr. Bowles has pretty clearly given his whole heart: "The contrast between the palaces of New Delhi and the miserable hovels of the poor laboring class . . . cannot last one day in a free India, in which the poor will enjoy the same power as the richest in the land."

The masses, then, make history; and they bestow the palm of victory, where political power is at stake, on that leader or movement that enunciates most clearly the ideas that the masses wish to hear. Naturally enough, therefore, the pickle we Americans are in is partly a matter of our having bet too heavily on "military answers" to the Communists' bid for power, partly a matter of our having failed to take a firm public stand in favor of the right ideas, and partly a matter of our having failed to live up to those ideas at home—so that even when we do enunciate the right ideas, the masses perceive that we are something less than sincere. Naturally enough also, therefore, the course we must follow—for we are, in effect, running for office out over the world—is plain to see. We must enunciate *and* implement the four great contemporary "revolutionary principles" (Hung-Gandhi with a very considerable tactical admixture of water): national independence, human dignity, economic advancement, and peace. Concretely, we must oppose colonialism and racial discrimination everywhere, eliminate from our propaganda all outmoded foolishness about free private enterprise, convince the masses (via "vastly stepped-up economic aid," which is "essential") that our economic system can compete with Communism when it comes to developing undeveloped areas (for the masses are "impressed" by the economic performance of Communism in Russia and China), and assure peace by taking the proper steps to "relax tension in world affairs."

Also, we must disabuse our minds of the tendency to confuse Social Democracy with Communism, or to think of the former as an enemy. For Socialism is a "thoroughly popular word in Africa, Asia, and South America." And democracy, of which we are the propagandists, "is the way to achieve the ideals which many millions of non-Communists throughout the world associate with Socialism." In short our posture vis-à-vis the world's masses must be one of "As You Desire Us"—*must* be, on pain of letting the Communists pick up the blue chips; and the world's masses desire us to be levelers. Let us, then, take a firm stand in favor of leveling the world over, and let us live up to that stand in our domestic politics.

And, *mirabile dictu*, we can in this matter, in despite of David Riesman, be other-directed and inner-directed all at the same time! The four revolutionary ideas that we must translate into reality abroad and at home are, after all, "the ideas that powered our own revolution"; and if they "sometimes sound strange to our ears," this merely proves "our isolation from our own past." They are "the very concepts on which America was built"; and it is "not surprising that we should expand our dream to all mankind." They are also the basic concepts of the French Revolution, whose "affinity" with our revolution Mr. Bowles regards as axiomatic. (Poor Gentz!)

In short, Hung = Gandhi = Robespierre = Washington = Lincoln = Roosevelt = Socialism. The way to beat the Communists is to accept leveling as the historical imperative of our age, prove that we can do it better, and assert proudly that we thought of it first. In short, the way to beat Communism is to be more Communist than the Communists.

THE FUTURE AS HISTORY. By ROBERT L. HEILBRONER

(New York: Harper and Brothers, 1959.)

What "we" have to do, according to this pretentious venture into deep thinking by a well-known Liberal ideologue, is to learn to "understand the grand dynamic of history's forces," to see the "future as a part of the sweep of history," above all, to seal ourselves off from "false hopes" and "an equally false despair." History (which includes, for Mr. Heilbroner, roughly speaking, everything that has happened since last night's dinner, as his "future" includes everything between here and the end of our collective nose) has a "drift and a temper," a "pattern," from which no "vital . . . effort can depart very far in its essentials." It poses "challenges" that are "irresistible, pitiless, unyielding," so that *often* "we" are not "the masters but the prisoners" of our time, "with no alternative but to bow before its demands." Why only "often"? Because we do not, as all that might seem to suggest, have to "remain passive before the enveloping changes of history"; we can, rather, "attempt to adapt our institutions so as to minimize . . . [the] impact of those changes." But the "often," in any case, gives the show away: there are "forces," "necessities," where Mr. Heilbroner and his political allies choose to see them, and "opportunities," "freedom," where what is involved is what *they* want to go and do.

I do not forget, of course, that the notion of "forces" in history is often a useful metaphor—useful, that is, to persons who keep themselves reminded that it is a metaphor. And to those who remember that what is "there" in history is *people,* who behave or misbehave, who do that which we wish them to or that which we would prefer to keep them from doing, and who keep on doing that which they do either because we permit them to or because we lack the strength or the will to keep them from doing it. I do not, by the same token, forget that there are at given moments in history states of affairs, situations, that given persons are indeed incapable of affecting. Nor do I forget that wisdom and statesmanship indeed consist in part in distinguishing between these situations and those we can affect. It is not wise or statesmanlike, either, to see stone walls where there are none, or to fail to distinguish between stone walls you can push over if you use your bulldozer, not your head, and those you can't push over. Or to fail to identify the stone walls that have been built of stones and mortar of which you are the only supplier—that is, (a) the ones you can learn a lesson from, and (b) the ones you can keep the other fellow from building any higher or any thicker. "Forces" in history are a profitable study only for men who approach history responsibly, which means regarding themselves, and other men, as agents in history, responsible for their own actions and the consequences of those actions.

Heilbroner is emphatically *not* such a man. He would have us simply accept "forces": the "accelerating sweep of science and technology," the "revolutionary extension of popular aspirations to the impoverished base of the human community," the "economic reorientation . . . away from the institutions and ideology of capitalism." The "forces" within whose interstices he would have us seek the poor historical destiny we have left are pretty clearly of nobody's making, certainly not ours, so that obviously there can be no question of our unmaking them. Our choice is limited to smashing ourselves against them, or taking a free ride on them, or helping them along and, in helping them, maybe managing to redirect them a little.

The world in which his "history" drearily unwinds is one in which (in Ortega's phrase) nobody is "running things," nobody failing to run them, certainly nobody running them badly or foolishly. Things just happen, and go on happening until they stop happening because some other things have started happening. His book should have been called not *The Future as History* but *History as Kaleidoscope*. The only questions he has to ask of "history" is where it is going, and which road we must take to be there to meet it.

Heilbroner offers us pure stick and no carrot: history from now on is *not* going to go as we should have liked it to. Capitalism, except in America, is through, as the West itself is through; Communism has amply demonstrated its ability to develop under-developed areas more rapidly than capitalism can, and that is what all the world except America and Europe is interested in. Despite the examples of American, German, and Japanese prosperity, Europe will go socialist because of the political, not the economic, inadequacies of capitalism. Most of the world will become authoritarian because rapid development does call for sacrifices, and these must be imposed from above.

As for America, either it prospers or it does not. (It will, provided it is prepared for an indefinite future of deficit-spending, which however means finding a substitute for military expenditure when, peaceful coexistence having come into its own, military expenditures can no longer be justified.) If it does prosper, the example of its prosperity will make the peoples of Asia, Africa and South America even more insistent that their standard of living be raised (besides which, what are we going to deficit-spend on if not "aid" to the underdeveloped areas?); if it doesn't prosper, capitalism comes a cropper even here. We have no real choice, then, except to deficit-spend; coexist with Communism; help the underdeveloped countries; lapse further and further into impotence and insignificance, telling ourselves we do all this because things are bad. Or, if you want to call it a choice, we can refuse to do all this and make things worse.

It all fits. What we have hitherto erroneously called the Liberal program is in fact a series of historical imperatives, to which nobody in his senses would even try to say "No." Also, however, the stick won't seem so bad, won't hurt so much, if like Heilbroner we take the longer, more detached view. Communism (in a curious "slip" that his editors should have caught, he says that it has betrayed its "original ideas" *less* than the Christian Church) seems so bad only because we dwell on its failures or glory in its shame. Its "cruelties, its use of terror, its indifference to personal liberties . . . [are] not so much the face of the new world as the shadow of the old." "It is only moral cowardice to single out the evils of communism, while refusing to admit to what may ultimately be the beneficial consequences of the tremendous economic movement it is effecting." Besides which, we can always hope that "with communism, as with capitalism, the completion of the industrial transformation may soften and mellow the rigors of the transitional phase." As for the rise of the underdeveloped countries, the "transition ahead will be ugly," *but*, let us "remember in our consequent concern and likely irritation that . . . [they once] suffered the impact of a Western dynamism they did not understand . . . and could not control." Besides which, "what is a closing-in of history for us is an opening-out of history for [them]" (i.e., even if it is not more blessed to give than receive, turn about's fair play).

An age dominated by eunuchs needs a philosophy of history appropriate to eunuchs. This is it; and I recommend it unreservedly for the Stalin Prize.

SPAIN AND THE DEFENSE OF THE WEST.
By ARTHUR WHITAKER
(*New York: Harper and Brothers, 1961.*)

The thesis of this book is that Spain, because of certain mistaken or sinful American policies, has become and will continue to be a "political liability" for the United States; that we must "dissociate" ourselves from the Franco dictatorship, alike in the eyes of the world and in the eyes of the Spanish people, by reversing those policies. All of which means: cease to do things that confer international political "respectability" on the Franco regime, and begin to use the leverage of our economic aid program on behalf of Spanish policy reforms in the direction of "freedom," "social justice," and the kind of "institutionalization" that would remove or at least lessen the present intolerable uncertainty as to Spain's political future; and thus as to the security of our Spanish bases. The book further argues that continuation of present American policies (e.g., trying to get Spain into NATO and, e.g., scheduling visits by American presidents to Madrid, and so strengthening Franco's hand domestically) is incompatible with our rôle as leader of the free world in its "struggle" against Communism, and violates our deepest "ethical" commitments.

Whitaker argues both that a girl like the United States is known by the company she keeps and that a nice girl like the United States ought, calculations of good repute entirely to one side, to want to keep good company. Both that doing anything except minimum business with Franco is a game at which we cannot win, and that even if we could win at it, we should be ashamed, "deep down" within ourselves, for even wanting to. Both that national effort in favor of "free institutions" and democracy "pays," and that we should owe such efforts to others even if it did not. Good policy, the author holds, is policy directed at good ethical purpose, let the chips fall where they may; Spain and the Spanish people—with love and affection for whom the book fairly drips—rightly expect that kind of policy from us and we must not let them down.

Spain and the Defense of the West is, then, mainly a policy recommendation; and we may assume that its appearance on the heels of an American presidential inauguration and under the aegis of the influential Council on Foreign Relations (where it was helped along by one of those huge consulting committees, bursting with important names that not everyone would have thought of in connection with the topic in hand, that the Council sets up—the sky the limit as regards "resources"—for its projects) is no mere happenstance. It is intended to *affect* policy, and, with such powerful backing and because of certain great strengths its author has been careful to build into it, is likely to do so. It will be widely read in quarters that "matter," and the more because it sets down in cogent and unambiguous fashion things, as to what to do about Franco, that have been gestating in certain heads, and awaiting midwifery, ever since 1953, when *The New York Times* gave the cue in the editorial in which, on behalf of a bewildered nation, it grudgingly "accepted" the air bases agreement with Spain: a strictly military arrangement if we must, but let us also gather our skirts about us; let us touch pitch if we must, but let us not be defiled. Not old virtuous us.

It behooves us, then, to take this new toy apart and see what makes it go. Let us see what the policy recommendation really amounts to; what kind of knowledge and thinking about, and "friendship" for, Spain, has gone into it; what its chances are of getting us the goods it promises us. And so be very clear with ourselves as to what the "issue" actually is (or ought to be) between those who will give it their support and those who will firmly oppose it.

Nor let us hesitate, in becoming clear about that issue, to go far afield on occasion if we must—e.g., by reminding ourselves, in connection with the political respectability and stronger hand we have allegedly conferred on Franco, of the political respectability and stronger hand we once conferred—and so far as I know have never repented of having conferred—on the late Joseph Stalin. And, e.g., by bumping questions up, where that might help us, to the level of general political and moral theory.

Let us, for instance, begin as far afield as the dedication ceremonies for the Valle de los Caídos, the Franco regime's memorial to the fallen on both sides in Spain's Civil War, and the address that the Generalissimo delivered on that occasion. In that address, which serves as a sort of *leit-motiv* for Whitaker's book, and elicits from him what many readers, especially American readers, will deem his most telling indictment of Franco, the Generalissimo did *not* (as Whitaker would have expected him to) deliver a message of "conciliation." Instead he drew and elaborated upon a sharp distinction between on the one hand "Spain" and on the other hand "Anti-Spain," against the latter of which he vowed, in future as in the past, to wage unrelenting war. Moreover, he included under "Anti-Spain," which he does indeed equate with "the Reds," not merely Communists but also all republicans, liberals, socialists, living and unborn, who might seek to reverse, in any sense, the victory for which the fallen on *his* side in the Civil War had given their lives. Worse still—and Whitaker is quite right in saying so—Franco has, instead of trying to provide a regime for *all* Spaniards, indeed continued to wage war on Anti-Spain. He refuses to let Anti-Spain organize in political parties that might dislodge him from political power; he withholds from Anti-Spain that most sacred of human rights, the political right to freedom of expression; he governs Anti-Spain by "force," that is, in the absence of the free elections by which, for Whitaker's money, both Spain and Anti-Spain would be governing themselves like other civilized peoples but for Franco's stubborn and perverse insistence on keeping alive grudges which, having reached the ripe old age of 31, ought, obviously, to be buried and forgotten. That is indeed what Franco went and did and what Franco has gone and done, and one way to state the issue Whitaker's book raises is to ask whether Franco should have behaved, should now behave, otherwise. And, on beyond that, whether we should put upon him the pressure we can put

—for I agree with Whitaker that we can put pressure, and plenty —to call off the war against Anti-Spain and get on with the clearly urgent business of building a Spain that will have *Lebensraum* for both "Spain" and Anti-Spain, or if you like for "all Spaniards." The issue, in a word, is whether our "ethics" necessarily puts us on the side of "conciliation."

Whitaker's answer is a clear, resounding "Yes," from which his entire policy recommendation flows as a matter of course; mine, as I have intimated, is "No," or at least "Not too fast," and not because I disagree with Whitaker about the merits of our putting pressure upon necessitous allies for the sake of principle (as we shall see, I am perhaps prepared to go *further* than he is about that), but because:

(1) I want us first to recognize, as Whitaker it seems to me does not, that the Spanish, on the day when we go about reforming them, will indeed be entitled to ask "Why us, when you weren't so choosey at the time of your alliance with the USSR? Is it that the Franco dictatorship is worse, less 'respectable,' than the Communist dictatorship in Russia? Or are we the first to undergo American surgery only because you have just lately got into the business of reforming the internal regimes of your allies?" The Spaniards, or at least Franco himself and those who feel themselves close to him, will, I say, be entitled to ask those questions, because they are good questions. And we ought to be prepared to come clean on (especially since we are obviously not going to be caught arguing that the Franco dictatorship is worse than the Stalinist) and answer these questions, to which I think we had better square off as follows: "Yes, we are new at this business; we should indeed have put pressure on Stalin, should indeed have made it clear over the years that we should have done so, have indeed over the years come to a new understanding of our responsibilities and their implications, do indeed regret that a lesser criminal should now be about to suffer when only a while ago we were ready not to say eager to break bread (and eat salt) with a greater criminal. We can only say that the business is not the less worthy because we are new at it." Such an answer, since it will make us sound a little less self-righteous than Whitaker

would have us be, will make the medicine, as we spoon it up, enormously easier for the Spanish to take. (The confession will not be entirely fair to those Americans of us who would never have entered an alliance with a Soviet Russia; but we will be gallant enough to bow our heads with the rest of us Americans —just as, in the present article, we shall be gallant enough not to ask Whitaker, and the members of that Council on Foreign Relations committee, what kind of noises they were making at the time of the Soviet alliance.)

(2) I should wish us first to move along (both prospectively, for Spain, and retrospectively, for the USSR) from "principle" as Whitaker understands it to "principle" as—we shall have more to say about this—it is correctly understood. Whitaker, I submit, confuses principle with Liberal ideology, which is to say that any overlap between his position and an ethical one would be not merely coincidental but miraculous. For principle as Whitaker understands it would bid us, as regards intervention in the domestic affairs of our allies, to subordinate everything to the requirements of a world-wide imperialism on behalf of free elections and free speech. Principle correctly understood would bid us, for that purpose, to subordinate everything (including our "image" in the eyes of certain allies that Whitaker loses sleep over but I don't) to the requirements of an imperialism on behalf of victory—victory, Professor Whitaker, not "struggle"—for a genuine and repentant West over the World Communist movement. I claim that the second of these imperialisms is consistent with what should be (to borrow a phrase Whitaker likes to borrow from a Rockefeller Brothers report) our "deepest ethical commitments," and that the first, in the premises at least, is inconsistent with these commitments—that is, wicked. I claim that the second is American (that is, rooted in what *are* our deepest ethical commitments), and the first merely (as Courtney Murray likes to put it) Eastern Seaboard Liberal (that is, with roots that are in America only by an accident of geography).

(3) I'd like us first to be very clear as to the meaning, in Spanish conditions, of "conciliation," as to the relation in those conditions between conciliation on the one hand and free elections

and freedom of expression in Spain on the other, and as to where the Franco dictatorship narrowly construed (that is, Franco himself) fits into the whole business. (I am not, let us understand, less eager than Whitaker to see the Spaniards all reconciled to one another, and to have a Spain for all Spaniards.)

Let us, by way of working our way into all that, let Whitaker pick up the marbles as regards certain arguments he would no doubt like to draw us into. For example, as to whether it is terminologically correct to classify republicans-in-general, liberals-in-general, and socialists-in-general as "Reds." It isn't. Or as to whether General Franco at one time favored an Axis victory, which is what Whitaker likes to talk about (in preference to the burning of churches and the murder of priests and nuns under the Spanish Republic) when he gets into a historian's mood of reminiscence (me, I am open to conviction about this but must say his demonstration very nearly convinces me of the opposite of what he would like to prove). Let's assume that he did. Or as to whether the Franco "Movement" began, as the Generalissimo would indeed like us to believe, as a movement against Communism. It didn't, though let not Whitaker confuse the question whether it began as a movement against Communism with the question whether it began as a movement that was as a matter of course anti-Communist; for the Franco movement was always as a matter of course anti-Communist. Or as to whether Franco has any business boasting, in connection with the bases agreement, that the U. S. and the "free world" finally came around to seeing it his way. He doesn't; the U. S. and the free world have not yet come around, as, I think, the Whitaker proposal itself clearly shows. The West still shrinks before the comprehensiveness, the clear-headedness, the vigor, of Spanish anti-Communism, of which Franco, for all his shortcomings in other directions, is a faithful expression.

Let us, I say, concede Whitaker these points, and go on to a consideration of his policy for "conciliating" Spaniards to one another, where we find that in the course of conscientiously setting down (as he does) all the *little* facts about Spain he overlooks the *big* and one would like to think inescapable fact about Spain, which, with its indispensable applications, is this:

(a) Spain is not America. Above all, the Spanish Civil War was not and is not the American Civil War. After the latter, "conciliation," that is, a regime for all Americans, was possible because the vanquished were prepared to accept their defeat at the hands of the victors. Which is to say, *not* because the victors were prepared to assure the vanquished that the issues the war had been fought over were unreal, or not worth fighting over. It isn't that the Spanish victors since the Civil War have behaved so differently from the American victors, but that the Spanish vanquished have behaved so differently from the Southerners—and have, what is more, never made any pretence of behaving otherwise. Their intention has been, ever since the last shot was fired, to undo the Nationalist victory, and to reverse the policies it represented. "Spain" and "Anti-Spain" may or may not be the happiest, certainly they are not the most "conciliatory," terms in which to state the continuing issues between the Spanish victors and the Spanish vanquished. They cannot be stated in terms of Communism, as Franco would wish us to believe, any more than in terms of Catholicism, as certain anti-Franco commentators wish us to believe; but that does not mean that the issues are not still there, or that Franco's insistence that they are still there is a matter of stubbornness or perversity. The issues are still there; they are, moreover, the deepest issues that can divide men, whether in politics or in political theory, because they are issues having to do ultimately with the meaning and practice of *freedom*.

(b) You cannot, therefore, exert pressure on Franco on behalf of all Spaniards, appealing as the notion is. Any pressure you exert must be exerted on behalf of *some* Spaniards against *other* Spaniards—in the knowledge that each of the groupings you must choose between is just as "anti" the other (*and*, in the long pull, *against* the other's "freedom," American style) as the other is of it—and with an eye to the predictable consequences of the pressure you are going to exert. You pays your money, and you takes your choice, and no kidding yourself (or other people) about having it both ways. The basic dividing-line, like it or not, is between those who are deeply convinced that Spain cannot repeat the Spanish Republic's experiment with freedom of expression, freedom of political parties, and free elections without producing another civil war and are therefore determined that the experiment shall *not* be repeated, and those, the people clearly that Whitaker feels at home with and listens to in Spain, who are willing to "chance" it because they have somehow talked themselves into believing that the divisions a regime of free expression would bring to light would, this time, be less sharp, less violent, than before. Now there is not, either in Whitaker's book or in the heads of those Spaniards who would be his favorite dinner companions, one shred of evidence to justify any such optimism. Political freedom, American style, is not, in Spain, compatible with order. A proposal to move things in Spain along toward political freedom is, therefore, a proposal for a bloodbath. You must exert pressure in Spain on behalf of the forces of order or on behalf of the forces of disorder. If you don't see that, as the danger is that America's policy-planners will *not* see it, the power that the economic aid program gives you is, as Huneker liked to say, a razor in the hands of a baby. That is, if you like, tragic; but its being tragedy does not make it any the less the facts of life. And your happening to disagree with the forces of order in Spain about freedom does not make them any the less the forces of order, who alone can prevent the new bloodbath.

(c) All that, moreover, is indispensable to clear thinking and sound policy-making about the Franco dictatorship—that is, about Franco himself. We must get it through our heads that it is not "freedom" that Franco stands in the way of in Spain; freedom you are not going to get no matter which "side" you exert pressure for. (In one case you get authoritarianism, in the other a blood-bath, which as you may have learned from *For Whom the Bell Tolls,* isn't freedom either.) What has to be saved from Franco is, paradoxical as that may seem, precisely the Spanish authoritarians; and not of course saved from Franco's authoritarianism but from his misgovernment, his laziness, his indifference not to freedom but to corruption. Which is to say (Whitaker is curiously timorous about this), *Franco must go* (be kicked upstairs, be made, e.g., a Prince of the Realm with no responsibilities except huntin' and fishin'). Any talk of liberalizing him, because as a matter of course that involves keeping him, merely fortifies him—by leaving Spain's authoritarian monarchists, who alone can create order in Spain, no alternative but to rally around him.

PEACE OR ATOMIC WAR? By Albert Schweitzer
(New York: Henry Holt, 1958.)

We stand constantly in the presence these days of a mode of argument that runs as follows: Proposition X, or Propositions X and Y, or Propositions X, Y and Z, if valid, would force certain conclusions that are *intolerable*. The propositions in question are, therefore, not valid. And the view of reality that has tended to make them seem plausible, or attractive, or unavoidable, must be a false view of reality. The task, therefore, becomes that of substituting for that false view of reality another view of reality which will yield up propositions whose validity we are entitled to take for granted because it does not lead to the conclusions declared intolerable. Nor do we require any criterion by which to evaluate this other view of reality than just that: we embrace it, *and all the tacit premises and clear implications* that go with it, because it assures us a means of escaping the intolerable.

X, Y and Z are, for this mode of argument, any variant of the following propositions: (1) The Soviet Union and World Communism must be dismantled because otherwise they will spread over the entire surface of the earth. (2) The great issue of our time is that between World Communism and the opposition to

World Communism; thus, that between the Soviet Union and the United States. (3) The issues at stake between World Communism and the opposition to World Communism, between the Soviet Union and the United States, are absolute, uncompromisable, save in the short term and on the level of unwarranted optimism, so that an ultimate showdown is off at the end unavoidable. (4) World Communism and the Soviet Union are not going to change in such fashion as to make that showdown other than unavoidable; and *we* can change in such fashion as to make that showdown other than unavoidable only by ceasing to be all that we have any right to value in ourselves.

And all these propositions are invalid—so, I repeat, runs the mode of argument I have in mind—because their acceptance leads ineluctably to conclusions that are intolerable; wherefore the view of reality that yields them up, that is, the view of the Communists and ourselves that we have entertained up to now, must go by the board. We must move to such-and-such another view of reality, and if someone says of that view of reality that it does not square with the facts, or that it also will lead to a state of affairs that is intolerable, well—and I come now to the major point —well, *we shall just have to take that risk.*

I oversimplify, you say? I exaggerate the weaknesses of the mode of argument in question, you say? No intelligent man would employ any such mode of argument, you say? Well, let's look into the matter a little, so that you can see for yourself that I do not oversimplify (usually the argument is both more brash, and *more* indifferent to patent difficulties than my schematic representation of it would suggest). I do not exaggerate those difficulties (they cannot be exaggerated). The hard task would be to find a man reputed to be intelligent who is not arguing along these lines (by confusing the extremely disagreeable with the intolerable; by abandoning all traditional notions of what is intolerable to civilized man; by telling any lie necessary about reality, historical *and* moral, in order to bring the argument off; and by insisting that *any* resultant risk, however frightening it used to be considered, is worth taking; and, above all, by ignoring all countervailing argument).

Let us take, for instance, that great and good man, Albert Schweitzer. X, for him, is the proposition that nuclear tests are a necessary part of the general defense against Communism and the Soviet Union. Y is the proposition that the rivalry between the United States and the Soviet Union may well lead to an atomic war. Z is the proposition that a Summit Conference, were one to be held, would accomplish nothing. Acceptance of these propositions, Schweitzer argues in his new book, *Peace or Atomic War,* leads necessarily to consequences that are—yes, just as we were saying, "intolerable." "The Summit Conference must not fail; mankind will not again *tolerate* failure" (italics, here and below, are mine). As for the tests, "We *must not* be responsible for the future birth of thousands of children with the most serious mental and physical defects. . . . Only those who have never been present at the birth of a deformed baby, never witnessed the despair of its mother, dare to maintain that the risk in going on with nuclear tests is one which must be taken under existing circumstances." Taking that risk, in other words, is intolerable. As for atomic war, it would be "the most senseless and lunatic act" that could ever take place, and "at all costs it must be prevented."

Having thus taken his stand, our philosopher-musician-theologian-man-of-science proceeds to tell any lie about reality, about his opponents, about the choices to be made, that suits his book. Those who favor continuance of the tests are deliberately engaging in "propaganda"; are guilty of "complete disregard" of their harmful effects on future generations and a "lack of compassion"; are conspiring against the "truth."

If the Rapacki proposal were adopted, the "maintenance of peace would be assured," and the "beginning of the end of *the spectre that overshadows the Soviet Union* would become an accomplished fact." The "testing and the use of nuclear weapons carry in themselves *the absolute reasons* for being renounced." As for "what will become of poor Europe if American atomic weapons no longer defend it," that is, what will happen if Europe is delivered to the Soviets—well, "perhaps the Soviet Union is *not quite so malicious* as to think only of throwing itself on

Europe . . . and perhaps not quite so unintelligent as to fail to consider whether there would be any advantage in upsetting her stomach with so indigestible a meal." "A Europe standing on its own has *no* reason to despair." To be sure, "East and West are dependent on presupposing a certain reciprocal trust in one another," and "we live in a time when the good faith of peoples is doubted more than ever before"; *but* "We *cannot* continue in this paralyzing mistrust."

Not even when the mistrust is clearly justified by the facts? Well, "another spirit must enter into the people." And therefore *will* enter into them? It will "if the awareness of its necessity suffices to give us strength to believe in its coming." Will it? Well, "We must presuppose the awareness of this need in all the peoples who have suffered along with us. . . . [We] must re-discover the fact that we—all together—are human beings, and . . . concede to each other what moral capacity we have. . . . Then there will arise the need for a new spirit which can be the beginning of a feeling of mutual trustworthiness. . . ."

Suppose that feeling does not arise? No answer, save that which is between the lines of every page: this is a risk you have to take, because the alternative is "intolerable." Not just very unpleasant, and perhaps less unpleasant than the predictable results of taking the risk? No, indeed.

In a word, the spread of the Communist movement over the entire world, *never once mentioned by Dr. Schweitzer as a possibility,* much less as *the* possibility that haunts the minds of his opponents, is "tolerable" in some sense in which the possibilities he stresses are *not* "tolerable."

These are, I repeat, lies; and Dr. Schweitzer is—not a liar, for to say that would be to say he knows better—a purveyor of false-hoods. But the intellectual crime to which I wish to direct at-tention is far less the misrepresentation of reality, which I deem to be derivative, than the playing of games with the word "in-tolerable." And the resultant rejection of the role of the intel-ligent and courageous man in history—that is, the careful and re-sponsible weighing of the goods and evils among which man is free to choose. For to reject that role is to refuse to be free.

AN HISTORIAN'S APPROACH TO RELIGION.
By ARNOLD TOYNBEE
(*New York: Oxford University Press, 1956.*)

Arnold Toynbee's new book offers us (1) a history of man's worshippings, (2) an explanation of the great turning-points in that history, (3) an analysis of man's present politico-religious predicament, (4) a prediction as to how man will extricate himself from that predicament, and (5) a long-run solution to man's religious problem, one aspect of which is a religious "message" of sorts. It would, therefore, be a bargain even at twice its price; and Suburbia, which in books at least has a sharp eye for a bargain, will predictably buy and absorb it in vast quantities.

First, then, as to the history of man's "worshippings," or in Toynbee's own phrase man's "religions" (this term he uses broadly enough to cover everything, e.g., Nationalism and Technology, to which, consciously or unconsciously and with or without religious experience, man has ever subordinated himself). Where I distinguish between "worshippings" and "religion," Toynbee distinguishes between "religions" and "higher religions." Here, though specialists will pick quarrels with him on matters of detail (and will no doubt win most of the resulting arguments), Toynbee the professional historian is in his element. He has a carefully worked-out story to tell, and he brings to the telling of it the vast learning, the profound sense of drama, the sympathetic imaginativeness, and above all the rich gift of phrase that have marked all of his historical writings. Human societies and communities, he declares, have at different times and places worshipped one or another of "no more than three objects . . . namely, Nature, Man himself, and an Absolute Reality that is not either Nature or Man but is in them and at the same time beyond them."

Chronologically, the worship of Nature comes first; when it fails—and we shall see in a moment what it is for a worship to fail—"man is left with a spiritual vacuum which he is impelled to fill; and he is then confronted with the choice of substituting for [it] . . . either a worship of himself or an approach to Absolute Reality, through the worship of God or quest for Brahma or for Nirvana." He chooses now the one of these two, now the other, and now—because he can always turn back to Nature—neither of them, and so he creates a "drama that, in our time, is not yet in its last act"; we can perhaps "make out the elements of the plot, but we do not yet know the dénouement."

The historian's task thus becomes, in the first instance, that of teasing out of the available documents and placing in correct order the choices man has in fact made, through the ages, in this locality or that one. And only the most erudite reader, I think, will fail to learn much from this phase of Mr. Toynbee's book; had he limited himself to this phase, indeed, the book would probably have done a little good in Suburbia, and no harm at all.

Mr. Toynbee does not, however, offer a mere record; he has, rather, invented an apparatus for explaining man's choices among objects of worship which, if I read him correctly, amounts to something like this: Man, in any place or any time, keeps on worshipping that one of the three objects he has elected to worship, until the consequences of his doing so become "intolerable," at which moment he turns to that alternative whose predictable consequences seem most attractive. The first form of "man-worship," which Toynbee calls the "idolization of the parochial community," endures until the "blood-tax exacted by the waging of ever more intensive, ferocious and devastating warfare has come palpably to outweigh any cultural and spiritual benefits that the contending parochial states may once have conferred on their citizens." The latter then turn either (as, for example, with the Roman Empire) to idolization of a universal community, under whose "all-embracing eyes" mankind can look forward to "living in peace and concord as a single family," or (as, for example, with Greece) to idolization of the self-sufficient philosopher. These alternatives having failed, the stage is set for the appearance of the "higher religions"—which, however, lead on to fanaticism, to religious wars, and to a new intolerableness, so that in the modern period in the West, man has embraced two new forms of man-worship: namely, Nationalism and Technology, whose consequences are today on the point of becoming unbearable.

Recognizably, this is merely the psychoanalytic theory of individual religious experience, the notion that the individual believes in his religion not because it is true, which of course it isn't, but because he needs it, or feels more secure with it than without it, kicked up to the cosmic level—and, I should have thought, no better after the kicking up than before it. Religious teachings, in a word, arise because men require them, and take the shape men require them to have. They are to be judged not according as they approximate to the Truth, or lead in fact to salvation and eternal happiness, but according as they put man on the spot or get him off it. Mr. Toynbee writes eloquently about Absolute Reality, about Suffering and Love, about the dangers of self-centeredness; but his reason for valuing these things always turns out to be this-worldly, a matter of whether they lead people to behave nicely, not kill each other off, and so find life bearable. This is to write about religion as a man born blind might write about color. For what we end up with, of course, is merely the cult of the bitch goddess of Success.

Mr. Toynbee's analysis of man's present politico-religious predicament, his prediction as to how man will extricate himself from it, and his religious "message" are pretty much what, in this context, we should expect. As the Machiavelli of *The Prince* was the prophet-planner of a united Italy, so the Toynbee of this book is the prophet-planner of the universal, one-religion, one-political-theory Liberal welfare state. The "control of atomic weapons," he writes, "is bound to be unified in the hands of some single authority sooner or later"; and we can "foresee that when world-government does come, the need for it will have become so desperate that Mankind will not only be ready to accept it even at the most exorbitantly high price in terms of loss of liberty, but will deify it and its human embodiments."

As Machiavelli proposed to rely, for the desired unification, upon Cesare Borgia, Toynbee proposes to rely upon something called a "discriminating liberalism," the essence of which appears to be a willingness on everyone's part to believe that the "missions of the higher religions are not competitive: they are complementary." That, stripped of their "non-essentials" (Mr. Toynbee takes a chapter to tell each of them what it must give up), they teach pretty much the same thing, and that, in any case, one of them is as good, or about as good, as another. The time, Toynbee thinks, "may come when the local heritages of the different historic nations, civilizations, and religions will have coalesced into a common heritage of the whole human family"—the sooner, one gathers, the better. And meantime, the trick to learn, it seems, is that of somehow believing your own higher religion without disbelieving anybody else's. And those of us who refuse to learn it will merely be in the way.

What if our religion forbids us to learn it? Ah, but it can't, because in doing so it would be insisting on a "non-essential."

ORDER AND HISTORY. By Eric Voegelin
(Baton Rouge: Louisiana State University Press, 1957.)

Israel and Revelation—Volume I

Forget it often though we do, *the* issue at stake between most American Conservatives and Liberals is that between "revelation" and "reason" (as most American Liberals understand "reason"). And there are two strategic errors the Conservative must not make in his continuing debate about that issue with the Liberals (I say debate not discussion because the Liberal, as a matter of settled practice, *refuses* to discuss).

The first is to let the Liberal substitute for the real problems as to the status of revealed truth his own question-begging restatements of them—that is, turn the debate into one about "values" or "value-judgments." The second is to compromise his insistence that the status of those truths turns exclusively on whether or not they *were* revealed—directly, by the One God, to His creature man—as the Conservative does when he acquiesces in the Liberal notion that revelation is a matter of "private" "religious" conviction, and so should never be mentioned in polite company. Both errors are now habitual with most American Conservatives; both greatly damage the Conservative cause.

Conservatism has, on such a showing, been poorly served by the political literature of recent decades. The textbooks from which our college students learn what little they are ever to know about politics tacitly equate the separation of church and state with the separation of religion and politics. Revelation, therefore, is never so much as mentioned in them; the "conflict" between revelation and reason is tacitly resolved in favor of the latter; right becomes anything in the way of law or principle that emerges from the decision-making process laid down in the Constitution; and commitment to the Decalogue is reduced to a "value preference," in the same category with a fondness for Bel Paese cheese.

The rare student who takes an "advanced" course in political theory does, to be sure, finally hear of revelation and its possible relevance to politics. But what he learns is that some sinister fellows like Augustine and Thomas Aquinas once tried to "enslave" "reason" to some alleged truths that had to be accepted because they had been handed down from on high—as also that Modern Man, having seen through the whole notion of truths handed down from on high, is on his own with what Burke calls his "private stock of reason." The Liberals have, in a word, had things all their way.

I am going to resist the temptation to say that this book will, by reclaiming for revelation the ascendancy many Conservatives would like it to have over political thought, alter that and point modern man down the path that leads to political sanity. The book has yet to meet the test of scholarly criticism in a score of "fields"; it is only the first volume of a six-volume work; many students of politics will refuse to read it, or dismiss it as inconsequential *because* of its attitude toward revealed truth. In other words, before it can have much influence it must change minds that belong to men who would greatly prefer to keep on thinking what they now think.

But if the next five volumes prove worthy of this one, if the book's scholarship is as sound as it appears to be, and if erudition and logic and wit and sweet reasonableness can sway men's minds, then I think it might rally the generation of scholar-politicists that *might* rescue modern man from the futility, the fury, and the destructiveness of modern politics. The book offers to religious Conservatives, in a word, a ray of hope; and it will behoove them to steep themselves in it, to cherish it, and to gird themselves for battle against the Liberal hatchetmen who will as a matter of course be told off to discredit it.

When men establish a government, according to Professor Voegelin, they analogically repeat "the divine creation of the cosmos," and thus, within their existential limitations, participate in the "creation of cosmic order itself." The kind of order they create, therefore, depends upon their relatedness to God, which in turn depends upon (a) the extent to which He has revealed Himself to them, and (b) the response to His revelation. And from this it follows that (from the political scientist's point of view) the first important event in world history was the leap from mere existence into "con-substantiality with the being of which [man] is a creaturely part"—a leap that occurred with Moses' experience of revelation. For the revelation to Moses—whether an historical, flesh-and-blood Moses or a symbolic representation of Israel's experience of order is, he thinks, inconsequential—was only the beginning of a progressive disclosure of divine will of which the entire Old Testament, correctly read, is an account.

Previous readings of the Old Testament, Professor Voegelin shows us, have been incorrect because the critics have approached it without a theory as to how in his literary creations man "represents" to himself his experience of order. The first task for the scholar-politicist becomes, accordingly, that of developing such a theory, and his second that of reinterpreting the crucial sections of the Old Testament in the light of that theory. So reinterpreted, it takes on new and ever-deeper meaning as regards the proper ordering of society (and, finally, its deepest meaning), which is that man—*all* men, not merely the people of Israel, and all men as individuals, not collectivities—moves through History, under God, for a purpose *outside* History. And, so reinterpreted, it yields up the breath-taking implication that any attempt to order society as if man did *not* live under God, or as if the purpose of ordering society were *within* History, is impious, doomed to be punished by destruction, and therefore self-defeating. The breath-taking implication, in a word, is that all modern political theory is an attempt to square the circle.

In *Israel and Revelation* we have, then, (1) a distillation of wisdom about the ordering of society from sacred scriptures that previous historians of political theory have simply ignored, (2) the articulation and fleshing-out of a theory (the "theory of symbolic forms") that enables us to find political wisdom where before we have seen only cosmology or theology or poetry, (3) an attempt to rescue world history from the chaos of meaninglessness to which, for our generation anyhow, it has been reduced by Spengler and Toynbee, and (4) an invitation to accompany the author on a journey—through the remaining literature of politics—that promises to be the most exciting intellectual adventure of our time. Because of (2), the author mines out of (1) a message that, insofar as one had previously understood it at all, one had associated with the New Testament. He enriches it by baring its roots in the fertile soil of experience; and doubly enriches it by showing us how it can have its roots simultaneously in experience and in revelation. For revelation, we understand at the end, is not the less revelation because its truths can be explained "anthropologically" (that is, in terms of the "need" for it generated in man by his history).

To say more than that to the prospective reader of *Israel and Revelation* would be to rob him of one or another of the most unforgettable moments he has ever spent over a book—and to impair the satisfaction, intellectual and aesthetic, with which he will read its concluding lines:

> The Ethiopian eunuch of the queen sitting on his cart and reading Isaiah, ponders on the passage: "Like a sheep he was led to the slaughter." He inquires of Philip: "Tell me, of whom is the prophet speaking? Of himself, or of someone else?" Then Philip began, . . . and starting from this passage he told him the good news about Jesus.

So let me leave it at that.

The World of the Polis—Volume II
Plato and Aristotle—Volume III

Man, according to an old wives' tale on which we were all brought up, has an incurable tendency to "anthropomorphize" the gods he invents, to attribute to them merely human qualities and characteristics and faculties, and so to confuse the "supernatural" with the "natural," the superhuman with the "merely human." One of the major theses of Eric Voegelin's *Order and History*, now half completed, is that this old wives' tale is the reverse of correct; that, on the record, man's besetting temptation is not at all to anthropomorphize his gods but divinize himself; that, if anything, man is *ab initio* more or less right about the gods, whom he *never* thought of as being like himself, but completely wrong about himself.

But, Voegelin's thought continues, there is this element of truth in the tale: man reaches a crucial turning-point in his development on that day when he clarifies his relatedness to God. It is indeed a matter of getting the divine and the human, the transcendent and the world-immanent, pried apart, separated, in a fashion in which they had not been separated before. But man is capable of doing this only when his experience of God has reached the point where he ceases to attribute to himself qualities and characteristics and faculties of the divine other than the one which is truly his—namely, the capacity to "respond" to God, to "grow" in attunement to divine will through revelation or philosophy, and so to *see* human nature as it really is. Man "clarifies" his conception of God simultaneously with his conception of himself; the clarification comes, when it comes, through his experience of God; but what has to "give" most at the moment of clarification is man's conception of man.

This is a crucial moment in man's "history" because it is then that man "discovers" history, enters history, and begins to be able to think clearly about his role in history as a creator and preserver, under God, of "right order." Only, mark you, begins. Having entered history, man lives forever between two temptations. On the one hand, there is the temptation to repudiate his responsibilities as creator and preserver of order, to write off "politics" as unworthy of his attention. And this Voegelin believes to be *the characteristic vice of Christian political thought and action.* On the other hand, there is the temptation to redivinize history, to forget that the purpose for which man acts is outside history and cannot be within history, and so defeat himself, because, in forgetting that, he loses his capacity to see human events in proper perspective. He still, in fine, has much to learn. He must, steering a meticulous course between those two temptations, develop a *political science,* a theory of prudential action in history that will prevent him from channeling his efforts either into enterprises that are bound to fail or into enterprises that, if successful, will predictably prove incompatible with the purpose outside history that alone authorizes action.

We have, to date, only three volumes of Voegelin's *Order and History,* and these are given over mainly to an account of pre-Christian man's unfolding experience of the divine, his gradual discovery (*pari passu* with that experience) of human nature, and, in the third volume in particular, *Plato and Aristotle,* the initial stages of his development of a political science. But primarily it is something much more than the most skilled and learned of antiquarian enquiries. It is a profound analysis of the contemporary crisis of Western Civilization *and* a courageous confrontation of the problem: What are we who value Western Civilization, we who seem at the moment to be so few in number—what are we to do? Always, mind you, with tacit insistence on the point to which I have devoted the opening paragraphs of this review: only those who approach the crisis with that experience of God that truly underlies Western Civilization can hope to find an answer to the problem, because only they can pose it in terms of realities. The others, those who approach it without experience of God, cannot bring it into focus because the divinized "historical" in which they are steeped does not exist. They are the "sleepwalkers."

Plato and Aristotle, like the three great books to which most of its pages are devoted (Plato's *Republic,* Plato's *Laws,* Aristotle's *Politics*), is at one and the same time a summary of a certain phase of man's experience of God and a statement of the problem of order. And it is, so to speak, a memorandum on political strategy to those who might conceivably be prepared to apply the truths of political science in the conditions of disorder that obtain in our world as in the Athens of Plato and Aristotle.

I can only suggest, in this brief space, what sort of thing Voegelin presents to us on this level of discourse. Not, let me hasten to say, any message of hope or optimism about the probable working-out of the present crisis—at least for our generations. ". . . [T]hose among us who find ourselves in the Platonic situation," he writes in one of his *obiter dicta,* "recognize in the men with whom we associate the intellectual pimps for power who will connive in our murder tomorrow"—which amounts, I take it, to a flat prediction that those to whom Voegelin is addressing himself must, in our time, expect to be murdered. Nor will he urge us on either in our continuing *polemical* fight against the Liberals or in our summons to the "West" for a crusade against World Communism (the former, he will assure us, won't get anywhere: "when the society in its broad mass is corrupt, [corruption] has become self-perpetuating through social pressure on the younger generation and, in particular, on the most gifted of [them] . . ."; as for the latter, it can only, in present circumstances, enhance the power of those pimps).

Nor does he show us an easy way out. In a situation of disorder, he will explain to us, there is *no* short-cut to the restoration of order: "political realism must operate through the [education and training] of men; and [that education and training can alone] secure social predominance for the [mature, good men]." In short, if right order is to be infused into society, this must come about through revelation and philosophy, proceeding always through persuasion. And, again, Voegelin calls upon us to reconsider our whole strategy; to realize that the time to act will be, at soonest, after mass democracy has run its course; and to cultivate—Voegelin at least sets us the example—our books and our prayers.

CRISIS OF THE HOUSE DIVIDED. By Harry V. Jaffa
(New York: Doubleday, 1959.)

Harry V. Jaffa's *Crisis of the House Divided* is: (1) a political history of the United States through the years preceding the Civil War; (2) an analysis of the political thought of the spokesmen (Abraham Lincoln and Stephen A. Douglas) for two of the alternative courses proposed during those years; and (3) a creative venture in political philosophy that—unless the United States be as sick intellectually as some of us believe it to be—will provoke the most profound and far-reaching debate of our generation about American politics.

Some of the book's readers (who this reviewer hopes will be legion) will no doubt wish that Jaffa had written his three books one at a time. Like Bergson, he is a subtle and seductive teacher of philosophy who, however, makes great intellectual demands upon his pupils. But what Jaffa proves, if he does not prove anything else, is that political history is inseparable from the history of political philosophy, and that neither can be grasped by the man who is not a political philosopher in his own right.

The man who refutes Jaffa's controversial theses (which *are* legion) will have to bring to his task all the skills Jaffa shows himself to possess, and to possess beyond any member of his generation whom I have encountered on the printed page: the skill of the historian with an encyclopedic grasp of his materials, of the all-seeing textual analyst, of the creative political philosopher, and of the literary artist who has mastered the nuances and rhythms of the rich and beautiful language bequeathed to us by Milton, Shakespeare, Burke—*and* Abraham Lincoln. (Of Lincoln's right to be mentioned in this context Jaffa leaves this reader—the Gettysburg address, incidentally, entirely apart—in no doubt at all.)

The central problem of *Crisis of the House Divided* is the status in the American political tradition of the "all men are created equal" clause of the Declaration of Independence. For Jaffa this is the same problem as the status of Abraham Lincoln *vis-à-vis* the Signers of the Declaration and the Framers of the Constitution; which, again, is the same problem as that of the very possibility of self-government, that is of democracy, as a realistic political alternative. These three problems, Jaffa brilliantly demonstrates, were Abraham Lincoln's own deepest preoccupations from the earliest moments of his career—preoccupations, moreover, with which he wrestled not as the smart political strategist of recent Lincoln historiography (though Jaffa is willing for us to think of Lincoln as that too), but as a political philosopher of the first order of importance.

As for the "all men are created equal" clause, Jaffa's Lincoln (and Jaffa) sees it as the indispensable presupposition of the entire American political experience; either you accept it as *the* standard which that experience necessarily takes as its point of departure, or you deny the meaning of the entire American experience. As for the status of Abraham Lincoln *vis-à-vis* the Signers and Framers, Jaffa's Lincoln sees the great task of the nineteenth century as that of affirming the cherished accomplishment of the Fathers by *transcending* it. Concretely, this means to construe the equality clause as having an allegedly unavoidable meaning with which it was always pregnant, but which the Fathers apprehended only dimly. As for the possibility of self-government, Jaffa's Lincoln sees it as turning on the following questions: What can be done about the Caesarist potential in the system elaborated by the Framers? What can be done to prevent the *passions* of a self-governing people from, in the long run, taking over from their *reason*, so that it ignores the duties correlative to the rights self-government is intended to secure?

Jaffa's Lincoln (and Jaffa) has a crystal-clear answer to these questions: Caesarism can be avoided, and the take-over by passions at the expense of reason circumvented, only through the ministrations and ultimate self-immolation of an anti-Caesar, himself as indifferent to power and glory as Caesar is avid for it—an anti-Caesar capable of transforming the fundamental affirmations of the Signers and Framers into a *political religion* that men can live by. And for Jaffa these three problems reduce themselves to the question—tacit, but present on every page of the book—of whether the Civil War was, from the standpoint of natural right and the cause of self-government, the "unnecessary war" of the historians of the past fifty or sixty years, or a war that *had* to be fought in the interest of freedom for all mankind.

Jaffa's answer to the question is that the war did indeed have to be fought—once the South had gone beyond slaveholding (Lincoln, he insists, had no wish to draw an issue over the slavery *within* the Southern States) to assert the "positive goodness" of slavery, and so to deny the validity of the equality-clause standard as the basic axiom of our political system. He insists that it had to be fought lest the possibility of self-government perish from the earth. That the war *did* establish the equality clause as the fundamental truth of the American political tradition, which by the very fact of the war's being fought transcended itself as Lincoln transcended the Framers. And that the present meaning of the tradition lies precisely in its commitment to equality as a goal ultimately to be realized. And, *within the limits* to which he for sound reasons of strategy confines himself, Jaffa's case for that answer seems to this reviewer as nearly as possible irrefragable.

His readers will, therefore, be well-advised to keep a sharp lookout *for those limits,* lest Jaffa launch them, and with them the nation, upon a political future the very thought of which is hair-raising: a future made up of an endless series of Abraham Lincolns, each persuaded that he is superior in wisdom and virtue to the Fathers, each prepared to insist that those who oppose this or that new application of the equality standard are denying the possibility of self-government, each ultimately willing to plunge America into Civil War rather than concede his point —and off at the end, of course, the cooperative commonwealth of men who will be so equal that no one will be able to tell them apart.

The limits I speak of are set by the alternatives that Jaffa steadfastly—plausibly but steadfastly—refuses to consider: namely, that a negotiated solution might have been worked out in terms of compensating the Southerners for their slaves and attempting some sort of radical confrontation of the Negro problem, and that the Southerners were entitled to secede if the issue was to be drawn in Lincoln's terms.

The idea of natural right is not so easily reducible to the equality clause, and there are better ways of demonstrating the possibilty of self-government than imposing one's own views concerning natural right upon others. In this light it would seem that it was the Southerners who were the anti-Caesars of pre-Civil War days, and that Lincoln was the Caesar Lincoln claimed to be trying to prevent; and that the Caesarism we all need to fear is the contemporary Liberal movement, dedicated like Lincoln to egalitarian reforms sanctioned by mandates emanating from national majorities—a movement which is Lincoln's legitimate offspring. In a word, it would seem that we had best learn to live up to the Framers before we seek to transcend them.

SOVEREIGNTY. By BERTRAND DE JOUVENEL
(*Chicago: University of Chicago Press, 1957.*)

A science, like a language, is a mode of thought and expression. The man who seeks to master a science must, therefore, first of all learn its grammar, and by so doing get himself across the line that divides literates from illiterates—those who are ready to learn from those who cannot learn because they cannot understand that which is said to them. And that man may count himself fortunate if the science he has chosen to master possesses a book of which teachers can say, "Read this, stay with it until you have made its content your very own, and you will have got your start."

With the publication of *Sovereignty* by Bertrand de Jouvenel, the science of politics becomes such a science; those of us who have witnessed the development of de Jouvenel's thought over the years have, for that reason, eagerly anticipated its appearance. And the reviewer's problem, as he turns its pages and relives the experience of each of a thousand passages that he has marked, is that of choosing among a thousand different ways of saying, "Forget about the other books on politics in the current lists, and see to it you don't miss this one."

De Jouvenel, like Immanuel Kant, like Plato himself, touches no topic without illuminating it, and, what is more, illuminating it in the way of the great teacher—namely, by simplifying that which illiterates in their illiteracy have overcomplicated, and by pointing up the complexities in that which illiterates have oversimplified. And Kant, by the way, is much in point; for were de Jouvenel a less modest man he would have called the book *Prolegomena to Any Future Work on Politics.*

To de Jouvenel connoisseurs—particularly to those who read Dennis Brogan's shamefully inadequate review in the *Times*—let me say at once that *Sovereignty* is in the vein not of his *Power,* which was the book he used to transport himself into the political universe about which he has written in recent years, but rather (among his works hitherto available in English) in the vein of his *Ethics of Redistribution. Power* is the work of an historian, not a political scientist; in writing it de Jouvenel learned (and taught others) to see, with awful clarity, the enormity of the political adventure upon which modern man has launched himself. "Sovereignty," once lodged in the "people," becomes *ipso facto* limitless and expresses itself *ipso facto* in huge concentrations of coercive "power" that is increasingly manipulated by men who, in the very nature of the case, have no standard to which they can refer what they do, save that of sheer appetite and desire, both of which are inherently without limit. And thence arises the infinite capacity of the modern state to destroy the good, the true, and the beautiful.

In the *Ethics of Redistribution* de Jouvenel began to grope for the tools of analysis that might, in due course, enable us to tell ourselves what we have to do in order to make sense of this adventure, and bring it, *per impossibile,* to some result distinguishable from death. And in this book he steps forward as a political theorist who possesses these tools of analysis, is convinced that they merit the kind of confidence that economists have long since been claiming for theirs, and is ready, therefore, to put them on display.

Like Aristotle, de Jouvenel has dreamt the dream of a political science that will be to the health of the body politic what medical science is to the health of the human body. Like Aristotle, therefore, he finds himself obliged to elaborate a "picture," or "model," of political situations in general—a model that will enable the mind to grasp the anatomy of political situations (as in medicine we grasp human anatomy) and transform it into an instrument that we can use in the course of building the therapeutic science that is our ultimate objective. De Jouvenel tries to develop here, in other words, an intellectual construct that can play, in the science of politics, a role equivalent to that of the market in the science of economics.

De Jouvenel sees politics wherever men seek to enlist the co-operation of other men with a view to increasing the resources, whether material or spiritual, at their disposal. He cuts right through, that is to say, the misleading distinction between "state" and "society," reabsorbs "sociology" into political science, and makes of the latter a general inquiry into the question, What fosters human cooperation, and what hinders it? It is, following out the analogy with economics (which asks and answers the question, What fosters, what hinders, the workings of the free market?), a good question, and in de Jouvenel's hands a fruitful one. But it is the kind of question that yields its maximum fruitfulness only if you both (a) ask it without "taking sides" while answering it, and (b) use it, having asked and answered it, merely as a tool for affecting matters on which (prior and subsequent to asking and answering it, and on ethical not scientific grounds) you *have* "taken sides." Only, that is to say, if you use it as a methodological device, appropriate to only one stage of political inquiry.

Let me explain that a little further. Aristotle asks with respect to each form of state, What would you have to do to preserve it, and what would you have to do to undermine and destroy it? But Aristotle means both parts of the question, really is "impartial"—at that stage of his inquiry—as between preserving states and undermining them, never yields to the temptation to be more helpful to would-be preservers of states than to would-be destroyers of states. Not so de Jouvenel; he ends up forgetting that men enlist the cooperation of others for evil purposes as well as good ones, that therefore there are forms of human cooperation we *want* to hinder rather than foster. Therefore, human cooperation, any old human cooperation, becomes a good which it is the task of political science to forward.

The point cannot be overemphasized, and for the following seemingly paradoxical reason: For those of us who are not ethical relativists, the purpose of political science must be to provide us with the knowledge we need in order to move political situations along in the direction called for by *our* ethics—in order, if you like, for us to be able to act politically with some confidence that we are not defeating our ethical ends.

As Aristotle saw, however, political science can provide us with that kind of knowledge only if it is itself ethically neutral (as, shall we say, toxicology is ethically neutral as between the poisons and the antidotes, the poisoners and the physicians). And de Jouvenel, who is certainly no relativist, commits, in this book, a twofold misdemeanor: he presupposes a "good" for his science, and in doing so, takes as his "good" one (any old human cooperation) which is—as he would see at once if he tested it against his own ethics—a patently false one. Or rather he commits a triple misdemeanor, because in due course he picks up a second good—that darling of the Liberals known as "progress"—that is also patently false. For from an ethical standpoint, progress is good only if it be in an ethically desirable direction—which is to say that some "progress" is good and some bad. To settle all the major issues of politics by appealing now to the good of cooperation as such, now to the good of progress as such, as de Jouvenel does, is both bad methodology and bad ethics. And that —from de Jouvenel above all the political scientists visible on the horizon—for this reviewer will not do.

To put the same point in another way: *Sovereignty* is a book to be instructed by, not one to be influenced by, because—dare the pupil say it frankly to the master, both in politics and in ethics?—its teachings on the level of political ethics are, quite simply, wrong. De Jouvenel does here to political ethics that which he accuses modern man of having done to politics. That is, he cuts them off from their proper orientation to true religion, and launches them upon the treacherous sea of relativism.

He sees—and describes more eloquently than any of his contemporaries—the evil of the modern politics; off at the end, however, he has nothing to say except "Settle for it." He sees, more clearly than any of his contemporaries, that the "open society," the society without an orthodoxy, leads unavoidably first to greater diversity of opinion than any society can carry, and then to persecution. Yet his teaching here is, "Let us keep our societies open, lest we fail to progress." He is aware, far beyond any of his contemporaries, that man cannot subsist without the warmth and certainty that attach to the face-to-face community based upon common religious and ethical beliefs; yet he denounces as totalitarian all who would encourage modern man to abandon Babylon (his name for open society) in favor of Icaria (his name for the community founded on shared belief).

His example, however, is better by far than his precept. He himself lives in a charming Icaria called Anserville.

WHAT IS POLITICAL PHILOSOPHY? By LEO STRAUSS

(Glencoe: Free Press, 1959.)

All histories of political philosophy are abominable, and for two excellent reasons. Nobody knows enough to write a history of political philosophy. And if, *per impossibile,* someone did know enough to write a history of political philosophy, the last thing he would take time for would be to write a history of political philosophy.

Why does no one know enough to write a history of political philosophy? Again for two excellent reasons. In the first place, the mastering of any single one of the books that the tradition has identified as the great ventures in political theory requires not that hasty reading over the week-end that will enable another chapter in a "history," but months and years and even decades of living with, of rethinking, of what I like to call "universal confrontation of the text." No lifetime is long enough to permit a man to do that with many texts. Indeed, the more texts a man tries to do it with, the *less* optimistic he becomes about the possibility of doing it with many more, because he understands better and better the vastness of the undertaking.

Secondly, the more a man learns about political philosophy the less interested he becomes in its history as such—as contrasted with the constantly recurring problems (the same problems, some of us believe, in every age) with which it deals.

This is not to say, of course, that no historical problems arise in connection with political philosophy, or that these problems (provided one knows why one raises them) are without interest. The Greeks, as Mrs. Disraeli was never able to remember, came before the Romans, Socrates before Plato, and Plato before Aristotle, and Aristotle before Cicero. Those who came after were able, had they the humility and wit to do so (which they did not always have), to pick up the problems where their predecessors left off. So, as we understand how the great men of political philosophy are related to one another with respect to the great problems, we do come out with a kind of history. But this "history" is worthy of attention not because it is history, not because it tells us what happened, but because of the light it throws on such urgent questions as: What *are* the real problems? What is the extent of our continuing ignorance of the solutions?

The Greeks came, we repeat, before the Romans; but above all the classical political philosophers and the medieval political philosophers came before Machiavelli, and Machiavelli before Hobbes, Hobbes before Locke, Locke before Burke and Rousseau and the Federalists, Burke and Rousseau and the Federalists before Kant and Hegel, Kant and Hegel before Marx, before Hitler, and before our present-day positivists and historicists—before, that is, the present-day denial of the very possibility of political philosophy. Now, whatever else there is to be said about our histories of political philosophy, and even conceding, reluctantly, that they make a certain amount of sense about the "story" from Plato to, say, Dante, nothing can be more certain than that they go to pieces when they come to Machiavelli. Of Machiavelli, as of each of his great successors, we have a long series of wildly conflicting interpretations, over against which you just pays your money and takes your choice.

Professor Leo Strauss, whose newly-published *What is Political Philosophy?* is the occasion for the present statement, has created over the past thirty years a vast and fascinating literature whose central purpose we can now see to have been from the beginning that of making sense of the great political thinkers of the modern period. Although *not* a "history" of them, I suppose one could now piece together out of his works a sort of history. I doubt that he would thank anyone for doing so, and this was certainly not his aim. What he has done is to take up the writers in question, one at a time, and to stay with each until—to use one of his own favorite phrases—he understands him *as he understood himself.*

As for those wildly-conflicting interpretations, his contention has always been that, if we fail to make sense out of the writings of a Hobbes or a Spinoza or a Rousseau, that is probably because we have not given ourselves the pains to learn to read them. The difficulty we have in reading them is itself a problem for political philosophy—perhaps, until we learn how to read them, *the* problem. We have been attempting to read them from the wrong vantage-point in time, and with the wrong question on our lips —namely, "What did they 'contribute' to political philosophy?"— where the right question is, "Who killed political philosophy, and how?" And that question we, corrupted as we are by the very thinkers we seek to understand, can hope to answer only by approaching it from a vantage-point philosophically prior to the murder; that is, from within the classical and Biblical tradition our suspects (as we may now fairly call them) have (as from within the tradition we clearly see) not *sought* to undermine and destroy, but *have* undermined and destroyed.

The Strauss investigation over the years emerges, with the publication of his two latest books, as that of a detective who starts out with a dead body, that of political philosophy (if you want to see it yourself, go take a look at pretty much any political science department), whose former owner may or may not have died a natural death. At the beginning we do not know whether a crime has been committed, or, if one has, what is the nature of that crime. The one thing we can be sure of is that if a crime was committed, the criminal or criminals will have attempted to cover their tracks. But also, wishing in the end to have the credit for having committed the crime successfully—thus wishing us in a sense to find them out—they will have left us the clues we need.

Like all good detective investigations, it is revealed to us with a considerable element of "suspense." The "master-mind" of the crime came to light only with the publication, last year, of *Thoughts on Machiavelli.* Only then did we learn that we were not dealing with a criminal but with a criminal syndicate; worse still, with a criminal syndicate that develops in each generation a new master-mind who carries the crime a little further and gives it a new "twist"; and, again worse still, that the greatest crime of the syndicate is not so much the murder (though a collective and continuous murder there has indeed been) but the creation of a state of affairs where committing the murder is no longer a crime at all, but a ticket to respectability and honor. Killing political philosophy is no longer "wrong"; it can't be, because everybody, including the nicest people one encounters at faculty-meetings, does it. That, if I understand Professor Strauss, is exactly how Machiavelli not only intended the story to come out, but took measures to make sure it did.

What is Political Philosophy? includes, among other things, the clearest statement we have from Professor Strauss of the method he has developed for reading the modern political philosophers. It contains, too, brilliant restatements of traditional teaching on the great problems of political philosophy and a running attack on relativism, positivism and historicism. Both of these should be not required reading but scripture for everyone who likes to think of himself as a Conservative. Taken together with the *Machiavelli,* moreover, it extends to any who wish to have it what has hitherto been a privilege reserved to a handful of students at the New School and the University of Chicago—that of learning political philosophy at the feet of *the* great teacher of political philosophy, not of our time alone, but of any time since Machiavelli. What is more, they will come away from reading him better, more virtuous men. For Professor Strauss, though (to use a phrase he is fond of) he would never seek to be edifying, *is* edifying in and of himself.

WE HOLD THESE TRUTHS:
CATHOLIC REFLECTIONS ON THE
AMERICAN PROPOSITION.
By JOHN COURTNEY MURRAY
(New York: Sheed and Ward, 1960.)

With the publication of his *We Hold These Truths* John Courtney Murray ceases to be mere teacher (at a college which performs a crucial function in the formation of American Jesuits), editor (of a distinguished theological journal), lecturer (before eager audiences all over the country), writer of articles (there is, to be sure, quite a bibliography of them: he is internationally prominent in one of the great continuing debates within the Catholic Church, and has contributed to many American journals of opinion), and becomes an *author*. But a reader readily sees why the event has been so long postponed: Father Murray's mind has been pregnant all this while with quintuplets, each with an equal right and an equal determination to be born, so that *We Hold These Truths* is *inter alia* a great act of distributive justice—for he has determined and contrived that all five of them should be birthed at one and the same time.

First, there is a book about the problems, perplexities, and "uneasinesses" of what Murray calls the "post modern" world, and the direction in which it must move—philosophically, morally, politically—in order to come to grips with its problems, dispel its perplexities, and free itself from its uneasiness. Here, he believes, our great danger is that of concentrating too much attention upon international Communism, which is merely "modern" politics carried to its logical conclusion (Communism, he argues, makes explicit and deliberate that which in modernity, in its non-Communist form, is merely implicit and "unintentional"). On the contrary, our truly urgent business is the Basic Issues, which are issues concerning metaphysical and ontological truth, summoning us to make decisions about the nature and structure of reality, the order of nature, and the economy of salvation. The present "civilizational fact," he insists, is *confusion;* the present civilizational experience is an experience of *disorder,* which, however, may impel us to the new act of thought that might make us clearheaded again and enable us to reestablish order in the world. Our alternatives he sees as reducing themselves finally to two, each of which may (though imposing upon us a single deed of choice) be stated in various ways. Taken on one of its many levels, that of "freedom," the alternative is between seeking freedom as the moderns did, in the sovereignty of the individual conscience (how "neolithic" they seem, he exclaims, those modern prophets of freedom: Milton and Mill, Madison and Jefferson!), and seeking it as medieval man did, in the "freedom of the Church" and the general style of political-moral thinking of which that phrase is both a symbol and a summary. On the level of government *sens pur,* it is a choice between government that is genuinely limited because limited by a standard intelligible to human reason, and the omnipotent and *therefore* spiritually impotent types of governmental authority with which in recent centuries we have had to deal. On the level of "democracy," it is a choice between the "democratic monism" of the Jacobins and something more or less akin to the democratic pluralism of the Framers of the Constitution of the United States. On the level of power and the uses of power, it is a choice between the violence in terms of which we have already become accustomed to transact our affairs, and a willingness to use force in emancipation from current sentimentalist inhibitions on behalf of justice. On what is for Murray (as it seems to this reviewer) the highest level, it is a choice between the act of "interior disloyalty" to reason and reality which is the essence of modernity, and the replacing of that with the premises and affirmations and methodological procedures associated with the great tradition. On the level of political theory, it is a choice between the "law of nature" of Hobbes and Locke and Rousseau and the "natural law" of the *philosophia perennis*—between the natural rights of man and natural right (which is a matter not of particularized "rights" but of justice).

The second of Murray's five books, accordingly, is a book about the "law of nature," the third a book about natural law. Even readers familiar with Voegelin and Guardini will read these parts with pleasure and profit and, if they be Americans, pride. For, hitherto, the task of pronouncing dead and ready for burial the "movements"—liberalism, positivism, scientism, scientific humanism—that even today dominate the intellectual-moral climate of the American universities, has been left to men of distinctively European formation. And it is good that we should at last be able to point to a fellow-countryman who can take care of himself (as, make no doubt of it, Murray can) on this level of controversy, and say that which needs saying. As for those readers who have not read Voegelin and Guardini and for this reason or that are not likely to, *We Hold These Truths* can open up to them, with great economy of time and effort, a universe of discourse of which it is already possible to say that the man who has not made himself familiar with it is beneath the level of his times (in Ortega's phrase) and so unable to look the latter in the eye. The second book, that on the "law of nature," would belong on the shelf with Leo Strauss's *Natural Right and History*, and the third, that on natural law, with the works of Heinrich Rommen—each of them, however, taking its place more modestly than the first book.

The book on the "law of nature," like one of the chapters in *Natural Right and History*, is a critique of the political philosophy of John Locke (there are passing references to Hobbes and Rousseau both of whom he is content to treat as standing or falling with Locke; when Rousseau categorizes the types of law, in his masterwork on politics, he conspicuously omits the "law of nature"). Like Strauss, Murray is quite clear that Locke's "law of nature" is a complete perversion of the natural law of the tradition, that Locke's political writings are poor philosophical performances, and that the "modern" age (insofar as it adopted Locke's natural-law position) has cut itself off from any possibility of advance along the path of true freedom and justice.

Unlike Strauss, however, Murray tends to move somewhat hastily to his (generally sound) conclusions about Locke; and, for all that it is good to witness a birching of the author of the *Second Treatise* by an ardent admirer of those American founding fathers who allegedly wrote under its influence, the book on the "law of nature" is perhaps that one of the five books that might, with the least prejudice to his enterprise, have been omitted—especially since he chose to sidestep the question that, as I have suggested, fairly cries up at you out of the volume as a whole, namely: Are we to conclude, if the Framers of the Constitution wrought so well, that they were *not* under the spell of Locke's "law of nature"? (If so, here certainly is a topic that wants another book.)

For the readers of a non-Catholic journal of ideas, the question that ought to be asked and answered at this point is perhaps this: To what extent is the work an expression of a "merely Catholic" point of view, or, from the standpoint of philosophy, of a "merely Christian" point of view? In the case of our first three books (on the crisis of our time, on the "law of nature," on natural law) our prior question resolves itself into the question, How careful has Murray been in these three books, to keep his natural law (which strictly speaking should, as this reviewer understands it, be discoverable by human reason unaided by revelation) apart from Christian theology? The answer to that question is, I venture, Not so careful as he might have been. This is to say that one can easily imagine a Leo Strauss suffering some pretty hard bumps as he puts himself through Murray's exposition of natural law; and that it injects a certain conspicuous ambiguity into the meaning of his book—at which I have called above the highest level. Is it a summons to "modern" man to return to "natural law thinking," or to return to the thinking of the Church? Catholics would of course like to see modern man return to both, but that does not dispose of the question I am raising even for Catholics—who though committed to both had best be clear in their heads as to where the one commitment leaves off and the other begins. As for non-Catholic Christians and unbelievers, my fear is simply that Murray may, by placing too great a burden on his natural law, frighten some of them away from the rational but perhaps not specifically Catholic "act of thought" for which in only some of the passages he appears to be pleading. To put the same point otherwise, I do not think it possible to tease out of *We Hold These Truths* an unambiguous answer to the question, Is natural law, unsupported and unsupplemented by specifically Christian teaching, an adequate basis for truly civil society?

Of the remaining two books one (in which Murray raises and answers the question whether Catholics can, and should, and do in fact accept the "affirmations" of the American Proposition) is indeed a quite proper series of "Catholic reflections"—though not, I think, in any sense that should make it the less interesting for non-Catholics or, since the question concerns one-third of the nation's population, the less important. Which brings me to the point for the sake of which I have clung thus tenaciously to the question whether Murray writes from a "merely Catholic" point of view, namely: That one of his five books that should be of the greatest interest to American Conservatives as such, the book on the American Proposition, seems to this reviewer to be not merely "not merely Catholic," but a major breakthrough in American political science. And one that might well give to American political scientists in general their first ever-so-startling lesson in how to write "objectively" about the content and meaning of the American political system, as we received it from the First Session of Congress, and how to use "objective" criteria in arriving at judgments about the system's present state of health. Here, in a word, is a book long overdue for those American Conservatives who find themselves, nowadays, hard put to it to say what it is in the American political system that they should be trying to conserve, and what it is in the present American environment that accounts for their (eminently justified) apprehensions as to whether its conservation is any longer possible. Murray's theses in these areas (their effect, as I have intimated above, is to move American system over from the column headed "Law-of-nature, natural-rights systems" to that headed "Natural-law systems") are so fresh, so brilliantly argued, and (in my view) so unanswerable as to warrant immediate grand jury proceedings against the authors of the entire existing literature of American politics—on grounds of incompetence, irrelevance, and inconsequentiality.

Acknowledgments

My deepest indebtedness in connection with this book is to the small circle of intimate friends, each of them a rare man in his generation because he still has time for conversation, with whom over the years its problems have been talked about, and talked about, and talked about: especially Frank Meyer and Brent Bozell, but also Revilo Oliver, Frederick Wilhelmsen, Charles Lichenstein, and George Casey. I think I know them all well enough to feel free to add: Let us have no foolishness about their not being responsible for the opinions I express. None of them can plead lack of "access" (as we political scientists fashionably call it) to the author, or—perish the thought!—anything other than sweet reasonableness and openness to persuasion on the author's part.

Further debts that I acknowledge with deepest gratitude in connection with this book are: To the trustees of the Relm Foundation, who recently made it possible for me to devote full-time, over a long period, to reading and thinking and writing, for their generosity. To William F. Buckley, Jr., affectionately, for encouragement not always easy to distinguish from slave-driving, and to Baron Bertrand de Jouvenal, affectionately, for encouragement not always easy to distinguish from blackmail, at every stage of the book's growth. And to the greatest living teacher of politics, whom I have ventured to imitate in the very structure of the book, for his teaching.

I am beholden also: To the *American Political Science Review* and the *Mid-West Journal of Political Science,* for permission to reprint portions of this book that have appeared in their pages; and to Harvey Mansfield and Vernon Van Dyke of, respectively, those periodicals, for invaluable editorial criticisms and assistance. To *National Review, Modern Age, Catholic World* and Collier's Encyclopedia, for permission to reprint other portions of this book. And to Richard Noble, Thomas E. Reilly, Jr., Charles A. Lofgren, Charles S. Shuken and Peter F. Erickson, who published an earlier version of my chapter on pacifism, for permission to reprint it here. And to Addison Potter and Morton Cronin, both colleagues of mine at Los Angeles State College, for numerous last-minute suggestions, and the time and energy that went into them. Finally, to my persistent editor, Jameson G. Campaigne, Jr., for his persistence.

Index

269

Index

Index

Index

272